Psychotherapeutic Strategies in Late Latency through Early Adolescence

Psychotherapeutic Strategies in Late Latency through Early Adolescence

Charles A. Sarnoff, M.D.

Jason Aronson Inc.
Northvale, New Jersey
London

10 9 8 7 6 5 4 3 2 1

Library of Congress Cataloging-in-Publication Data

Sarnoff, Charles A.
    Psychotherapeutic strategies in late latency through early adolescence.

    1. Bibliography: p.
    Includes index.
1. Adolescent psychotherapy. 2. Adolescent psychology.
3. Adolescent psychopathology. I. Title. [DNLM:
1. Psychosexual Development—in adolescence.
2. Psychotherapy—in adolescence. WS 463 S246p]
RJ503.S28   1987   616.891'14   87-19474
ISBN 0-87668-937-3

Manufactured in the United States of America

To Carole

Contents

Acknowledgments

I would like to thank the organizations and educational institutions that have been helpful in the advancement of the present work, parts of which have been in preparation since 1964. For providing dialogues and forums through which issues could be presented and details challenged, I am grateful to the Staten Island Mental Health Society, Brookdale Hospital, Long Island Jewish/Hillside Hospital, the Detroit Psychoanalytic Association, the American Psychoanalytic Association Interdisciplinary Colloquia on Anthropological Fieldwork and on Symbols, the New Jersey Psychiatric Association, and the Psychoanalytic Center for Training and Research of the College of Physicians and Surgeons of Columbia University. I wish also to thank those educational institutions that, by their invitations, kind attention, and the questions of their members, aided in the preparation of this book. Among these are Princeton University, the University of Texas at Dallas, Columbia University, Dartmouth College, the University of Colorado at Boulder, Emory University, Tufts University, Adelphi University, Harvard University, the Long Island Psychoanalytic Society, the American Psychoanalytic Association, and the Association for Child Psychoanalysis.

Great Neck, New York, 1986

Introduction

Latency, which was published in 1976, described the typical internal psychological structure of those 6- to 12-year-old children, who produced states of latency (e.g., periods of pliability, calm, and educability). The ability to predict the influence of childhood behavior, that diverges from latency calm, on adult character is a matter of concern. This ability could not be learned from the information contained in the 1976 book, *Latency.* It requires information beyond the scope of that book. That which would be required would be data on the normal development of cognition, symbols, and fantasy during the period of transition between latency and adolescence. One would need to know the answers to the following questions: How do normal and pathological development of the ego structures of latency influence adolescence? What are the developmental transitions that transmute the object relations, cognition, and symbol structures of latency into their derivatives in adolescence and adult life? What are the pathological aberrations that could distort these processes? What is the effect of aberrant behavior during latency on psychological functioning during later life? Can one predict, on the basis of divergent childhood behavior, pathology in adolescence? What are the lines of normal development for cognition, symbols, and fantasy during the period of transition between latency and adolescence? The current volume has been written to answer these questions. Such developmental information serves as a background against which psychotherapeutic progress could be judged and predictions of outcomes can be postulated.

There is a salient question implied here: Is there a relationship between the psychological events of the late latency years and pathological development during adolesence? The answer is "Yes." *Psychotherapeutic Strategies in Late Latency through Early Adolescence* describes the relationship. Remarkably, the relationship referred to has been relatively unexplored in the field of child development. Although it could easily be seen, explored, and used as the basis for theory and practice, this relationship has not as yet been considered in the mainstream of useful knowledge. Instead, preselected perceptions have tended to shape the way therapists see and interpret the world. New data can only be introduced when old conceptions have been put aside. One such conception is the tendency to view adolescence as a phase that arises *de novo* with the advent of puberty. If antecedents to adolescence were recognized in this theoretical concept, they would be placed in prelatency. Within the context of such theories, child development was seen as progressing apace from the years 1 to 6. Then, as if by some wondrous act of levitation, it soared like the classic winged seed of the dandelion to float untouched by cognitive growth or life events far above influence during the latency years. Finally, it came to rest on puberty's bosom, where it began to grow again. It is the purpose of this book to set aside this prejudice, which prances on the pages of our literature as hallowed fact, and to replace it with the observation of children.

A finding of direct observation of late latency through early adolescence is an awareness that early adolescence is an outgrowth of latency. Adolescence should not be characterized as the time of a sudden spawning of mature personality features. The major task of early adolescence is not the resolution of those psychological problems that were left unattended and unresolved when the child passed at the age of 6 from early childhood to the supposed unimportant wasteland of psychological events called latency. Adolescence receives prelatency fantasies after the fantasies have undergone processing, attempts at mastery, and modification during latency and early adolescence.

Late latency–early adolescence is viewed in these volumes as a stage of transition. It is a central and seminal developmental stage. Adolescence proper and the years beyond can be seen as the product or outcome of this stage of transition.

In the current volume emphasis is placed on the following observations and conclusions that aid us to see relationships between latency and adolescence: (1) similarities of structure and function; (2) the influence of characteristics of latency that persist into adolescence; (3) the unbroken continuation of lines of development, with origins during the latency years, that influence adolescence; and (4) physical maturational changes and cognitive maturation that undermine latency force the child to seek new objects for drives and create the milieu of paired chaos and reorganization, which is the emotional venue of adolescence.

In addition, we explore the resolution of the residua of persistent latency structures during adolescence. Included in these are personality features whose persistence reflects a failure to grow (e.g., evocative symbolization) and those that, through maturation, will form the basis for fundamental mechanisms of adjustment (e.g., future planning). In addition, we deal with new human resources that evolve from latency structures in early adolescence (e.g., the cognitive basis for the ability to fall in love).

As the child enters adolescence, he leaves behind the subtly fashioned masking symbols through which he had expressed much of his sexuality during latency. In place of fantastic symbolic representations confronted in his inner world, he moves toward sexual expression with real objects in the world of his peers. At first he is limited to reality-derived symbolic representations, which are formed into fantasies shaped by the newly awakened object orientation of the genitals. The sexual drive seeks realistic objects in daydreams that are at first fashioned of raw, unmitigated lust. These distortions of reality become the basis for the child's early adolescent interpretation of the world. Gradually, as relationships with objects in the real world progress and begin to dominate the sexual life, the feelings and needs of the partners begin to be taken into account, mitigating the narcissism and rawness of the manifest fantasies. Eventually the needs of others and the demands of society blend into and mold the planning and expectations of the adolescent swain. In the process, the sexual preoccupations of the child are transmuted from Hollywood's love myths, rapine, and sadism to the state of being in love. The latter, for the purposes of this book, will be defined as the activation of the capacity to incorporate the needs and preferences of the loved one into one's expectations and planning on an unconscious level (see Chapter 6). This incursion of the partner's needs occurs in each instance before a fantasy of need fulfillment emerges into the lover's consciousness. The ability to achieve the latter state of relatedness does not arise out of thin air. It is the product of a drawing together of cognitive functions that mature and develop in concert during the transition from latency to adolescence. Many of these functions are the direct precedents of the ego functions of latency. Others are the products of transmutations of latency ego functions. The transmutations take place under the influence of the increasing object orientation of the ways in which early adolescents view and organize their perceptions of the world. The transition into early adolescence is accompanied by maturational changes that have manifold influence on later life.

The transition from latency to adolescence is congruent with maturational changes in the personality structures that created latency.

The transition to early adolescence is accompanied by the following maturational and developmental changes: (1) cognitive (i.e., evocative to communicative symbols and speech), (2) physiological (i.e., the development of orgastic potential), and (3) psychological (i.e., ludic demise, the loss of the power of play symbols to discharge drives).

These maturational changes influence:

1. the development of object relations;
2. the overtness of private masturbatory activity;
3. the experiencing of new and uncomfortable affects;
4. relationships with opposite sex peers;
5. initiation of the march-of-adolescent dating patterns;
6. adjustment to the burgeoning of the sexual drive coupled with the loss of latency-age defenses;
7. intensification of narcissistic vulnerability and responsive grandiosity;
8. new exposure to uncomfortable affects, with the effective loss of the ability to control affects, that occurs with the reorganization of the structure of latency to serve the task of future planning at this age;
9. new directions in symbol usage (ludic demise and the appearance of communicative speech, tertiary elaboration, and emphasis on the communicative pole in symbol formation), which—when internalized through their incorporation into the needs of the observing object in the mind's eye—contributes to social consciousness and identification and forms the cognitive basis for the ability to fall in love.

Early Adolescent Cognitive Growth

There has been a great deal written about cognitive growth in adolescence. Few studies touch on the maturation of the cognition involved in the capacity to fall in love. The usual orientation, that of Piaget (1945), has primarily been toward an understanding of the interface between the mind and the world of the observable. That which can be measured, perceived, verified, transmitted, and repeated becomes the primary topic of concern for those who study the science of cognition. Cognition is then "assumed to include perceiving, remembering, judging, informing, exchanging, and understanding the 'psychology' of others" (p. 321). The formal mechanisms involved in the activity that is studied are devoted almost exclusively to the interpretation of the environment as a result of "circular interchanges between the nervous system and the social milieu" (p. 322). Such approaches are of great value in the understanding of the learning process and of the comprehension of those areas of socialization having to do with the influences of society on the child. They fall short in explaining love and other affect-weighted areas of interest to the psychotherapist. They do not take into account the drives, the inner strivings, and the inner-oriented cognitive apparatus that is developed in early adolescence. These process a wider net of circular interchanges, including the dynamic links between the perceptual and the processing apparatus of the nervous system, the social milieu, and the derivatives of the drive-dominated unique inner life of man (e.g., the derivatives of the id).

In keeping with this assertion, areas of study involving the organization of fantasy must be pursued if we are to understand the growth of the child's cognition in early adolescence and the pathological possibilities which are pendent to it.

Early Adolescence and Daydreaming

Somewhere in the study of the development of adolescent cognition we must make a place for daydreams. A study of the adjustment of the ego to the environment and the environment to the ego is not enough if we wish to speak of falling in love. We must find our way to a deeper understanding until we discover how an adolescent tunes his ego to his id and inner world, while responding to the lusts of peers who clamor at the gates of nubility.

A theory of cognition should encompass an understanding of the developing child's capacity to interpret the interaction between his inner and outer world and should organize and apply this understanding in psychotherapeutic situations. Included in the skills to be studied is the ability to transmute needs into action in three areas of relationship. These are communication, discharge-oriented object relations, and "ties that bind."

The emotional life of the adolescent is most often described in terms of the content of his fantasies and the demands of society and peers. As a result, it is thought that these factors alone form the outer boundaries of the terrain. For the child therapist, a more complete picture can be provided if we include, among the areas of concern, a description of the maturation of cognitive structures, whose origins are to be found in preexisting structures first arising in latency. Once that is done, it should be possible to study the development of techniques that serve as bridges to the outside world, across which drives can be expressed.

Part I deals with phenomena in the borderland between latency and adolescence. Starting in late latency–early adolescence, with its emphasis on narcissism, it follows the development of the child into adolescence proper and emphasizes the adjustment of newly acquired cognitive skills and object relatedness to the demands of the world.

Chapter 1 deals with the precursors of adolescence. Here we note changes in late latency that are responses to three factors:

1. Psychological/emotional—This includes: the return of pre-latency fantasy content to overt representation in those instances in which fantasy content has not been mastered and resolved by the structure of latency; ludic demise, which is the decline in the ability to use playthings as symbols through which drives can be discharged; decline of the structure of latency; and the shift from dependence on the reality one can feel to dependence on the reality one can touch.
2. Puberty—This includes the physical changes of youth, the psychological impact of menarche, and the impact of the first ejaculation.
3. Social and parental pressure towards social behavior with appropriate sexual partners, including dating and parental encouragement of sexually differentiated social behavior.

Chapter 2 deals with narcissism and reactive omnipotence. The origin of early adolescent narcissism is to be found in residua of narcissistically cathected latency fantasy and self-directed attention spurred by pubertal changes in the body. Reactive omnipotence is a response to breaches in the vulnerable walls of adolescent narcissism. The mobilization of feelings of omnipotence salves injured narcissism. The passing of reactive omnipotence is essential if maturity is to be reached.

Chapter 3 introduces the shifting symbolic forms of late latency-early adolescence. The symbolic forms most important in latency are evocative mode symbols. The forms that are most important in adolescence are communicative mode symbols. These are the symbols involved in aesthetics, creativity, future planning, and pursuing love objects. A shift to the more mature symbolic form is an indicator of emotional health. The developmental transition from the evocative type of symbol to the communicative type of symbol is a central component in the transition from latency to adolescence. The shift to the communicative mode with emphasis on the needs of objects in reality can be examined by studying the origins of communicative speech. Communicative speech is verbalization tuned to the needs of the listener for empathy, clarity, and completeness on the part of the speaker. The beginnings of tertiary elaboration—which is verbalization dominated by a knowledge of the background, point of view, and philosophy of the listener—is also a source of insight into the communicative mode.

Chapter 4 emphasizes anorexia nervosa. The occurrence of anorectic symptoms during the period of emergence from latency is a common event. Anorexia can be seen as an attempt to reverse maturation through a return to the cognition, reality testing, and the configuration of the body in latency. Latency skills that make it possible to live life without surrendering to reality and the undemanding nature of the latency-age body configuration make regression to the latency state a sanctuary from adolescent turmoil. Hypercathexis of fantasy, as in latency and return to the latency-age body configuration, provides a potential agenda of responses that rivals asceticism and withdrawal as techniques for dealing with increased sexual and aggressive drives during puberty.

Part II deals with sexuality and falling in love. It traces the maturation of sexual potential through masturbation, object seeking, and a study of the response of the object world.

Chapter 5 describes adolescent sexuality with emphasis on masturbation. It notes that sexuality undergoes maturation and development during early adolescence and prepares the child for the requirements of adult life. In the successful adolescent, sexual energies shift from pleasurable discharge, concentered all in self, through outlets using fantasy channels, to the use of genital organs specifically developed for the discharge of the drive. Biological maturation readies the genital organs. Culture and cognitive maturity define the limits and effectiveness of their use. Success is indicated by the extent to which a loved object is found and the degree to which fulfillment of the needs of the self and its drives also satisfy the needs of the object.

In the sexual sphere, the work of adolescence consists of: (1) the undoing of latency constraints; (2) disengagement from latency fantasy activity as an organ for sexual discharge; and (3) the integration of thought, action, drive, and object into an acceptable pattern for discharge using a new primary organ. One of the primary steps in this process is the rapprochement of sexual fantasy and genital masturbation so that both occur in concert.

The function of masturbation in adolescence is twofold. First, it is a technique for the discharge of sexual tension. Second, masturbation plays a vital role in providing outlet for fantasy and an arena in which an individual can work through and get acquainted with sexual feelings prior to essaying sexual experience with real objects.

Chapter 6 deals with the maturation of internal cognitive structures during the transition from latency to adolescence. Use of the communicative symbolizing function and strengthened object relations combine to influence utilization of object-oriented fantasy content to produce a bridge to the object world.

Internal changes in the strength of drives and in cognition produce a supporting pontic on one side of the bridge. To stretch a span to reality from the pontic requires the dynamic influence of three processes that make it possible to engage the loved one in the real world. These parts of the bridge to the object world consist of masturbation, projection of reassuring images, and maturation of the observing object of the mind's eye.

Masturbation here serves as a means of mastering intense affect and providing a stage for trial action. There is an aspect of masturbation that adds a plank to the bridge to the object world. The realignment of masturbatory fantasy and the act of masturbation that occurs during late latency–early adolescence serves an important purpose. The maturing organism learns to test, experience, bear, and finally enjoy the welling sensations of orgasm before he is called upon to experience them after having established a relationship with an object in reality. The content of the masturbation fantasies in turn provides patterns for the life search for a partner.

Projection of reassuring images is a part of the late latency–early adolescent cognitive shift toward the communicative mode. In early adolescence, projection becomes a useful mechanism serving socialization, altruism, and the ability to fall in love. Adolescents dare to face a world populated by reassuring fantasy projections. When they identify with new objects contacted in this way, the characteristics of the objects become internalized. This process of projection–reinternalization contributes to the contents of character and of the superego.

Failure during late latency–early adolescence to achieve such a communicative mode for projection produces grandiose states and paranoia.

Through *maturation of the observing object in the mind's eye*, when communicative symbols, communicative speech, and tertiary elaboration are aimed at pleasing an observing object in the mind's eye that represents a loved one, there will be produced fantasies and planning that take into account the needs of the loved person on a preconscious level. Thus, one's thoughts and actions are shaped by an inner awareness of the loved one's needs. This is the state of being in love.

Chapter 7 describes the process through which the object world responds. The influence of the demands of peers and society on the utilization of the communicative and drive structures that mature in early adolescence is discussed. The object world's response has a strong influence on the final shape of the personality. It is the source of the reality influences that put their stamp on the ultimate form. From the standpoint of late latency–early adolescence, the interactions of drives, talents, and needs—which make up the adolescent thrust—and the responses of the object world follow a predictable pattern to end in an acceptable product. Disorders in this unfolding are a form of psychopathology distinct to this age period. They are quite apart from the formal emotional disorders such as psychoses, neuroses, and adult character disorders. Transient homosexuality during early adolescence is discussed in this chapter.

In the third part of the book, clinical aspects of psychotherapy take center stage. The first three chapters in Part III are devoted to the clinical aspects of the process of psychotherapy in adolescence.

Chapter 8 presents assessment of this age group. In assessing the late latency–early adolescent child, there is focus on areas different than those commonly dealt with when assessing the mental health of younger children or adults. Early adolescent development is not marked by the expected homogeneity of development of the latency-age child or the stability of adulthood. Early adolescents move toward maturity through a multitude of disparate paths. Any one of these could lead to a healthy adult adjustment or chaos. At times, even an unruffled early adolescence can be a sign of a rigorous defense against progress in drive expression, pleasing parents while leaving the child unprepared to deal with peer sexual partners in late adolescence and adulthood. Subtle indicators such as persistent omnipotence and a history of accidents of fate, such as the setting of initial sexual experiences, can have more importance in determining the developmental outcome of a child than superficially chaotic patterns of adjustment that may be short-lived but overwhelming at the time of a clinical interview.

Chapter 9 discusses therapeutic strategies in late latency through early adolescence. The late latency child's therapy is based on play therapy, the use of toys, and talking. The adolescent psychotherapy patient differs from the late latency-age patient by dint of the fact that ludic symbols play no important part in the associations of the early adolescent. This maturational step makes play therapy inappropriate for the adolescent-age group. Talk and fantasy dominate their lives and therapy.

In psychotherapy, the difference between the early adolescent and the older adolescent is more subtle. The cognitively mature adolescent who willingly seeks therapy, who is verbal and psychologically minded, is likely to benefit from the free-association based interpretive process that works well in the form of psychoanalytically oriented psychotherapy for adults. Unfortunately, few early adolescents fit into this category. The average adolescent associates to more limited topics in therapy, such as personal relationships with real objects, incomplete separation from parents (removal), and narcissistic interpretations of close relationships. The latter are often colored by the inner fantasy life of the child.

For the most part, late latency–early adolescent patients require that the psychotherapeutic strategy applied to them be adjusted to take into account the characteristics of the early adolescent life stage. There is a distinct phase of transition between the ego structure of latency and the adultiform ego organizations of adolescence. There are transitional characteristics which require special handling. These include removal, thought disorders, omnipotence, the involvement of parents, socially defined immaturities (e.g., lack of comprehension of the role of educated professionals in providing expert help in areas of need), and the persistence of evocative polarities in symbolic usages. The latter is of special concern since it limits free association. Such impairments of the therapeutic usages of free association are dealt with separately in Chapter 10. The latter half of this chapter is devoted to techniques and strategies, which are presented for the use of beginning child therapists. Covered are the basic theory of psychotherapy, problems unique to the early adolescence, and the presistant use of evocative polarities which interfere with communication during treatment.

Chapter 10 emphasizes adolescent masochism. It contains information on the effect of the maturation of the use of symbols and language on the *uses and abuses of free association*. This chapter deals with psychotherapeutic aspects of masochistic fantasies and their derivatives during adolescence. These derivatives consist of masochistic bragadoccio, masochistic perversions, adolescent shyness, aspects of prepubescent schizophrenia, incipient masochistic character traits, and the misuse of free association during psychoanalytically oriented psychotherapy sessions. In children with these conditions, there is an inability to turn attention cathexes from memory and fantasy. This detracts from the child's ability to invest reality with the right to call the tune. Repetitive preoccupation with the presentation to the therapist of the "joy" of suffering results in a stagnation in associations. Free association and the new insights it produces are blocked when the child replaces therapeutic goals by enlisting the therapist as a witness to pain bravely borne rather than fulfilling his role as a helper. These sources of vulnerability to masochism in adolescence must be pursued, understood, and analyzed, if progress is to be made in psychotherapy.

Chapter 11 is an epilogue that has been added to trace the influence of developmental impairments of late latency–early adolescence on later adolescence and adult life. The psychotherapy of late latency–early adolescence requires a component consisting of alertness on the part of the therapist to the need of the patient to prepare in advance for the tasks and troubles of the transition period between late adolescence and adulthood. The reflective self awareness of the late latency–early adolescent child is turned toward the impact of the resolution of early adolescent problems on the tasks and troubles involved in mastering adult sexuality, resolving one's identity, choosing a career, marriage, and parenthood. This final chapter contains a description of these late adolescent tasks and troubles from the point of view of a younger person gazing ageward.

Part I
The Adolescent Brink

Chapter 1

The Precursors of Adolescence

This chapter and the six that follow will be devoted to the delineation of the transitional phenomena of late latency–early adolescence and the psychotherapeutic strategies involved in this period. All too often, child psychotherapists design their theories and organize their therapeutic work around latency and adolescence, each in isolation. As a result, the period of the transition between latency and adolescence tends to lose in importance. The developmental phenomena of the transition, which have marked implications for adolescent and adult functioning, are deemphasized in theory and clinical practice. The transitions of the adolescent brink are cognitive (e.g., evocative to communicative symbols and speech); physiological (e.g., the appearance of orgastic potential), and psychological (e.g., ludic demise). They are subject to pathological turnings and influences. These phenomena are usually considered to be automatically resolved when maturation and social influence move the attention of all concerned to other problems. Untended and unchanged, the transitions, when they have taken a wayward turn, either fail to progress, succumb to inhibitions, or are mastered through harmful mythologies that set at ease minds deserving of better explanations and directions. This can result in symptoms and character traits in later life which, like fossil traces, carry over remnants of past problems.

Emotional maturity in adolescence is not turned on like a light bulb, but is the result of a long process of development with origins in late latency. For some of the time, it is accompanied by striking physical maturation. There is, of course, a tendency to link the two phenomena as though they were facets of a single phenomenon. This has led to the tendency to view adolescence—the transition phase between the stable ego structure of latency and the stable ego structure of adulthood—as a stable process comparable to latency and adulthood and limited in time to the period of physical growth and undifferentiated from it.

Actually, adolescence is neither. It is more a period of transiency than of stability. Beginning with the late-latency time period, a multitude of ego structures are tried, developed, and discarded. Physical and emotional maturation should be differentiated.

To effect this, physical maturation would best be called *youth*, that is, the period between the onset of physical sexual maturation (ages 11 to 13) and the attainment of full adult growth (ages 17 to 19). As in the case of a number of other arbitrary clinical terms, the time period described would deal only with an easily observed superficial aspect of the growth phenomenon (i.e., the growth spurt and the development of primary and secondary sexual characteristics).

Emotional maturation would best be called *adolescence*. If we follow this categorization, we shall find that some of the phenomena usually considered to be part of adolescence begin before the time period during which physical growth occurs. A description of these follows.

The Shift from Latency to Adolescence

The first stages of emotional growth that mark the beginning of the move away from the ego organization of latency are manifested in a change of cognition. There is a shift from self-cathexes and intuition to an intensified cathexis of the object world and reality testing. Foremost among the mental elements involved is the shifting, into the service of object ties and reality testing, of certain symbolic forms. These include the shift of the waking arena for the expression of fantasy away from latency symbols and toward object ties patterned after the prelatency relationships with parents as objects of fantasy activity; the shift in emphasis from evocative to communicative symbols, and the appearance of communicative speech and of tertiary elaboration. The acquisition of these cognitive skills paves the way for the acquisition of the ability to fall in love. They make it possible to include the needs of the loved one in the future planning of the lover on the level of preconscious planning.

In addition to the development of the shifting symbolic forms of late latency–early adolescence, there are maturational and social pressures that give rise to the developmental state of adolescence. Of necessity, the occurrence of these factors is early (from age 8 to age 14). The three primary factors which initiate and shape the move from latency to adolescence are

1. Psychological/emotional, characterized by the return of overt prelatency fantasy activity; ludic demise; decline of the structure of latency, and the shift from dependence on the reality one can feel to dependence on the reality one can touch
2. Puberty, the physical changes of youth and the psychological impact of menarche or the first ejaculation.
3. Social and parental pressure toward social behavior with appropriate sexual partners, including dating; parental encouragement of sexually differentiated social behavior (e.g., "makeout" parties, training bras)

The Return of Prelatency Fantasy Activity

One of the major problems to be worked through in adolescence is the resolution of fixations to oedipal and preoedipal fantasy structures. These guide, even lock, the drives into patterns of discharge that become characteristic for a given individual. As a result of the persistence of these patterns, adults repeat painful relationships derived from these fantasies.

Children are thought to "enter latency" as a result of the repression of oedipal wishes. This repression is produced through involvement of the system consciousness with earlier (e.g., anal phase) drive manifestations which had been recathected through regression. In "entering adolescence," the child must reconfront, with symbols drawn from reality, that which was only temporarily resolved through fantasy symbols during the latency years.

The nature of symbols available to the child changes during the transition from midlatency to early adolescence. Psychoanalytic symbols (those with repression of the link between that which represents and that which is represented) dominate fantasy play and dreams in midlatency. Small manipulatable replicas (called ludic symbols—see Piaget 1945), such as toys, dolls, and two-dimensional images, can be used as symbolic representations in latency play to manifest latent fantasy content. In the same context, verbal images are used in daydreams. During sleeping dreams, visual components dominate. In both nighttime dreams and daydreams, such symbolic representations continue to be used life-long. The use of ludic symbols in play wanes from middle to late latency. This is the ludic demise. As a result, fantasy becomes less effective as a latency defense, and play therapy begins to lose "play," which is the very source of its name and perhaps its primary means of communication with the secret and unconscious world of the child. However, though play ends, fantasy continues. By early adolescence, reality objects are often recruited to serve as symbols. Through this step a door is opened, either to living a fantasy-dominated life or to establishing a bridge to the object world and perfecting future planning. In the transitional phase between midlatency and early adolescence, attempts to resolve problems through autoplastic fantasy activity continue even after ludic demise has begun. During this *phase* of transition, fantasies are less masked and representations become more explicit. Masochism becomes represented by fighting or physically hurting oneself. Bisexual fantasies in boys are manifested, for example, by effeminacy or wearing items of the mother's clothes; or are defended against, for example, by lifting weights to ensure a manly physique. Scoptophilic fantasies are lived out through illustrated sexual magazines and Peeping Tomism. Fixation at this level results in such characteristics as residual effeminacy, transvestitism, and scoptophilia.

In early adolescence the search for symbols reaches into the object world. Thinly veiled expressions of oedipal wishes become scenarios for which there are recruited, from family members and close peers, the reality object symbols used to play out the fantasies. At this point, sustained fantasies involving the parents as objects appear. The boy fantasizes that his mother or an older woman will help him with his sexual urges. The girl feels warm with father, or manifests fears of burglars attacking her, from whom father will save her. Intense jealousy of father and fear of besting him, or concern that he will strike one or do injury, become directly manifest in boys; children of fathers who were excellent in school dare not exhibit academic proficiency. The core fantasies that lie in the unconscious of these individuals are the oedipal fantasies that dominated in the 4- and 5-year-old. If the child fails to resolve, decathect, or modify these core fantasies, he may well react to new objects as though they were the old ones and thus replace reality with his own fantasies. These steps in the move toward restoring prelatency fantasy style begin at about age 8. It occurs before the vast increase in drive-mobilizing sexual hormones that occurs at puberty. Therefore, it cannot be attributed to hormonal changes alone.

Prelatency fantasy style is characterized by a relatively direct representation of the core fantasy. Sexual role-oriented wishes are expressed with direct representation of the parent as the object (e.g., "when I grow up I'll marry daddy"). During prelatency, ludic symbols which are close simulations of reality dominate. However, in dealing with stress, distorted representations are available for the formation of manifest symbols from as early as 26 months of age. The use of distorted representations takes the forefront during latency. The fantasy activity of latency is characterized by marked displacement and symbolization, so that vast distances exist between the latent and manifest contents (unconscious and conscious) of the fantasy. The parent becomes a king in a distant land or an amorphous monster. Sexuality is reversed and becomes hostility. The core fantasy is distorted by the structure of latency; the fantasy style of early adolescence expresses the fantasy more directly through the use of real objects to live out the fantasy.

After the phase of transition described, early adolescent fantasy style develops to the point of more nearly resembling the fantasy style of prelatency than any other psychological process. The two fantasy styles can be differentiated on the basis of the presence or absence of narcissistic emphases in the child's conceptualization and use of symbols. For the most part, *prelatency fantasy style* emphasizes the use of symbols for the evocation of inner needs and feeling states. This use of the evocative polarity is continued in latency with its markedly distorted manifest symbols. *Adolescent fantasy style* and its mature cognate, future planning, shows a return to the reality representations of prelatency, with emphasis on the use of symbols in their communicative and adaptive polarity. Psychotherapy during adolescence requires the encouragement of the use of symbols in their communicative context. Ludic demise is accompanied by a shift in emphasis in the thought processes of the child from the intuitive, magical, symbolic mode of thinking to the more reality-oriented use of interpretations associated with abstract conceptual memory organization. In going from play therapy to insight therapy, the psychotherapeutically effective maneuver used goes from catharsis through play to insight through verbalization.

"Masters of the Universe" or "Superman" can serve to block insight and minimize discharge through catharsis in play therapy by providing ready-made fantasy figures and stories that shoulder away from center stage the private symbols that a child might have used for evocation and mastery. Such contaminations of play therapy are called *cultural capture*. The therapist should try to get the child to substitute his own symbols. Once the child has gained a firm footing on the far side of ludic demise, the same popular culture figures can serve as useful passive symbols, such as those found in mature sublimation through the enjoyment of the creations of others. These symbols and the tales in which they dwell may become the basis of discussions that reveal the child's interests and complexes.

Once children have changed their symbols from toys in the evocative mode to communicative reality symbols, one runs the risk of a reinforcement of intuitive and magical modes of thought if the use of psychoanalytic symbols in a play context is encouraged. Adolescents usually reject play as childish and resist such activities, thus minimizing the danger of a regression induced by the therapist. The most common situation in which there occurs this sort of regressing activity on the part of the child therapist can be seen at those times when a formerly excellent playchild who has found communicative speech and self-reflective awareness is confronted by material that requires exclusion from consciousness. Under these circumstances, the child patient may become silent as a defense. The therapist, in an attempt to reinstate a therapeutic environment, encourages the child to play. This encourages regression and should be avoided.

During the transition from latency to adolescence, unprovoked swings between play and communicative speech may occur. These are accompanied by more magical and intuitive thinking when play symbols are dominant. At such times the therapist is forced to switch his cognitive orientation to coincide with the child's state of cognitive regression.

All symbols at all stages of development have the potential to serve in both evocative and communicative roles. In the analysis of any individual symbol, an estimate of the degree of emphasis on the evocative or communicative pole is appropriate. Such analysis can be applied to all symbols at all ages and stages. The development of ludic demise is supported by the maturational shift to communicative symbols.

In prelatency, the child is buoyed by a sense of omnipotence; there is a sense of being indestructible. No wonder the child may say *anything*, in spite of the capacity, available since 26 months of age, to use masking psychoanalytic symbols. Contrariwise, the age of latency is haunted by a sense of humiliated smallness. It is ushered in with the introduction of castration fear, fear of loss of love, and the incest barrier. Fantasies that involve objects (parents) in sexual and aggressive contexts become unbearable. The poor reality testing and cognitive function of the child permit the use of repression, fragmentation, displacement, symbol formation, and synthesis of symbols into story patterns. Through the use of these mechanisms, disguised fantasies replace real-life confrontations. The drives are discharged without danger to loved ones. Situations that relate to or stir up the core fantasies (pregenital, oedipal, and genital) are resolved by the formation of seemingly unrelated conscious fantasies. The configuration of ego functions that produces this activity is an important part of the ego structure of latency. The formation of benign fantasy in this context provides a buffer to permit the continuation of the total structure of latency.

Loss of latency-age fantasy defenses leaves the child exposed. Failure or default of these mechanisms results in a breakdown of the structure of latency as a means of mastering current problems and forces direct confrontations with the parent and reality. This is the paradigm for the parent–child confrontations of adolescence, when maturational improvement in reality testing and cognition (improved reality testing, ludic demise, increased drive, social pressures, improved abstraction ability, and reinforcement of object influences through sexual maturation) permanently deprives the child of the use of fantasy as the sole means for solving problems.

Between ages 7½ and 8, there is a marked improvement in cognitive function, with operational use of the capacity to comprehend cause-and-effect relationships between objects that are concretely present. The magical power of words can no longer be used to cause changes in relationships between real things and between real people. Throwing water does not cause rain and the killing of a distant king wreaks no vengeance on a father in the here and now. The structure of latency fails in its function, and it crumbles. Reality becomes more and more the obligate outlet for the discharge of the drives—the stage is set for the turmoil of adolescence. Now the demands of the world and of the drives expressed in prelatency fantasies must be faced and resolved.

Puberty

Puberty begins between 11 and 14 years of age. With puberty, youth begins. *Puberty* is defined as the time of the onset of the external physical development of the adult biological sexual apparatus. Then there begin the development of secondary sexual characteristics, enlargement of the primary sexual apparatus, and the development of pubic, axillary, and body hair and, in boys, the beard. These and other bodily changes are the results of a marked increase in the amount of sexual hormone produced by endocrine glands. Such body changes accelerate and intensify the process of parental and social encouragement of dating and parties with emphasis on kissing and eroticism. In addition to producing the physical changes of puberty, the increased production of hormones stimulates the sexual drives. Stimulation of sexual or aggressive drive is one of the factors that can be implicated in breakdowns and the eventual destruction of the already crumbling structure of latency.

Puberty provides dramatic experiences for the child. The youngster is supplied with an internal mental awareness of bodily changes that organize the psychic elements of the long-developing adult emotional sexual apparatus. Newly developed body organ functions guide the attention and the fantasy with planning of the child in an outward and object-oriented direction.

The opposite of self-serving omnipotence is the object-oriented altruism required to care for and raise a child. The opposite of narcissism is the ability to sacrifice one's energies and time in the service of reproducing and sustaining the human race. The child's harbinger of the taxes to be paid for the privilege of having and using life is contained in the experiential impact that accompanies the first menstrual period (menarche) or the first ejaculation.

Menarche. Three aspects are basic to the impact of menarche: (1) There is the period of expectation of menarche and its effect on the psychology of the late latency–early adolescent. (2) There is the effect of menarche itself, with its realistic statement of womanhood, which identifies the child with adult sexual potentials and which either squelches or intensifies conflict in relation to bisexual body image fantasies. (3) There is the influence of menarche on the reactions of others in the child's environment. They waken to her as a sexual object. She in turn acquires a cognate physical resource that makes adult sexuality and sexual communication possible on a nonsymbolic organ level. Object relations are thus reinforced.

During the period of expectation of menarche, which starts as soon as the girl first hears about and develops a concept of menstruation, there lies in wait in a corner of each girl's mind, ready to spring to the center of attention, a preoccupation with menstruation. There may be hidden fantasies that somewhere within oneself there is a bit of a boy, perhaps even a penis, ready to grow. These are bisexual fantasies left over from the confusions of the prelatency period. Boys have corresponding fantasies.

This upsurge of pregenital bisexual conflicts and fantasies produces periods of identity diffusion and emotional disequilibrium in the girl. This period of expectation has been extensively studied by Blos (1962), Deutsch (1944), Fenichel (1945), A. Freud (1936), Hart and

Sarnoff (1971), and Kestenberg (1961, 1967). All consider the bisexual phase of late latency–early adolescence to be a normal reaction to the expectation of menarche. The illusory penis is seen as a psychic reality maintained in order to protect the little girl against narcissistic depletion. It is worthwhile for the therapist to be alert to such conflicts when working with premenarchical girls.

Menarche is anticipated by children in terms of fantasies experienced in earlier years. Thus, there is fear of oral deprivation derived from the thought that once one reaches womanhood, one is one step closer to being on one's own. There are feelings of revulsion at the thought of messiness, or even fear that the process cannot be controlled. This mobilizes defenses in the direction of controlling everyone in the immediate environment as a way of working through the passivity involved in the expectation of an uncontrolled flow of blood. Concern with bodily changes and catastrophic responses to slight bodily injury are a signal to the child therapist of a preoccupation in the patient with an event that in both fantasy and reality nullifies any thought of being a boy.

Almost universally puberty is a time of inner turmoil as a result of a combination of the psychological factors just described and internal sensations derived from the bodily changes of puberty. Kestenberg (1961) has described the ebb and flow of these sensations as a result of the increasing flow of hormones that initiates the bodily changes that presage the onset of menarche. Girls can become so preoccupied with the nipping-in of the waist, which is one of the first signs of puberty, that they develop obsessional symptoms and refuse to go to school. Confusion of body image occurring at this time can interfere with the child's capacity for abstract thinking, resulting in impaired progress in mathematics and difficulties in spatial relations and chart and map reading. Kestenberg (1961) recognized that confusion of body image and sexual identification produce vague and clouded thought processes in conflict areas and beyond. It is imperative that psychotherapists work through these areas with youngsters who present with this symptomatology. Social pressures may intensify the problems (Kestenberg 1967), sometimes evoking relatively dormant bisexual fantasies. Educational activities such as sex education movies may mobilize bisexual fantasies. For example, a child dreamed that she grew a faucet to control her menstruation, with the association that the faucet in the dream looked like a penis, after seeing a sex education film that in her case raised more questions than it answered.

Other factors involved in stirring up conflicts around pregenital bisexual fantasies in the premenarchic child are parental conversations and the maturation of friends. The influx of bisexual fantasies stirred by these inputs concentrates the fantasy life of the individual around sexuality. Kestenberg (1961) has viewed this circumstance from the potentially positive aspect that for some children, this organization of fantasy provides an opportunity to work through and even resolve earlier conflicts. These results might otherwise not have been reached.

With the first menstruation an unambiguous reality event intrudes on the confusion to define the sexual role and identity. Kestenberg (1961, 1967) and Blos (1962) describe the first menstruation as the necessary organizer which, for the young girl, serves to crystallize and define body boundaries. To the extent that there has been confusion about identity and body image, this clarification is paralleled by a consolidation of the feminine role and clearer thinking. Likewise, to the degree that the girl finds a feminine role unacceptable, the menarche, with its finality of meaning, intensifies and organizes fantasies related to feelings of castration and impaired self-esteem. These fantasy systems are in turn responded to by a panoply of defenses producing disparate symptomatology.

Deutsch (1944) described the first menstruation as traumatic, regardless of prior instruction. Kestenberg (1961) emphasized its positive aspects in contributing to the acceptance of femininity. P. Blos (1962), in contrasting the preadolescent and adolescent girl, sees vagueness and ambiguity giving way to clarity of perception following menarche. The complexities of the reproductive apparatus of the female, unlike those of the male, are hidden within the body. The prepubertal girl is told that there is something within her which is as "fancy" as that which is on the outside of the boy. The nondemonstrable nature of the female internal sexual apparatus permits the child much leeway in fantasy; the illusory penis fantasy is a case in point. Menstruation provides a concrete proof of the existence of a complex system of organs deep in the body. Hart and Sarnoff (1971) described children who bemoaned their inability to define their body image—to know what was inside. The first menstruation provided proof of femininity. It was most striking that following menarche, there was a change in their acceptance of themselves as feminine, and they emerged with a better-defined body image. Thinking was clearer; they dealt more directly with genital conflicts, oedipal strivings, and their own realistic future roles as wives and mothers.

Menarche does not always bring with it the resolution of conflicts. In those who cannot accept a setting aside of bisexual fantasies, the first menstruation intensifies the problem. This aspect of the impact of the menarche relates to childhood experiences, feminine identifications, and to the mother's acceptance of the girl's role as a woman. Kestenberg (1961) described a direct correlation between emotional disturbance and proneness to view menarche as a threat. The genital conflict and castration complex come to the fore and stir up intense emotions: anger, depression, feelings of inferiority, and guilt over increased masturbatory urges. If the cloacal theory is strongly cathected, then the child must deal with feelings of shame and disgust (Deutsch 1944). She must, furthermore, resolve guilt mobilized by increased aggressive and sexual drives.

Kestenberg (1961) emphasized the role of menstruation in enabling the girl to differentiate fantasy from reality. Feminine tendencies will be mobilized and, it is hoped, will master the genital trauma. There is intensification of sexual excitement, with fantasies of defloration and rape. Wishes and fears related to pregnancy and childbirth appear. Many menstrual cycles occur before fuller "reintegration" (Kestenberg 1967) can be achieved as the young adolescent emerges from the disequilibrium and diffusion of prepuberty.

Menarche has clear impact on the people around the child, producing a gamut of reactions both personal and ritualized. Even before menstruation begins, attitudes of the parents shape the nature of what will be told to the child.

Deutsch (1944) reported frequent neglect on the part of mothers in giving instruction prior to menstruation, although other aspects of reproduction were dealt with. This is an additional indication of how emotionally charged the subject is. It is not unusual for fathers to feel estranged from their daughters during the time of menarche (or to show a desire, as one man described it, to "take her out for the evening on a date"). Often the reactions of people around the child add to her difficulties. People in the immediate surroundings respond with characteristic behavior which reflects not only their concern for the child, but for themselves. These self-oriented responses are not easily recognized.

Reports concerning the behavior of people in less sophisticated times, when magic predominated over intellect and logic as we know them, make unconscious motives for behavior in response to menarche clearly manifest (Frazer 1922). In general, in primitive cultures, menstruating women were treated as though they were dangerous. They were not permitted to touch growing things, and that which they had touched had to be discarded. They were secluded, and considered unclean. In addition to these responses to menses (fear, enforced seclusion, feeling of uncleanliness), menarche was responded to at various times and places with a number of irrational demands upon the child, such as suspension aloft, exclusion from contact with sun, sky, and earth, and prohibition against scratching herself.

Frazer (1922) believed that "the object of secluding women at menstruation is to neutralize the dangerous influences which are supposed to emanate from them at such times. . . . The danger is believed to be especially great at the first menstruation. To repress this force within the limits necessary for the safety of all concerned is the object of the taboos in question" (p. 702). He noted a "deeply engrained dread which primitive man universally entertains of menstruous blood. He fears it at all times but especially on its first appearance; hence the restrictions under which women lie at their first menstruation are usually more stringent than those which they have to observe at any subsequent recurrence of the mysterious flow" (p. 698).

This is a useful but not necessarily sufficient explanation for the intense response to first menstruation among primitive peoples and their more culturally advanced counterparts. Ancient and modern myths, legends, and folk tales contain in transmuted form the customs of primitive man. From the contexts in which symbols of primitive menarche customs appear (Sarnoff 1976), we can conclude that fear of menarche derives from fear and uneasiness at the presence of attractiveness, sexuality, and reproductive potential in young girls, with their implications for incest. Isolating girls is like returning a cake to the oven or a negative to the developing tray until it is done. This is a forerunner in cultural evolution of the social attitudes that result in stilted sex education at puberty and a denial of the id and the unconscious, resulting in social planning and theories that disregard the drives. The message for the child therapist in this material lies in the warning to look to parental attitudes toward the sexuality of the child in situations of angry interchange and passivity problems between recently pubertal girls and their parents.

Menarche affects others in the child's environment; they are alerted to her debut as a sexual object. Conversely, in acquiring the organ resource needed for adult sexuality, the girl gains the potential for communication on a nonsymbolic organ level. Object relations are reinforced by menarche. Long-developing changes in the symbolizing function are organized to create the communicative symbolic structure of the adult emotional sexual apparatus. As a result, drive discharge is offered release in a reality context that exceeds evocative symbols in efficiency and productivity. The way is open for the participation in sexual discharge with real objects.

In addition to the organizing impact of menarche, there is an aggressive response in the girl, who may see the first menses as a manifestation of weakness, messiness, and loss of control. It is a phenomenon that stirs up castrated feelings (see S. Freud 1918). A part of adult reaction to menarche is in actuality a response to the confusion and anger that the child feels in approaching and experiencing menarche.

The First Ejaculation. For the boy, the first ejaculation is the herald of maturity comparable to menarche. Studies of primitive customs, the psychoanalytic literature, and books devoted to myths, symbols, and rituals reveal little in the way of interest in the topic. It appears that the only ones who care at all about it are pubescent boys. The phenomenon does not even have a name.

This state of affairs belies the true circumstance. Child therapists should be aware that the first ejaculation has an impact on the evolving personality. The end of a long developmental path is marked by the first ejaculation. The sexual drive no longer need seek symbolic expression. Erection, orgasm, and ejaculation provide the child with a means for articulating the drives with reality objects.

With the first ejaculation, the tendency to act on poorly displaced and symbolized fantasies diminishes. Exceptions to this are found in some highly narcissistic individuals, who develop perversions without partners; for example, transvestites and exhibitionists.

Erections have always been present, so they cannot be used by a pubescent youngster as a sign of sexual maturity and readiness for object-directed sexuality. The ability to ejaculate alone carries the import of a capacity to communicate, procreate, and involve oneself in reality. Of course, the ejaculation of which I speak cannot be silent or unrecognized for what it is. The influence of peers or parents must be felt in interpreting the potential in the issue to which reference is made.

The heightened narcissism of early male adolescence can in part be explained: it is the result of an inward turning of cathexes toward fantasy and symbols rooted in the pubertal increase in drive energies. Turning inward is forced by the absence of an available physical mechanism (ejaculation) for the outward expression of sexual drive towards objects. Latency-style fantasy play continues to be cathected and expressed through the primitive body–self symbols of late latency. With the onset of the first ejaculation, a discharge pathway involving reality becomes available. At that point, fantasy is opened to reality influences.

The actual act of the first ejaculation is not as important as the context in which it occurs. The context helps in organizing sexual identity more than does the phenomenon of ejaculation itself. Menarche comes as a surprise; its context is not the product of the action or the wish of the girl. Indeed, its onset cannot be blamed on her in any way. In contrast, the first ejaculation always occurs in a situation of sexual excitement and within a context that can become a source of pride or concern to the child involved. In a youngster whose prepubertal fantasy life was rich in bisexual and homosexual fantasy activity, the occurrence of the first ejaculation in a heterosexual context can be very supportive and positive. If the context of the first ejaculation was of a homosexual nature, the effect on the child can be devastating. His first contact with sexual reality confirms his fear that he is homosexual. This is made more meaningful if taken in the light of the observation of Coren (1967): "When a reality event occurs which mirrors the internal conflict of a child, specifically the repressed id impulse, the psychological trauma is very great, particularly to the reality testing apparatus, and necessitates a rapid shift in defense mechanisms which often fails" (p. 356). The fantasy at the time of the first ejaculation seems to be the clue to its impact. As Freud (1919) stated, ". . . in the main [guilt] is to be connected not with the act of masturbation but with the fantasy which . . . lies at its root" (p. 195). Jacobson (1964) has described this aspect of the first ejaculation: "The boy's first ejaculations commonly . . . evoke guilt conflicts of such intensity that frequently the pleasure of becoming a man is overshadowed or smothered by long-lasting fears of this step" (p. 102).

In summary, the first ejaculation, like the menarche, is an organizing experience that serves as an increased contact with reality and the object world. It is one of the maturational pressures that impels the individual toward a dissociation of masturbatory fantasy from masturbatory activities and an increased articulation of the drives with reality objects. Should the fantasies accompanying the first ejaculation be comfortable for the child—either because they themselves or sexuality is acceptable to him—the maturational step is taken in stride. In those with severe bisexual conflicts, a first ejaculation in a heterosexual context is a reassuring experience. As with the girl, it helps the boy to define his identity. If the child is anxious about bisexual fantasy, and the first ejaculation occurs in a homoerotic context, the child will experience an intensification of the disorganization and confusion that accompanied the bisexual conflicts of prepuberty. There is evidence that children who are conflicted about ejaculation, usually on the basis of severe castration anxiety, may fail to achieve a consistent shift from narcissistic, poorly symbolized sexual fantasies, associated with latency-style acting out of the fantasies, to articulation of drives with reality objects. These individuals, when in the state of regression that is associated with this inhibition, manifest perversions without partners.

Social and Parental Pressures

With the onset of adolescence, sometimes before, and certainly hurried by the presence of secondary sexual development, society or parents take a keen interest in encouraging their children to develop an interest in the opposite sex. In effect, the threats and barriers that impeded the expression of sexuality and forced the child to take on latency defenses, are now replaced with encouragement. It is important to note that parental and societal dictates, by their intrinsic nature, make objects acceptable as compared with the sexual inhibitions associated with objects during latency. Sexual interests in people outside the home are encouraged. Incest is still forbidden. Reality testing is effective in extirpating fantasy figures that had represented parents as objects for drive discharge. Parents and society point toward new and approved objects to take the place of the fantasy objects—peers of opposite gender.

New objects are provided. Unfortunately, though, no direction is given that would help prevent the adolescent from relating to the new object using old fantasies as models; and this constitutes one of the major problems of the period of adolescence. "Removal" (q.v.) is left incomplete. This is one of the major deterrents in the move toward sexual maturity.

The Transition to Adolescence

In studying the shift from latency to adolescence, we have dealt so far with the three forces that press toward adolescent levels of emotional maturity. We now turn to the cognitive changes that support the transition to a goal which in name is late adolescence, but is essentially the functional ability to fall in love.

As the child passes into late latency, more and more potential activities are permitted him. Masturbatory prohibition is lessened. The child is permitted to cross the street by himself. He is given some control over his own money. The superego's demands (ego ideal) begin to soften. The child turns toward real objects as the latency years draw to an end. The pressure of the sexual drives accompanying the approaching puberty adds additional stress.

During a period concurrent with late latency (the time from 9 to 12 years of age) there commences a maturation whose product is the cognitive organization of early adolescence. This maturation completes the organization of fantasy representations in which fantastic objects are replaced by realistic objects during fantasy formation. This is followed by a modification of the organization of the drive discharge mechanisms of the ego from seeking realistic objects in fantasy to seeking objects accurately perceived in reality.

The cognitive maturation of early latency (the second cognitive organizing period—see Sarnoff 1976), which culminates in late latency, prepares for a heightened awareness and exploration of reality. The cognitive maturation of late latency (the third cognitive organizing period), which prepares for early adolescence, emphasizes the utilization of reality for drive discharge. Finally, the cognitive maturation of late latency–early adolescence (the fourth cognitive organizing period) prepares for the establishment of a lasting bond with the object *who* in reality will be used for drive discharge. This is effected through the development of the cognitive skills required to fall in love (i.e., the development of the capacity to place the partner in a unique relationship, in which narcissism is replaced with the ability to take the needs of the significant other into account prior to the organization of a fantasy or future planning from its component parts on a preconscious level). An understanding of the components of this maturation is necessary for the child therapist in establishing psychotherapeutic strategies for dealing with problems in narcissism, immaturity, and object relations of patients in late latency–early adolescence (see p. 62).

The Third Cognitive Organizing Period of Latency

Changes in Intensity and Direction of Object Relatedness. Before the portion of adolescence that coincides with youth, there is a noticeable increase in drive energies above the levels experienced during the latency period. In males, erections become more frequent. Minor bodily changes portend the beginnings of maturity. Sexual fantasies become more intense, and more overt. Fantasy contents begin to relate to planning around the search for objects in reality to be used for the discharge of drives. In content, the earliest of these fantasies entail looking, seeing, and fulfilling one's curiosity about the form and appearance of the mature male and female. This curiosity relates to the parents and the future self of the child. Since parents are forbidden objects, the child must displace curiosity and, later, interest to photographs and peers. This results in an experience of separation from parental figures; it is an early form of removal.

In going from early to late latency, there was a shift from thoughts about fantasy objects to thoughts about reality objects. During late latency–early adolescence, the emphasis on reality objects becomes more intense. Eventually fantasy as object gives way to reality as object, a characteristic of adolescence.

Deaffectivization of Words. In the child who is developing normally, improvement of the apprehension of reality is contingent upon a shift in the emphasis of the cognition used in memory from affectomotor hallucinatory memory to a memory organization based on verbal conceptual elements. Words eventually come to serve as cryptic traces of affects which have succumbed to the "infantile amnesia." Early in this transition, words retain remnants of the affect they represent. This is a transitional step in the deaffectivization of words (Ferenczi 1911, pp. 139 and 145). When affect is removed from word representations of things which have been seen and remembered, greater neutrality and clarity can be brought to bear in solving problems related to the management of the things. Links to fantasy are lessened, and planning is carried out with a focus on the future and reality.

Deaffectivization of words proceeds through the latency period. The fantastic objects that populate early latency have more in common with primitive emotionally charged words than with affectively neutral words. With the onset of late latency, words with a less charged tone representing a neutral reality objects are introduced as fantasy objects. Use of essentially deaffected reality-based objects, with implied double meanings, when used as symbols, makes acceptable the discharge and planning fantasies of this period. It is made possible by repression of the links of these symbols used as fantasy elements with incestuous objects. Essentially fantasy can still be used for discharge if neutral (deaffectivized) words are used as objects or as representations of them.

Children Who Write Novels. Since seemingly neutral words and situations can be used for discharge, it is possible for the psychotherapist of childhood and early adolescence to use associations to books, movies, television, and reports of events in the lives of peers as media for the working through of unconscious fantasies and complexes. Psychic determinism controls the selection of topics. Interpretations, constructions, and reconstructions can be made from patients' associations, and these effectively lead to further associations if sufficient ego distance is maintained in framing the interpretation. Linked, but hidden, affects can be uncovered and used as a starting point for associations into the past ("When did you first feel this way?") and at times traced to their original causes.

A common clinical manifestation of the use of neutral (deaffected) words to represent highly charged complexes is the early adolescent writing of novels. Such topics as "the Girl who became a cowboy" and the spaceboy who overcame the forces of the overpowering and all-seeing "leader," which reflect adolescent concerns, are typical. The symbols and settings chosen are sufficiently removed that their valence for attracting affect is diminished while the armatural themes of the tales draw closer to latent fantasy content.

The child does not always tell the therapist of the work in progress. Usually, the information comes from a delighted mother who feels that "muse" is communicating with genius in her child's head. The child should be encouraged to remember the chapters in the session. Direct interpretation of the material is impossible; it can be treated as a dream or used as a source of data to sensitize the therapist to the complexes currently being dealt with by the child. Such novels are hardly ever finished. Parents should be forewarned of this possibility, lest they feel that this sign of progress be taken as a sign of regression in the therapy. The children leave their works when they have served their purpose, that is, when the door to reality opens permitting the discharge of drives through the recruitment of peers. These novels are a part of the contributions of imagination to life. Imagination based on latent fantasy with roots in early life experience forms a trial action containing the child's unique identity in confronting the object world. The use of the novel form is evidence of the child's awareness that, in the felicitous phrasing of Duncan (1968), "Art creates symbolic roles which we use as a dramatic rehearsal in the imagination of community roles we must play to sustain social order" (p. 222). One should not confuse the role of the novel in society with the role of the novel in the life of the early adolescent. Whereas art reflects the social order and guides group behavior, the child's novel is an experiment in the expression of personal fantasy. It is the task of the child and the therapist to replace the child's restructuring of the object world, carried out in the service of resolving old conflicts and imma-ture wishes, with reality-oriented future planning.

Children Who Use Words as Objects de Novo. One of the problems with the use of words shorn of past associations by repression of affects is the child's expectation that words have an existence of their own. This is frequently seen at 7 years of age, but in some cases may be seen in late latency–early adolescence. These children lie about misdeeds. They feel that their words are as good as the words of a witness against them. In the absence of direct knowledge by an adult accuser they feel immune. This is a manifestation of an omnipotent overvaluation of one's own words, and is a poor prognostic sign.

There are two directions in which the process of maturation in relation to the use of words as objects may develop: normal and pathological.

Normal development is characterized by moving a step forward in finding objects in reality to use in place of neutrally toned words as fantasy objects. The objects in reality so recruited bring new experiences and potentials into the life of the child, and add to resources for future planning. In this way, for those with potential for health, there is produced a metamorphosis toward the object world of the roots of imagination of the child. This is only a step away from involvement with objects in reality.

Pathological development occurs if, instead of replacing fantasy objects with real objects, the process of deaffectivization of words is emphasized. Instead of reality being strengthened as a source of objects to be used for the discharge of drives, fantasies without affect may be cathected at the expense of reality. It is at this point in development that flattened affect, thinking disorders, and delusional thinking can be used consistently in diagnosing schizophrenia. At age 11, manifestations of schizophrenia indistinguishable from the adult form first appear.

The preference for words over people is a manifestation of ongoing poor relatedness; it is often detectable at a very early age. The use of fantasy as object in latency often creates differential diagnostic problems, which are reduced once the child enters adolescence. Its presence reflects ego pathology (hypochondria, schizophrenia, organic brain syndromes, and manic–depressive disorder) at the most severe extreme and narcissistic character traits in less severe cases.

The Preadolescent Vicissitudes of Projection. The mechanism of projection is a compound of simple component defenses. Sometimes it is possible to change a component defense without modifying the essential nature of the complex defense of which it is a part, as in the case of projection. Projection consisting of repression associated with symbol formation gives way to projection consisting of denial associated with the attribution of motives to real figures. This occurs as a component of the third cognitive organizing period of latency. As a result, fantastic interpretations of reality are in a position to be checked against reality and the object world itself in place of autoplastically generated symbols. In addition, repression, displacement, and symbolizations of affects and motives become less involved in the discharge of drives and more with communicative modes. There is a shift from defensive to sublimative projection. Through the projection of the ego ideal, the superego is opened to influences from the peer group and the environment.

Changes in Body Image. The great changes in body conformation that occur during prepuberty produce states of doubt and confusion; children wonder what and who they are. Latent bisexual fantasies and fears are stirred when youngsters experience growth patterns which they consider to be aberrant. It is common for young boys to develop breast buds, which are a growth of tissue under the nipple, during prepuberty. This becomes a source of great concern, for the boy interprets it as a sign of femininity, whereas it is actually a part of male growth. The child's interpretation reflects his own doubts. Impairment of abstract thinking, which blocks an appreciation of the intrinsic meaning of puberty for sexual identification, may occur in prepubertal girls who have strong conflicts in regard to sexual identity.

The increasing changes in body configuration that mark this period produce a situation of self-awareness similar to that experienced during the first year of life. At that time, there was a cognitive inconsistency. Memory skills progressed and regressed under the influence of illness, parental rejection, and maturation. The infant finds a new discovery each morning in his body, since some of what had been known of it can be lost with regressions in memory skills. This is certainly the epitome of an uncertain sense of self, and doubtfulness, in relation to identity. A quite similar situation prevails in prepuberty. Changes in the sense of self and form occur. Whereas in early childhood fluidity of self-image was paralleled by fluidity in cognitive structures, in prepuberty fluidity of self-image is based on true fluidity of body form. The fluidity of self-image in prepuberty and early adolescence produces a distorted sense of self, coupling awkwardness and uncertainty. This provides a poor base from which to move into adolescent social competition. Often, doubt and self-rejection derived from this become the source of the rejecting thoughts that children in late latency–early adolescence project and attribute to peers. This circumstance can produce behavior patterns of fear and withdrawal in social situations in otherwise well-functioning youngsters and trigger defensive narcissistic traits and behavior.

Intensification of Narcissistic Investment in Fantasy. The shift in objects used for drive discharge from those in fantasy to objects in reality characterizes a healthy development in object relations. It is slowed by a countering increase in narcissism during late latency. Improved cognitive apprehension of reality intensifies the latter reaction. The more one sees oneself realistically as a small piece of a big world instead of its center, the more will such narcissism be mobilized. As a result, the substance of the child, *including his fantasies,* is self imbued with a quality of importance transcending the importance of reality. As mentioned above, the confusing changes in the body image that occur in prepuberty draw the child's attention to himself while they also heighten his need to see himself as important. The presence of heightened narcissism in early adolescence interferes with the finding of objects in reality for the discharge of drives. As we have seen, the step in moving from early latency to late latency is accomplished by the introduction of reality objects into fantasy thoughts. The step in moving from late latency to early adolescence should be the recruitment of reality objects, first to populate fantasy and then to join in reality as one moves into adolescent and adult life. The upsurge of narcissism interferes with this step.

Narcissistic cathexis of fantasy results in the intrusion of fantasy thoughts into the child's involvement with reality objects. Such intrusions on reality interfere with removal of object cathexes from parents to peers. At times the narcissism serves a useful purpose; often, fantasies and their affects are more familiar and comfortable than contact with new reality situations. Dreams of great achievement produce willingness to undertake truly difficult tasks. Fantasies provide an orientation through which to relate to reality objects during the time that the reality objects are becoming familiar. Thus, narcissistic invasion of reality situations with fantasies may serve a useful purpose, for the fantasies give reality a chance to impress and win the thoughts and schemes newly involved in future planning and setting up object ties.

In order for reality to gain a foothold, internal changes must take place. Adolescent narcissism must ebb. A set of cognitive skills that enable the personality to become attuned to and incorporate the needs of the world must be developed (the fourth cognitive organizing period). The achievement of these changes are the task of late latency–early adolescence. Sometimes, the child therapist must, in addition to his role in uncovering the unconscious and strengthening the ego, shepherd, and point the way toward the completion of these tasks for his patients.

Chapter 2

Narcissism, Puberty, and Omnipotence

Prominent among the factors that retard the advance of object relations in the pursuit of real love objects is the increase in narcissism that accompanies early adolescence. As currently used, the word *narcissism* has two definitions: The first, which is the usage in this chapter (see also S. Freud 1914) consists of the concept of libidinal energies directed, turned, or drawn toward the self. Object-seeking that conforms to fantasies, and the cathexis of personal fantasies at the expense of reality are manifestations of narcissism. The more that one's fantasies, self, and ideas are held in esteem by oneself and the more that acceptance is reinforced by recognition from the world, the more positive is one's affect. Loss of such support results in depression, feelings of emptiness, and a sense of low self-worth. A narcissistic digression into fantasy in one's search for a model after which to pattern the sought for loved one will result in the finding—or imbuing—of new love objects with characteristics derived either from the image of the self or from past experiences or wishes. Thus does the welling-up and intrusion of narcissism during pubescent adolescence halt progress toward relating to an object in reality.

The second definition of narcissism denotes a defensive and reactive heightening of self-esteem to cope with inner feelings of low self-worth, depressive mood, and empty feelings. These defensive maneuvers are mobilized when there is a loss of self-enhancing libidinal (i.e., narcissistic) supplies. This loss can occur with parting from a loved one, academic or business failure, and humiliating situations or insults. Grandiose ideas, plans, and views of self are manifestations of narcissism conceived of in this way. In this chapter the term *omnipotence* (see Ferenczi 1913b), and occasionally *grandiosity*, will be used for this concept of reactive narcissism. Thus the frequent confusion between the two concepts will be obviated.

Maturation: A Two-Edged Sword

Each move toward mature living in a reality context strengthens the adaptive potential of the person. The price for this gain is a loss of infantile narcissistic gratification. The all-powerful child, carrier of infantile omnipotence, succumbs to reality and becomes one of the crowd. With each strengthening of reality testing in late latency, there must be a concomitant surrender of implied power. The lost power can be identified with that experienced when the child used the defenses that dominate adjustment during the latency years. These defenses create fantasies, use magic, and field power-plays in dealing with the resolution of complexes and handling problems. In placing fantasies above reality, they become an exercise in narcissism. Moves toward reality entail a loss of this manifestation of narcissism.

Even puberty brings synchronic progression and regression. The changes in the body that surround puberty, especially menarche and the first ejaculation, propel the child toward the object world and diminish narcissism. Since pubertal events call attention to the self, the pubertal process itself entails an increase in narcissism. The children dress up, pose before mirrors, flex muscles, and strut. This interferes with the move toward the object world. There is a darker side, too: It would not be undesirable if the child were propelled toward reality with a heightened self-esteem. What is unfortunate is the loss of narcissistic pride in the face of the unknown elements of puberty. Body changes, fear of adult expectations, and unexplained and unexpected new experiences are potentially belittling events that humiliate the child and shatter the self-image and self-confidence that make up the child's armor against fear of a newly dawning world.

Passivity

Each surrender to the outside world cuts into narcissistic enhancement of the self and causes feelings of low self-worth. The negative and forceful reaction of young adolescents to positions of passivity may be explained on the basis of the humiliation felt by the loss of control to powerful authorities. Strivings for independence become more intense as a result of awareness of impending physical maturity and social expectations. As a result, the children often reach beyond their social skills and the limits set by their parents. Battles between early adolescents and their parents ensue. The children defend their dawning independence. The parents watch for the safety of their children. Unaware that they are not at cross purposes, children and parents fight. Demonstration of the presence of shared goals can be a helpful intervention by the therapist.

Two complications of parental overinvolvement are (1) fathers whose erotic interest in the child produces projections of advanced levels of sexuality into the activities of the child, and (2) mothers whose desire to infantilize the child impairs the acquisition of the skills for evaluating danger in new situations. The first may actually suggest or stimulate interest in sex in the child and result in the very activities that were feared. The second guarantees that there is something to fear if the child tries independent planning and action.

Expectations and intimations of independence are a frequent source of depression and confusion in early adolescence. There is an area of human adjustment in which independence and loneliness overlap. "It's lonely at the top" and "Uneasy lies the head that wears a crown" are sayings that reflect this. Young adolescents detect this connection, while they still strongly need their parents. Striving for independence and expectations of the future then become at once stirring and frightening. This insight is often suppressed, so that it hovers in the shadows of awareness. It is possible to help the child with this problem through the therapeutic intervention of explaining that independent people are less apt to be taken advantage of and, if joined with other independent ones in a relationship of mutual respect, can shape their world and defend their turf more effectively. In this way their needs will be met more efficiently than if they surrender independence out of a fear of loneliness. Often these fears are experienced as narcissistic wounds. Defensive mobilization of grandiose ideation and feelings gives rise to haughtiness, criticism of others, disdain, fantasies of expensive cars, and bragging about parent's holdings. It is well when such behavior appears in sessions to seek out concerns about the awesome demands of adult life as they are experienced by the child in late latency–early adolescence.

During the normal resolution of narcissism, bursts of rage may also appear. These are the by-product of the adolescent acquisition of sharing skills. There is sacrifice of narcissistic supplies involved in the acquisition of the capacity to fall in love. Deep depressive mood swings relate to the sacrifice of self and narcissistic supplies inherent in developing the capacity to share. Another early adolescent phenomenon in which developmental progress is accompanied by narcissistic loss is the shift in symbol use to those which emphasize the communicative mode at a sacrifice of self-expression. Evocative symbols give way to communicative symbols at a cost in the child's self-esteem comparable to that of a star who must share the limelight.

In people who fail to resolve the heightened narcissism of pubertal adolescence there are found residua in later life. These may be manifested in a view of the world seen through lenses distorted by past fantasy masquerading as life experience, or there may be invocations of past persecutors to explain current failures.

Even the necessity of sharing may give rise to rage in reaction to the implied need to give of oneself (i.e., give up narcissism). For early adolescents who can express themselves directly, the problem can be resolved through discussion and insight derived from confrontations. However, trouble lies ahead for those who are conflicted about feeling or expressing their rage. They are prone to use generalized disdain and hypochondria to take the focus away from any anger that may occur in response to the deflation of narcissism. They lose narcissistic supplies even as a result of an unacceptable rage within. The ventilation of such feelings is an important psychotherapeutic goal.

Those who transform their rage to disdain and then act out aggressive fantasies have no difficulty with expressing aggression. They are troubled by their inability to admit that they do not wish to share and thereby are inhibited from acting so that they would have to admit to being ungracious losers. They mobilize disdain and act out grandiose aggressive fantasies, which serve as a defense. They are able to express hostility through acting out their grandiosity and disdain for others by criminal acts and psychopathy.

Hypochondriacs and criminals have in common a reactive self-conceit, which is a manifestation of grandiosity. Both groups consider themselves to be special. The former group only *thinks* this. They set up hierarchies in the mind's eye, in which they occupy the positions of kings or, withdrawing from struggle with their image of reality, they draw into themselves and place primary importance on the implications of their body functions and sensations, and let the world go by.

The latter group acts out the sense of grandiosity. They show through action their unawareness of the human needs, life history, and existence within a family context of their targets. Victims and injured bystanders serve only as one-dimensional entities in the population of their fantasies—they are merely set pieces to be "rubbed out" of the imagery if they fail to play the game.

A 15-year-old high school student was arrested on the complaint of a neighbor from whom the boy had stolen large amounts of sound equipment, which was found set up in the boy's bedroom. The youngster told of lunch-hour forays into the local hardware store, where he stole such items as hammers and screwdrivers from "under the noses of those peasants" (his words). When the neighbor insisted on pressing charges of breaking and entering and burglary, the boy complained bitterly about the "brutality of those people." His mother was known to tease and bewilder his friends, and to laugh behind her hands at the sight of the befuddlement of the children.

There is here an element of the encouragement of narcissistic behavior by parental example, thereby enhancing adolescent narcissism. The following case incorporates hypochondriacal body hypercathexis with criminal devaluation and disdain for the victim.

Bill, who was in his early forties, was seen in the prison ward of a city hospital. He had recently been released from a prison in western New York state after serving a sentence for murder. At the age of 14, he had shot a friend with a target pistol. He was released from police custody because of his youth. A year later he shot a man with whom he had been involved in an argument. He had shot at some distance, and the spent bullet lodged itself in the man's clothes. A relative in local government managed to get the case dismissed because "no harm had been done." Within two years, and after many scrapes, he killed someone with a blunt instrument. As a result, he was sent to prison. He was a model inmate, and had no physical complaints. After he was released from prison, he took a train to New York City. During the trip he developed a severe headache, which persisted. Once in the city, he went to a bar. There he was picked up by a man, who invited him to share some wine at his apartment. On the way to the apartment they picked up some bottles of wine. Once inside the man's home, the wine was drunk and the man kissed him. "I knew what he was doing, but I just let him do it," said Bill. Interaction proceeded to the point at which the man began to perform

fellatio on Bill. At that moment, Bill picked up one of the wine
bottles and with one swing smashed the skull of his host.
"What were your thoughts and feelings?" he was asked.
His swift reply was, "I was glad my headache was gone."

The Enhancement of Narcissism by Puberty

Of all the two-edged maturational swords that cut across adolescent
development, puberty is uniquely cryptic. By its very nature, puberty
is in the vanguard of progress; yet within the processes of puberty,
there are forces that strengthen narcissism. Puberty readies the biology, while psychological development brings up the rear and struggles
to catch up. Menarche and first ejaculation, which are facets of puberty, open portals to the object world. On the surface, children swept
towards object relations seem hurried to their destinies by pubertal
changes and the implied obligations of nubility. Only starvation can
halt the flow of pubertal maturation. Failing this, puberty brooks no
stay and marches on.

Hidden within the process of puberty, though, there lies a source
of pressure that tends to impair the development of a psychology to
support the kind of object relations needed to propel the psychological
products of puberty toward fair couplings and parenthood. And that—
working unsuspected within the process of puberty—is the capacity of
physical change to draw narcissistic energies inward toward the changing self. In the process, the development of a cognitive set of modalities
(symbols used in a communicative mode) that would be prerequisite
for the ability to share, and to fall in love, is drained of the force needed
to motivate its completion. Although puberty propels, there is a narcissistic enhancement that occurs with puberty that interferes with the
giving up of a preexisting remnant of latency. The use of symbols and
fantasy as an organ for the discharge of drive during the latency years
(i.e., the structure of latency) implies that drives can be discharged
without objects. This is an example of narcissism, or the absence of
object relations *sui generis*. Any experience that supports a continuation of this latency style of symbol use (e.g., evocative pole emphasis)
will interfere with the development of object relations. Any interference with the primacy of symbols and fantasy over reality during late
latency–early adolescence will also diminish the supports of narcissism. Such an undermining of narcissism will in turn be responded to
by a mobilization of omnipotentiality and grandiosity.

Terms such as *borderline* or *narcissistic* personality disorders have been applied in recent years to the adult outcomes of a persistence of this reactive omnipotence. The origins of these "disorders" (called narcissism, though they would be better understood as *omnipotentiality*) are usually relegated to moments in early childhood. I consider the appearance of these features in adults to be examples of "narcissistic traits"—in conformance with current usage— but I emphasize the implication of the defensive nature of the omnipotential symptoms at play here. The origin of these adult traits can be found in failures to resolve conflicts about continuation of preadolescent narcissism during the time period from late latency through early adolescence.

The Early Roots of Adolescent Narcissism

There is a developmental trend in the extent to which narcissism dominates the interchange between drives, masturbatory core fantasy, and reality during latency through early adolescence. This can be used in evaluating and treating states of narcissistically tinged libidinal cathexis and reactive omnipotence during early adolescence.

In the latency years, there is discharge of drive energies through fantasy and whole-body play. The masturbatory component in this is not readily apparent. The substitution of symbols for objects in reality indicates the degree to which this process in latency is an expression of narcissism.

With puberty there is marked augmentation of the residua of latency-stage narcissistic libido, which is a gradually developed effect of one's awareness of bodily changes. The discharge of drives becomes involved with the stimulation of the genitals, whose gradual enlargement and increasing orgasm readiness provide the body and self with an ever more effective organ for discharge. This calls attention away from symbols and objects. Early in the process of transition, the symbols contained in the masturbatory core fantasies require less distortion for their information. This is an aspect of ludic demise. States of sexual excitement occur which display elements of both latency play and masturbation in their manifestations. In these states, youngsters act out incestuous masturbatory fantasies with little distortion. The evocative pole dominates in the poorly displaced symbolic representations chosen. For instance, boys may dance about excitedly in their mothers' clothes and jewels; wrestling and self-mutilation replace the vastly more distorted fantasies of the latency years. Sexual objects in reality are not yet in clear focus.

Further progress finds the child seeking masturbatory behavioral states in which people and things outside the mind no longer need be present. The child remains in one place; movement is limited, and the body is withdrawn from participation in fantasy. Action is limited, so that fantasy is experienced only mentally. Fantasy content comprises symbols drawn from reality, which function within the mind. There is marked narcissism here. The reality objects which are incorporated as symbols in fantasies are primarily used in the evocative mode, and serve the narcissistic self. At the phase here described, they serve as a nidus around which develops a configuration of the reality image to which the child will eventually relate. In the meantime, ejaculation and orgasm, rather than the acting out or implementation of fantasy, is the means of gratification. This union of fantasy and masturbation gives way in the normal course of events to preoccupations with, approaches to, and application of fantasy in the pursuit of sexual intercourse.

When biological maturation provides the possibility of sexual intercourse with real objects, the cognition and the psychology of the child are far from ready to bring maturity to the process. The child can only conceive of participation within contexts derived from fantasy. This is an example of the hypercathexis of fantasy at the expense of reality objects and their needs. It is a very practical example of narcissism retarding progress in object relations while at the same time contributing slightly to its success. Fantasies that are familiar and have been mastered in the past can be used as bridges to new and unknown objects of the object world. Once the real objects are recruited to play a role in these fantasies, their own characteristics can be impressed upon the memory and their wishes can become new experiences that alter the expectations and planning of the child. Such a gradual replacement of fantasy with reality is possible for those whose narcissistic upsurge has been sufficiently light to set aside the cathexis of fantasy. In those whose narcissistic investment in fantasy and self does not permit this, removal of the drive discharge wishes from incestuous objects and fantasy is not accomplished spontaneously. The psychotherapist who works with children in late latency–early adolescence should be aware that a phase-specific upsurge in narcissism can delay, or cause to fail, the achievement of reality-oriented object relations, leaving the child prone to narcissistic traits in adult life. To evaluate this, one should determine the extent to which symbol use has shifted to a communicative mode; whether adequate removal (shift of object from parent to peer) has been accomplished, and the resolution of narcissism has been negotiated. The treatment of these developmental lags depends upon a number of psychotherapeutic techniques, among which are

1. Confrontation and discussion of the evocative use of symbols.
2. Detecting the child's recruitment of the therapist into a part played in a fantasy, after which reality and the origin of the fantasy can be interpreted (this is a form of transference).
3. Demonstration of the internal origins of fantasy through the detection of other manifestations of the fantasy throughout the experience of the child, which will devalue the fantasy and demonstrate the origin of the contents of the child's projections. Analysis of the masturbation fantasy through free association puts too much emphasis on the fantasy at this developmental period. Because this will heighten narcissism, it is better left for a time when maturation and consolidation of the personality will be proof against regression.
4. Support and clarification of mythologies and misconceptions in regard to the world's expectations.

The Psychological Experience of Puberty

In the preceding chapter and here, we have discussed the open door to object ties that results from menarche and the first ejaculation. They form one of the bridges to the object world, and facilitate reality-oriented object relations. A prime feature of puberty, then, is the "enablement" of adult sexuality. There are, though, other aspects of puberty that inhibit the development of reality-oriented object relations. The role of the therapist in working with these puts great emphasis on correcting misconceptions and providing reassurance. The following discussion will emphasize the ways in which the enablement of sexuality paradoxically enhances narcissism and may be instrumental in inhibiting the move toward reality-bound object relations.

The Advent of Pubertal Adolescence

Two of the factors that influence the advent of adolescence are biologically based; they are the maturational increase in reality testing at age 8 that undermines the structure of latency, and the intensification of drives that occurs with biological puberty.

A definition of puberty was presented in Chapter 1. Briefly, puberty is the onset of the development of intensified primary sexual characteristics and the first development of secondary sexual characteristics.

Pubertal development depends on, and is concomitant with, an increase in the secretion of the sexual hormone. In addition to producing physical changes, sexual hormones produce psychological changes, which are manifested in intensification of sexual drives. Fantasies as a result are more intensely cathected. There appears an increased pressure for reality expression of fantasies with origins in prelatency that have been held in check by the structure of latency. Improved reality testing skills and the concomitant breakdown in the structure of latency as the result of ludic demise combine with intensified cathexes to push for the expression and gratification of drives with an object. Psychologically, puberty adds to the intensity with which objects are sought. Because pubertal changes tend to intensify narcissism, puberty does not guarantee that the search for an object will be free of the influence of fantasy.

Girls. In girls, puberty is at first an exciting thing in which an undeclared contest among peers develops. They vie to be the first to develop breasts. To others, changes in body contour become a source of concern, especially those who fear growing up and are afraid of mature responsibility.

Menses may intensify the psychological trauma of puberty. It is one of the final steps in the feminine body identification. As such, any penis envy or unconscious wish to be a boy that may have been present is now shattered by the periodic reminder of the presence of the female sexual apparatus. As one child who had completed her analysis reported, "It's a good thing I no longer want to be a boy, with this [menarche] coming on, I'd sure be depressed if I were the other way."

Often, the menses are seen unconsciously as lost babies by the girl. In the child who has not fully resolved the penis envy, menstruation may be accompanied by reactions of anger and resentment. Then there are physical complaints in the form of incapaciting illness, menstrual pain, and discomfort. Is it any wonder that puberty heightens narcissistic concern for self? Remarkably, this comes just at the time that pubertal maturation and improved reality testing are propelling the child toward reality objects for sexual gratification and discharge.

From the maturational standpoint, menstruation is solely an indicator of the presence of a maturational intensification of cyclical hormonal secretion. There is no obligatory developmental event associated with it. Therefore, the regressing, narcissism-enhancing portion of its impact is all the more impressive. It does not indicate readiness for conception—that is related to the appearance of ovulation (egg production) during the cycle. It does not indicate the presence of the capacity for orgasm, which is independent, usually becoming available from a maturational standpoint a few years before menstruation begins. Children have reported genital sensitivity and orgasm at 8 to 12 years of age. Puberty does not introduce orgastic capacity; however, the secretion of hormones does increase the urge toward utilization of orgastic potential. Typically, in the absence of neurosis, or religious or other cultural restrictions, first intercourse begins about two years after menarche.

Boys. In boys, pubertal changes are more limited in scope. During the beginning stages of puberty, erections become more frequent and there occurs the capacity for ejaculation with orgasm. Although there is evidence (Levine 1951) that some infants practice masturbation, with ejaculation and orgasm, in the nursery, for the most part ejaculation and orgasm first occur at puberty. Ejaculation is experienced more privately than most of the physiological events of puberty. As already described, its primary psychological effect is to open the awareness to love objects in the sphere of reality.

Body change is not as dramatic as it is in girls until well into the adolescent years. On the surface, increase in body weight, deepening of the voice, increase in physical strength, and beard growth are watched with care, compared, and worried about at the expense of heterosexual object seeking. Increase in the size of the genitals is sometimes a source of interest and concern while undressing in locker rooms. These pubertal changes enhance narcissism. The presence of pubic hair becomes of great importance, and a measure of competition builds up around it, as well as comparison of sizes of penises both flaccid and erect. Implied contest with others puts one in jeopardy of negative comparison. This is the milieu in which narcissism can be undercut and omnipotentiality mobilized defensively in the service of self-enhancement. Puberty may then become a time of strutting, as well as fear and genuine pride. Bragging about sexual conquests, criticism of the therapist's car ("How come you don't have a Porsche?"), belittlement of peers for poverty, and embarrassment about the slightest variation in one's parents from the commonplace in speech, taste, or manner are evidences of self-enhancement in the face of narcissistic mortifications. Extraordinary degrees of hostility and disdain and withdrawal from contact with peers, out of fear of unfavorable comparisons or rejection, are prognostic indicators: They warn that the reactive omnipotence of late latency–early adolescence may color the adjustments of later life. The products will be feelings of emptiness, a high degree of vulnerability, and castle walls of grandiosity to keep at bay the precipitants of wounded narcissism.

Factors in Puberty That Create Wounded Narcissism

Throughout the foregoing material, there is presented evidence that puberty draws attention to oneself, enhancing narcissism. Parallel to this is a potential for undermining the pride that is an inherent concomitant of narcissism. For instance, the girl who was grateful that she no longer wanted to be a boy with the approach of menarche would have been an example of this. For her, menarche would have been a blow to her self-image. An unexpected and unexplained burst of seminal fluid can bewilder a child. Failure to grow, or a total absence of knowledge about changes in the body, can terrorize.

A girl of 12, who was seclusive and lived with a prudish foster parent, suddenly lost her usual sweet and compliant demeanor and became disruptive in the classroom. She had breast development but had not yet reached menarche. One element in the presentation of the case by a therapist alerted the supervisor to the fact that this was not a disruptive response to depression or a rage reaction to a current event: the child had tried to bind down her breasts. When this symptom was pursued, it was found that she thought that something was wrong with her and she tried to hide it. Educational lectures given by the therapist resulted in an immediate remission of behavior to her former style.

The bewilderment that comes from plunging unprepared into an uninspected life experience, such as puberty, can make life seem not worth living. Even with later education to set matters right, a permanent skewing of defenses can place a mark upon adult character. Typically, youngsters in such conditions develop skills in dealing with reality, but suffer from a tendency to escape into fantasy, which often reaches such proportions that the fantasies in turn influence life decisions. Such turning to fantasy becomes a part of their characterological defenses. In essence, the fantasy style of latency is perpetuated to be used selectively as a defense. Both fantasy and the contents of fantasy themselves are introduced to provide an omnipotent defense against injuries to narcissism. This pattern, which is strongest in the first years of life and intensifies in the latency years, should be resolved for the most part during late latency–early adolescence. Resolution is part of the strengthening of reality testing that marks this period. Failure to achieve this at the time of early adolescence leaves the child with the potential for narcissistic character traits in adult life, seen clinically as reactive omnipotence.

The Dynamics of Omnipotence

In early adolescence, omnipotence (reactive defense against loss of narcissistic supplies) becomes an important available defense in dealing with narcissistic mortifications. Drive-expressive behavior, with an emphasis on fantasies that enhance self-esteem and provide self-gratification, buffers the child's activities in relation to the great denizens of the powerful world. Fantasy dominates the actions and the interpretations of the world of those whose adjustment emphasizes omnipotence.

With the weakening of the structure of latency, the child is left with little in the way of defense in dealing with overwhelming affects and narcissistic mortifications. Omnipotence and grandiosity are mobilized as defensive techniques in adolescence. They take over the chores of the structure of latency in dealing with withdrawal or loss of narcissistic supplies until the child grows old enough and experienced enough to handle reality and the articulation of drives and wishes with gratifying objects in the object world. In those who cannot effectively deal with these tasks, omnipotence (narcissistic character traits) persists in adult life. This will provide character traits such as a high degree of vulnerability to insult, depressive episodes, a marked tendency to disdain, periods of deep loneliness, and a recurring sense of "an empty place inside." The feeling of emptiness, or a "hole," is rarely reported by patients in early adolescence; those few I have seen have been relatively mature physically. Where these feelings would usually appear in adult therapy sessions, one finds a parallel relationship to feelings of loneliness and humiliation, to which the child relates as to a love object. These feelings increase as the child grows older, and the affect comes to be represented by the symbolic hole or emptiness, which is then related to as a thing.

All is not negative for these people. The person who says "I'm special—I won't do any ordinary job" is spurred to seek fame and riches in order to support the actualization of his fantasies. However, their footfalls are not sure, and mood swings and false pride cause breaks and lurches on their road to success.

The increase in narcissism and narcissistic sensitivity during early adolescence has three sources: heightened self cathexes related to the physical changes of puberty (as discussed before); residual narcissistic cathexis of one's own fantasies that dominated psychological adjustment during the latency years (the cathexis of fantasy was so great then that fantasy vied with and exceeded reality as an arena for the discharge of drives), and heightened reflective self-awareness, which places the person on guard against potential humiliations and narcissistic injury.

The state of heightened narcissism in late latency–early adolescence thus produced is normally manifested in evocative symbol use and self-concern. (The resolution of this normal state—the development of altruism—will be traced in the next chapter.) Heightened narcissism is the Achilles' heel of adolescence. Any challenge to the child (e.g., anger out of control, small size, separation and loss, induction of a low self-image) can produce a loss of narcissistic supplies. This in turn is responded to by grandiose defenses.

During late latency–early adolescence, the child can no longer use the discharge and defensive powers of the structure of latency. Other outlets take its place. Primacy of the genitals develops, and symbols assume the role of intermediaries between fantasy and reality. As a result, there is a reversal of the process that initiated the development of the structure of latency and the latency states that ensued. The pressures of the Oedipus complex resurface and sensitize the boy to oedipal interpretations of parental activity. The father is seen as threatening and the mother's behavior is interpreted as seductive by the boy. The opposite situation enhances the predicament for the girl. To avoid the implied conflict, a defensive cognitive regression to prelatency, intuitive symbolic cognitive functioning occurs. Persistence of the hypercathexis of fantasy that fueled the structure of latency potentiates the importance of this regression. In the process, the child lets slip reality. Libidinal regression accompanies this cognitive regression. As a result, in the fantasies borne by the intuitive symbolic mode, oedipal themes give way to struggles for power.

The more the parent attacks, the more regression is required. The child shifts into a defensive sense of omnipotence in which there is little reality-oriented activity. Clinically a child can regress to a state in which self and object differentiation are minimized.

How often do we hear a youngster say, "Why do I have to learn this, I'm not interested in it" in referring to a school subject, whether it be science, math, or foreign languages. What the child is saying is that he cathects the world so little that those things which the world values have no value for him as an object of learning. He will learn the names of movie stars and of singers, and even songs, but not what he must learn that he cannot identify as evocative of himself.

This is one of the areas to be watched as a prognostic sign by the child therapist. If left untended and the role of knowledge uninterpreted, a chronic form of learning disorder will ensue.

This omnipotence has anal-stage roots. The refusal to cathect the value of what is outside finds a paradigm in the denial that one sees when a child is scolded for a break in toilet training.

A youngster of 14 could see study as a means for gaining prestige and a good job. He could see no value in the things to be learned. He would try memorization. More often, he was involved in postponing work. First, there were telephone calls to be made to girls. Then there was television to be watched. His father would berate him. This made things worse. He could work even less then, for he was forced by his inner rage into greater regression. He found that he could read anything in his school books with understanding, except that which was assigned. He said that pleasure was more important than work. I pointed out to him that he could only do what he was supposed to do at the wrong time. For the first two years of his treatment, he had spent at least fifteen minutes of each session defecating—he saved up the stool for the session. He could make the connection that he produced what he wanted to, when he wanted to, as an expression of his power, albeit regressive, in the face of his father's demands that he produce at his father's speed. He had done the same thing in the transference in using the bathroom rather than the therapy session he had traveled quite far to attend.

We can see in this case adolescent omnipotence as a regression to the anal stage as a defense against oedipal feelings. The characteristics of the omnipotence are of importance, for they explain the loss of value of the world to the child, as well as a type of learning disorder seen in adolescence.

The Resolution of Omnipotence

The predominant developmental events of early adolescence involve resolution of problems presented by maturational moves in the area of reality testing, sexual capacities, and reactive omnipotence. The resolution of omnipotence is primarily identifiable with early adolescence, although, as Pumpian-Mindlin (1965) has pointed out, such activity is to be found in middle and late adolescence. He described the *"resolution of omnipotentiality* . . . as [resulting from] . . . 'acting out' of the omnipotential fantasies in reality, thereby submitting them to testing. Gradually, as they are tested against reality, the diffuse omnipotential energies are channelized to modify omnipotential fantasies in accord with the demands of reality" (p. 9). This mechanism is effective throughout adolescence. Running parallel to it during early adolescence is the shift to communicative use of symbols, speech, and stories.

Reality testing is the converse of reactive omnipotentiality; its strengthening undermines omnipotence. There are for this purpose maturational influences that counter reactive mobilization of omnipotence. First among the maturational elements involved is the step from concrete to abstract thinking. Essentially this produces a setting aside of interpretation and memory of events through slogan, substituting in its place observation and recall involving the intrinsic nature of things. This occurs at about age 12. Of primary interest to us is the reorganization of the functions of observation and memory function as it relates to orientation of self in the world of percepts. Piaget (1945) set the timing of the phenomenon in his description of the transition from concrete operational thinking to abstract operational thinking. It is useful to add to his concepts, which are related primarily to interpretation of perceptions, the concomitant maturation of the memory function, which includes the transition from affectomotor through verbal–conceptual to abstract conceptual memory.

Verbal conceptual memory replaces with words the slogans and word concepts the recall of which during the first years of life was dependent on memory for total experience of affect perception and movement.

Concrete operational thinking implies that a person can deduce a cause-and-effect relationship in the action of a force on an object if the activity is taking place in a concrete situation within the sight, sound, and feel of the individual.

Abstract conceptual memory is the ability to codify in memory the intrinsic nature of events, processes, speech, and objects. Magical thinking and superficial similarities are filtered out by this process and therefore cannot be added to the body of memory that is used to interpret new experiences. Through scanning of the contents of this area of memory, newly arrived events and experiences come more and more to be understood realistically.

Abstract operational thinking denotes a person's ability to deduce cause-and-effect relationships and apply principles previously learned to new situations, and especially to forces and objects which are conceptualized through word symbols. Briefly, this means that a person with abstract operational thinking can work with ideas.

The abstract conceptual memory organization contributes to the development and maintenance of abstract operational thinking. When operating together, reality testing is enhanced by the addition of the intrinsic abstract to the interpretation of perceptions, events, and concepts. Enhanced reality testing in turn undermines the narcissistically cathected misperceptions from which the reactive omnipotence of early adolescence draws its enhanced and false images of the self.

Psychotherapists must be alert to this maturational step in the development of abstract thinking, for it allows the introduction of adultiform interpretations in psychotherapy. Teachers especially know of it, since they introduce a new form of study at this time (ages 12 to 14). Before, when reports were assigned, the child was told to look something up and to report on it. The child went to the library, copied down what was written, and then reported what he copied. With the coming of abstract concept memory organization and abstract operational thinking, the child can gather data and assimilate it to form a concept or a point of view. He can recognize what disparate abstract verbal concepts have in common and draw conclusions. He can perceive illogicality and recognize the inapplicability of fantasy derived from early life experiences as a guide to responses to the problems and experiences of people living now, in reality. Whereas the improvement in reality testing that arose with the development of concrete operational thinking led to the recognition that displaced fantasy could not be used to resolve problems with parents, although it could be used to discharge drives, the improvement in reality testing that comes with the development and application of abstract memory and operational thinking results in deemphasis of the use of fantasy to explain the actions of others, or to plan and execute the life goals and experiences in one's real world. This is a technical way to describe some of the inner workings of the shift from primary to secondary process thinking. There is now the potential to base the interpretation of the world more on reality than on interpretation through regression and fantasy-dominated memories and recollections of past experiences. One of the keys to the resolution of adolescent omnipotence is this strengthening of reality testing.

Not all youngsters gain from this increase in the maturational potential for reality testing. Individuals who are strongly drive-discharge-oriented and have a pervasive ego disorganization will have less improvement in function with the passing of latency than those who are drive-dominated in few areas, in whom this new maturational factor appears to promote improved reality testing. It is not unusual for individuals to spend their adult lives with entire areas of functioning still dominated by fantasy. The most immutable of the omnipotent early adolescents is the one who has no object ties to the world at large, or is limited to fantasy objects. Omnipotence may then continue into late adolescence, and often tints adult character with traits of reactive omnipotence.

Frequently there occurs in adolescents brilliance of mind without the capacity for sustained work or a reality-oriented goal for the use of the mind. Children write for the sake of writing, have sex for the sake of sex, or invent in the service of their own self-aggrandizement and to prove that they can do almost anything. In essence, they exercise their minds for the sake of the exercise, with scarcely another object in view.

One very bright youngster was in the habit of saying that anything that man's mind could conceive, man could do. He meant himself.

Another young man planned his life and career (medicine) on the basis of the theory that such a career would solve all his problems. He ignored the fact that he did not have the grades to get into medical school. In spite of this, he put aside all other realistic opportunities in pursuit of that which he believed would cure his troubles.

A late adolescent (reported by Pumpian-Mindlin 1965) invented a machine which did what no one believed possible. He lost interest when it came to the patenting and marketing of the device, which his teachers testified would be a boon to all mankind. He was not interested in its relation to the world and its needs. He was interested only in his own self-gratification and the aggrandizement of his self-image, which derived from the act of invention. He was more interested in enhancing his sense of omnipotence than in directing his talents to serving others.

On leaving early adolescence, the adolescent himself and his needs become less important and the world of objects and people and external forces and needs become more important in shaping plans and actions. All this occurs because the child gains the capacity, which he may not necessarily use, to recognize that the fantasies he would like to force on reality do not fit. He can now test the validity of abstract concepts and fantasies, and their application to the world in which he lives. The fantasy that places him in the center of the world at high school graduation must be set aside if he is to take his place realistically in society.

Should maturation fail, it is likely that the person will develop depressions in the late 20s and early 30s. This occurs in people who realize too late that they have chosen the path that leads to disappointment and failure on the basis of an overvaluation of themselves that was required in support of a reactive mobilization of omnipotence.

Summary

There is a relationship between the omnipotence of adolescence and "narcissistic" traits in adulthood. Puberty is accompanied by an intensification of narcissism, and the counterprocess of a move toward object ties. Injury to narcissism, including the impact of reality, can trigger reactive omnipotence. The resolution of narcissism and of reactive omnipotence enhances reality testing and object relations. The factors involved are many, and they are in a ramifying relationship, which is elaborated in the following chart.

I. Factors Enhancing Object Relations (drives turned from self to objects)
  A. Improved reality testing
  B. Ludic demise
  C. Weakening of the structure of latency
  D. Social pressures
  E. The shift from evocative to communicative mode in symbols, speech, story telling, reporting, and loving
II. Factors that Enhance Narcissism (drives directed toward the self)
  A. Persistence of latency-style fantasy. (This decathects reality and elevates self-esteem.)
  B. Pubertal changes drawing attention to self
  C. Physical changes creating a situation reminiscent of early development. These enhance vulnerability.

III. Factors that Undermine Narcissism (These create uncomfortable moods and a sense of humiliation against which reactive omnipotence is mobilized.)
   A. Awe of the future
      —sexual requirements
      —adult burdens of responsibility
      —impending separation from parents
   B. Inability to deal with misunderstood pubertal physical changes
   C. Passivity (independence urges confronted by social ignorance and authority)
   D. School experiences
      —teasing
      —new topic challenges
      —academic discipline required for excellence
IV. Responses to Injured Narcissism (When narcissism is undermined, omnipotential defenses add a controlled, narcissistically charged coloration to self-esteem and to attempts at relatedness.)
   A. Disdain
   B. Fantasies of power
   C. Hypochondriacal hypercathexis of body functions and malfunctions
   D. "Elitist" definitions of the signs of success

In this chapter we have dealt with the origins of early adolescent narcissism, the vulnerability of adolescent narcissism, the mobilization of omnipotence that salves injured narcissism, and the passing of omnipotence, with emphasis on the dynamic aspects of the process. A shift in the purposive mode in symbol formation is an important consideration here. One of the signs of improved reality testing is the selection of symbols to be used for fantasy and planning from the object world and reality. This does not guarantee the stifling of reactive omnipotence. Omnipotence can still be supported if the reality-derived symbols are dominated by evocative overtones. Future planning and self-image enhancements can be reality-oriented and still serve omnipotence if the meaning of the symbol and the need it represents are personalized and used in an evocative mode. Expensive cars and elitist settings are real, and can be used in the service of reactive omnipotence because of the superficial message they can be arranged to give. The resolution of omnipotence requires a shift of symbolic forms to those that are dominated by a communicative polarity. The shift from an evocative, self-oriented pattern to a communicative object-oriented pattern of thought strengthens the *testing* of reality at the expense of the *sense* of reality. From this there results a dimming of the potential for the development of reactive omnipotence. An adjustment to reality is forced. If this is unsuccessful, and there is loss of the capacity to regress to evocative modes, reactive depressions may result.

Chapter 3

Shifting Symbolic Forms during Late Latency–Early Adolescence

One of the prime maturational elements leading the early adolescent towards object relatedness is the shift of emphasis in the use of symbols and speech from the evocative to the communicative mode. In the evocative mode, symbols are used solely for self-expression and for the mastery of uncomfortable trauma and prior affect states. In the communicative mode, symbols are used as a tool for contact with reality and the control of the future. The effective transit of symbol use to the communicative mode is a vital step in development. It is important for success in work and is a primary constituent in the development of the ability to fall in love. It is also a vital element in effective free association in insight-oriented psychotherapies.

Psychotherapy in the latency-age child is often impaired by an age-appropriate cognitive limitation which dampens the ability of the child to communicate unconscious content to the therapist. The latency-age child has not yet fully developed the capacity to use psychoanalytic symbols in a communicative mode. When the child plays in a therapy session, or writes a poem or story, his primary intent is drive discharge involving narcissistic gratification through fantasy. Through evocative symbols he seeks the expression, or evocation, of inner feelings. The child's primary intent is not communication with the therapist.

Eventually, during middle and late adolescence, the evocative mode will contribute coloration to the symbols involved in creativity. This gives the impression that evocation contributes to object relations. This should not distract one from an awareness that symbols used in the evocative mode interfere with accurate communication of content. Communication often has a low priority for the late-latency child. During late latency, symbols used in an evocative mode slow natural developmental progress towards object relations. The presence of evocative symbols slows the development of the communicative thought processes required for effective psychotherapy and for adequate developmental progress.

The shift of symbolic forms from those that emphasize the evocative pole to those that emphasize the communicative is part of the larger group of transitional processes leading to communicative emphasis and enhanced object relations. Communicative emphasis is enhanced by transitions in symbolic forms (evocative to communicative symbols); the development of enhanced communicative potential in speech (social speech), and the revamping of story material to conform to the experience and orientation of one's listener (tertiary elaboration).

One of the tasks of the child therapist is to hasten as well as shepherd and encourage this natural process of development. An example of an area sensitive to the therapist's approach is that of bewilderment about the physical changes of puberty. The child is apt to draw into herself or himself in the face of such changes. Physical change draws narcissistic energies inward, toward the changing self. As a result, the development of symbols used in a communicative mode, which would support the ability to share and to fall in love, loses impetus. The therapist who can detect the child's bewilderment and clarify the sources of confusion helps to put the communicatively oriented developmental processes back on the track.

Evocative Symbols Dominate Latency-Age Play

Nonverbal Forms. A use of the evocative mode in the selection of latency-age symbolic forms causes the play of the child to be dominated by nonverbal elements that are difficult to understand and decipher. In addition to dreamlike personal fantasy elements, there is passive acquisition with rote use of nonverbal symbols, signs, toys, fantasy characters from children's entertainments, and mythic images. These are the characteristic representations from which are selected the evocative symbols used in latency-age fantasy activity. The latency-age child selects pertinent aspects of these representations for their highly personalized meanings. Ludic symbols can be used to evoke feelings and repressed affectomotor memory elements that have rarely been shared with others.

A girl of 7 brought to sessions a toy called the magic mirror. It was called that by the manufacturer because its design permitted it to be turned into a racing car. The girl played with it because of powers she read into the "magic mirror" name. It could be used to get rid of her mother when she was angry.

Of these nonverbal forms, certain culturally based mythic symbols (e.g., Batman, G.I. Joe) appear to be communicative. They share superficially a vocabulary relating to universally accepted themes. Actually, they are selected by the symbolizing function of the child with little emphasis on communicative value, and such symbols provide external foci of attention (countercathexes), which divert the conscious awareness of both therapist and child from conflicts and relegate personal memory elements to a state of repression. At the same time, they sweep the expressive skills of the child into apparently socialized channels of expression. This phenomenon, which I call cultural capture, implies that the child evokes inner feeling states and memories through the tales of his culture. Through the use of such tales, instinctual pressure is released through fantasy surrogates while the private evocations of the child are sequestered and repressed. This occurs at the expense of the exploration and communication of conflict. When fantasies containing such elements are discovered by a companion or a therapy-oriented observer, only superficial meaning is perceived; unconscious contents remain uncommunicated. Universal human experience may serve as a basis to help the observer to interpret the meaning of the symbol. The intent involved in using such symbols is to withhold the sharing and communication of meaning.

A boy of 8 was brought to therapy for uncontrolled behavior in the classroom. The first few sessions went well, with conflict material easily detected from the play of the child. A change of hour was requested so that the child could watch his favorite television program, "Batman." A change was made to a later hour. Quickly, the content of the sessions shifted from fantasies involving cutout figures that represented symbols from his own dreams to detailed presentations of episodes in the life of Batman. Questioning of the mother brought out the fact that the story line for each session exactly matched that of the program of the same day. The contribution of the child's unconscious to the selection of the material to be presented was slight. It was decided to interdict further television watching immediately preceding the sessions. Thereafter, the boy reverted to symbols that were an evocation of his own experience and traumas.

Symbol Polarities.   Each of all possible symbols possesses a potential dual polarity of expression. Each can be analyzed from the standpoint of the emphasis placed by the symbolizing function on the evocative or the communicative value of the representation used as the manifest symbol. The healthier the latency-age child is emotionally, the more he is apt to stop and ask the therapist if the meaning of the play is clear. Play that embodies repetition compulsion places more emphasis on the evocative pole of symbol use, whereas play that embodies reparative mastery places more emphasis on the communicative pole of symbol use (see Sarnoff 1987a, Chapter 12). Reparative mastery is a therapeutic goal. From a clinical point of view, the psychotherapist should use as a therapeutic strategy the encouragement of symbols with an emphasis on communicative potential.

The Shift from Evocative to Communicative Symbols

The shift from evocative to communicative symbolization is accompanied by the development of *the observing object in the mind's eye.* This psychological element of the personality is formed as an advanced level in the progressive development of self-reflective awareness, and is derived from the internalization of experience. It is characterized by the presence of an internal watching element that superimposes the needs of potential love and transference objects on a child's symbols and speech. The child who is never told to clarify a point, or is never questioned for meaning, fails to develop an observing object in the mind's eye. Like any superego element, the observing object requires the support of ego functions sufficiently mature to carry out its demands. The requirements include the maturation of communicative skills; these skill changes (which have been mentioned) include a shift to the communicative pole in symbol formation and perfection of social speech and tertiary elaboration.

Internal shifts from the evocative to the communicative mode in symbolic forms are forced by the following:

1. the end of drive expression through play symbols alone (ludic demise)
2. the enhancement of the perception of reality that accompanies the shift to verbal and abstract conceptual memory organizations (especially the latter)
3. awakening to the effectiveness for drive discharge of communication with love objects in reality; this is mediated by puberty (including menarche and the first ejaculation)

In normal circumstances, a need to communicate transmutes the speech of the child so that communicative elements dominate at about 12 years of age (social speech).

An observing object in the mind's eye plays a special role in monitoring tertiary elaboration. It demands that universally shared symbols and meanings take part in communication. The cognitive transformations of late latency–early adolescence make it possible to serve the needs of the audience (the reality world of objects) in selecting symbols. Because of the emphasis placed on the communicative aspect of symbolization at this time, aesthetic considerations influence speech with great force. Symbols push toward mature, adult forms which require verbal emphasis. In the shift from latency to adolescence, there is a change in the nature of the symbolic forms used in spontaneous fantasy formation. The evocative, personal experience and/or rote symbols of latency give way to the communicative, aesthetically determined symbols of adolescence.

The Nature of Symbols

Before proceeding further, it will be useful to define symbols according to the structures and functions we shall be discussing.

What is a Symbol? *Symbol* is a generic term describing any stimulus that carries to an observer the meaning of something other than the stimulus.

Symbols are the products of the *symbolizing function*. The symbolic form used at a given time is characteristic of the maturational stage at which it occurs, as well as the motivational circumstances involved. Symbolic form is the product of maturation, social influences, and intrapsychic forces and events. The structure of symbolic forms undergoes an ontogenesis. As symbols grow, so grows the ego.

What is the Symbolizing Function? It is one of the mechanisms of the ego. It is a complex mechanism the development of which parallels that of certain simpler functions. In the first two years of life, these are:

1. capacity to perceive similarities (e.g., establish mental linkages and/or perceive abstract relationships)
2. capacity for displacement along the linkage between concepts or objects based on perceived similarities
3. capacity for delay—to permit displacement
4. Motivation for displacement

Once these four ego units are developed, generic symbols can be formed. With the subsequent development of the following, psychoanalytic symbols can be produced. By 26 months we find:

5. capacity for reality testing to maintain and support a distance between the signifier and the signified
6. capacity for repression

Psychoanalytic symbols become operative at the age of 26 months. Intuitive use of these symbols provides the psyche with an organ through which drives can be discharged through fantasy. The use of this potential reaches a peak during the midlatency years. The primary sources of representations to be used in this way are the symbols of dreams and play. After the age of 12, with

7. improved reality testing and
8. ludic demise, reality elements predominate among those representations that will serve as symbols. However they continue to be used in the evocative mode through late latency-early adolescence.

The shift from the evocative to the communicative as the dominant mode is the work of early adolescence. Shifts between the modes can occur normally at any age or stage. Often the therapist of the latency-age child must encourage the shift to communication as a therapeutic technique. The shift to the communicative mode permits the discharge of acceptable drive derivatives. In adolescence, this discharge can occur with objects in reality used as symbols in the communicative mode. Prohibited derivatives continue to use dream symbols, passively acquired cultural (mythic) symbols, and fantasy. Unacceptable derivatives are unwelcome in communicative zones. They make up private thoughts and dwell in the zone of evocation. Dream symbols and fantasy symbols in the adult offer persistent psychological areas of vulnerability through and around which regressions can organize.

Products of the Symbolizing Function

The symbolizing function has a number of different products, all of which are grouped under the term symbol. This single term should not blind us to the fact that there are more than twenty-five different types of symbolic forms, of which we are interested in six. This is why I often use the term *symbolic forms* rather than symbols.

The following differentiation of four forms, and the two modes, is important for the work at hand, since if I say "symbol" and mean the fourth type, and the reader thinks it means the first type, there will be no communication.

The Four Symbolic Forms

The four basic symbolic forms that should be differentiated for our purpose are called indices, signs, symbols, and psychoanalytic symbols. We must be indebted to Ferdinand de Saussaure and Piaget (1945, pp. 98, 169) for their early contributions in this area.

Index. Denotes that the signifier is a physical part or an aspect of the signified. (Fingernail clippings are used in magical rituals to represent the whole of the victim.)

Sign. Denotes a sharp physical distinction between the signifier and the signified; where the choice of the signifier is arbitrary or determined by convention (i.e., involves a social relationship, as in language, which is a system of verbal signs). (Flags, i.e., patterned cloth chosen to represent a nation, signals, and words relate most closely to this category.)

Symbol. Here too there is a sharp physical distinction between the signifier and the signified; however, the choice of the signifier is "motivated" (i.e., involves, and is the product of, individual thought and involves signifiers coupled with signified elements—*referents*—which can be related through points of resemblance). The relationship between signified and signifier is conscious. Metaphors, such as "You are the angel glow that lights a star," consist of such conscious symbolic linkages.

Psychoanalytic symbol. A symbol, as defined above, in which the awareness of the relationship between signifier and signified has undergone repression, as in a cave or a clam representing female genitalia in a dream.

Evocative and Communicative Symbols

It is my contention that among all symbols, and especially within the category of psychoanalytic symbols, there are two subgroups that play an important role in the transition from latency to adolescence; these are the evocative symbols and the communicative symbols.

Latency and adolescence have distinct and characteristic emphases in their symbolic forms. The child in latency creates his fantasies with emphasis on evocative symbols, whereas the adolescent creates his fantasies with emphasis on future planning, using communicative symbols. In the intermediate zone of late latency–early adolescence, there is a continuous shift of emphasis of symbolic forms between evocative and communicative polarities.

Evocative symbols are defined as psychoanalytic symbols that express memory, or past feelings or fervors. They conjure up the past for the child, without particular emphasis on communicative or cultural aspects. *Communicative symbols* are those which express recalls—as do evocative symbols—while simultaneously, with an eye to the sensibilities of the observing object (the audience), they entertain, hold interest, and communicate. The division into evocative and communicative symbols is, thus, arbitrary; but these categories represent age-correlated emphases which are accurate: symbols in latency *tend* to be evocative, symbols in adolescence, communicative. The shift from emphasis on the evocative pole to emphasis on the communicative pole is a characteristic shift in the cognitive transition that accompanies the change from latency to adolescence.

It is wise always to be aware that each psychoanalytic symbol has the potential to evoke or to communicate. Which end of this polarity is emphasized in a given symbol must be determined on the basis of a patient's associations or the observer/therapist's evaluation of context. Evocative purpose is more common in latency, and communicative purpose is more common in adolescence, in keeping with the role of symbols in these different stages.

It is proper to say that a given symbol manifests activity related to the evocative pole while retaining some communicative characteristics. Psychoanalytic dream symbols are primarily evocative. The ordinary conscious symbols in daily use are primarily communicative. When one speaks of an evocative or a communicative symbol, it is understood that a portion of the symbol's role relates to the alternative mode.

Historical Overview

The Evocative–Communicative Polarity in Symbol Forms. Once one's ears become attuned to resolving psychoanalytic symbols into evocative and communicative forms, it is possible to recognize that the differentiation of symbolic forms into two categories has been observed and reported in one manifestation or another in the scientific literature many times during the past three-quarters of a century. The literature reveals an interest in the nature of these forms, as well as insight into their roles and positions in the developmental progressions that accompany the growth and evolutionary sequences in which they appear.

In the ontogenetic growth sequences of psychoanalytic symbols, which has a major thrust at age 26 months, evocative symbols precede communicative symbols. The transition from evocative to communicative symbols is a continuous process that begins when remembered words replace evoked feelings, images, and gestures. The greatest developmental surge in this process occurs during the transition from latency to adolescence, when symbols in health become consistently communicative.

In the following extracts from the psychological literature, we shall trace the development of the distinction between evocative and communicative symbols.

In 1903, Reinach introduced the concept that the arts of prehistoric man and modern man were intrinsically different. He described a difference in the use of symbols from the standpoint of a characteristic emphasis on evocation in the symbols of primitive art. In describing the art of primitive man, Reinach clearly had in mind two types of creative symbols, those which evoke inner sensations and those which blend the evocation of inner sensations with communicative intent. He said, "The prehistoric sculptor was never preoccupied with the intent to please but with the intent to evoke"* (p. 265).

Reinach's view of the type of symbols used by primitive man is reinforced by Di Leo (1970), who states in describing the cave paintings of Altamira:

---

*It is from this phrase that the term evocative symbol is derived.

Archaeologists and art historians are in agreement that the art
of primitive man was not intended as communicative but that its
purpose was magical; it was almost completely confined to
animal representation. Its aim was, by creating an image of the
animal, to gain power over it. These pictures were to be found in
hidden places and caves—not where they could be seen by others.
In a way, the child's drawings are similar in that they too are a
personal affair and not a communication—at least not an inten-
tional one. [p. 142]

Thus, Di Leo takes Reinach's point of view, and associates the
evocative symbolic style of the paintings of primitive man with the
drawings of children. He goes on to point out that "the use of graphic
means for communication begins with the stylization of art during the
New Stone Age . . ." (p. 142).

***The Phylogenetic Paradigm of the Shift from Evocative to Communi-
cative Symbols.*** Campbell (1959) sought to discover in the evolution of
art the time at which the graphic productions of man were guided by
aesthetic (i.e., communicative) considerations rather than by chance
placements of symbols on a background. He discovered the point of
change to be about 6000 years ago, with Samarra style pottery. Before
this, throughout the entire hunting period of mankind, he noted the
following:

We do not find, even in this latest stage of the hunting period,
anything that could be termed a geometrical organization, anything suggesting the concept of a definitely circumscribed field
in which a number of disparate elements have been united or
fused into one aesthetic whole by a rhythm of beauty. Whereas,
suddenly—very suddenly—in the period that we are now discussing, which coincides with the appearance in the world of well-
established, strongly developing settled villages, there breaks into
view an abundance of the most gracefully and consciously organized circular compositions of geometrical and abstract motifs . . .
[p. 141]

We may conclude from this that there has been a group of students
of prehistoric art who found that the graphic works of prehistoric man
consisted of symbols that were meant to *evoke,* producing a magical
control of nature. Although the world of objects and its content seem
to be the substance of their work, all such magical drawings and

gestures are not truly directed at objects in a relationship. The drawings and gestures are evocations of "magic power," the effect of which
does not transcend the boundaries of the mind. Symbols did not
emphasize an aesthetic, communicative meaning pole until the development of a high level of cultural and political organization some
6,000 years ago. Those among the students of prehistory who have an
eye for child development have noticed that the evocative symbols of
primitive man share with the evocative symbols of children the lack of
communicative influences.

The Evocative–Communicative Polarity as Viewed by Behavioral Scientists

In the works of psychologists who have delved into this field, we can
find references to carefully worked out clinical studies of the shift in
the symbolic form from evocative to communicative symbolization
with the onset of adolescence.

In the literature of scientific psychology itself, there are at least
two references that presage understanding of the fact that psychoanalytic symbols can be divided into the subgroups (evocative symbols and
communicative symbols).

Henry Krystal (1965) wrote of evocative and communicative symbols in his paper about the painter Giorgio De Chirico. Apparently
De Chirico suffered a major emotional decompensation, which resulted in a change in the nature of the symbols that he was able to use
in his art.

> The symbolism of reunion with the love object previously por-
> trayed by symbols referring to an idealized God-like figure of his
> father which incorporated the good mother as well were perma-
> nently given up and replaced by calculated mechanical and
> empty robots which took the place of the objects. . . . Early (in
> his career) the painter portrayed his depression and anxiety states
> on perceiving his isolation and depersonalization. This affect
> could be communicated and made a great impression on both
> audience and critic. As the artist mastered his anxiety at the price
> of relinquishing fantasy objects and loosening of associations,
> his painting lost appeal to his viewers. [pp. 224–225]

Krystal points out that in his early works, De Chirico was involved in
the communication of his mood to an audience:

His great discovery was that painting landscapes in the way he perceived them communicated his mood to an audience in an appealing way. [p. 213]

After 1917, De Chirico's paintings were largely rejected. In 1915, he had suffered mental exhaustion and had been hospitalized and discharged from the Italian Army with a psychiatric diagnosis.

[He then] settled in Italy and started painting in a new style using predominantly manikins without faces, sometimes associating these with unrelated objects such as gloves, maps, arrows, draftsmen's tools, food articles and other items. . . . The most conspicuous thing about this latter period was the fact that the pictures had lost their feeling and passion, were not coherent and evoked no empathy. [pp. 222–223]

Krystal goes on to relate the appearance of food in these paintings by De Chirico as evocative of oral needs. In the article one finds the description of a regression from communicative symbols to evocative symbols as part of psychotic process in an adult. Of importance to us is Krystal's demonstration that it was possible to describe a change in a clinical state as the result of a modification of the product of the symbolizing function in an area of its communicative potential.

More specific and extensive differentiations of evocative and communicative symbols with an exploration of the ontogenetic timing of the shift to the more communicative mode in late latency are found in a work of Piaget (1945). He recognized that it was possible to subdivide the secondary (i.e., psychoanalytic) symbols of childhood into at least two groups, ludic symbols (play) and oneiric symbols (dreams). Both of these symbolic forms are recognized as occurring during states in which the individual is "without the possibility of accommodation to reality" (p. 209)—i.e., purely evocative. When the child's activities emphasize the exercise of already experienced adaptations to the outside world, repeated for the pleasure of repetition or solely for the exercise of skills, Piaget called the activity *play*, or *dreaming*, depending upon whether the child was awake or asleep. The symbols used are evocative, and Piaget recognized that ludic and oneiric symbols occur in states of mind in which there is emphasis on the exercise of prior experiences without further adaptation to the real world.

Where there is adaptation of language or action to the real world, the symbols are communicative and the child's activity is called *work*. Ludic and oneiric symbols characteristically function primarily in the evocative mode.

Piaget recognized that there could be changes in the nature of secondary (psychoanalytic) symbols. These could occur when the individual matures, and in situations that encourage regression. Piaget stated that "unconscious symbolic thought is by no means a permanent expression. . . . It operates only in exceptional situations, such as: children's play, the dreams of both children and adults, and sometimes in states of completely relaxed thought" (p. 211).

(Furthermore, he mentions that states of completely relaxed thought occur during psychoanalysis.)

Characteristics of Ludic and Oneiric Symbols

There are characteristics that differentiate ludic and oneiric symbols according to form and structure:

Ludic symbols are experienced as play, with rare breakthroughs of a sense of reality that could make it feel almost real. The child feels in control of them. They usually relate to material substances. They commonly first appear around 24 months and rarely become porous to the affects that they defend against.

Oneiric symbols feel "real." They often go beyond the control of the child. They consist of visual mental images rather than material substances. They commonly first appear between 26 and 30 months. They frequently become affect-porous, as in nightmares.

There is a developmental differentiation between oneiric and ludic symbols. The former, as well as the evocative mode in symbol formation, persists into adult life in such manifestations as dream and "couch" symbols, and the visual symbols found in "modern art." Ludic symbols, however, are lost when adolescence begins; communicative reality symbols replace evocative (play) ludic symbols in adolescence.

Ludic Demise

Ludic symbols, with their extraordinary emphasis on egocentrism in the waking state, diminish in occurrence and importance as part of the transition from latency to adolescence. Piaget (1945) has not sharply defined the timing of this event. He indicates that the shift from egocentrism to the primacy of the outside world as the factor influencing the thought of a person is the most important element in the disappearance of ludic symbols. This is known to occur at about 8 or 9 years of age. Clinically, the shift away from ludic symbols does begin to occur at this point; however, it gains momentum a few years later at the age of 11 or 12.

Even before that, however, there is in human development a continuous shifting between evocative and communicative polarities. Affectomotor memory gives way to verbal memory. Naming speech gives way to the communicative use of words, and evocative verbalizations give way to communicative verbalizations. Likewise, narcissism yields to altruism. Piaget emphasizes such repeating polarities, which with each repetition result in greater communicative value and socialization of thought. For instance, he comments:

> Whereas imitation (reflections of prior memory or learned experiences) can only reproduce the action as such either externally by miming or internally by the image, in the verbal account there is in addition a particular kind of objectivization peculiar to it and connected with the communication or socialization of thought itself. [p. 223]

In essence, Piaget has here juxtaposed the intrinsic aspects of the evocation–communication polarity. He has described it in terms of the early childhood polarity of affectomotor recall versus verbal recall. Our emphasis deals with a later working through of the same polarity, that is, with the shift in the evocation–communication continuum (or polarity) which occurs at the end of a stage (latency) during which some verbalizations have been caught up in rote memory and have been pressed into the service of evocation.

The passing of the ludic symbol, with the retention of the oneiric symbol, as one enters adolescence is directly related to the fact that there is more communicative and work orientation in the adult than there is in the child, except during sleep.

Communicative Speech

Evocation–Communication Polarities

Adults are never truly free of the influence of evocations of previous experience. These influences are especially prominent during dreaming sleep. This is true of waking evocations of previous events even when realistic current communicative symbols are being selected and used. This is attested to by material described by Darnton (1975), who pointed out that of the stories written by a newspaper writer those most likely to elicit responses from readers and editors contained elements in common with old fairy tales. There is apparently an influence on communicative speech that derives from inner earlier experiences and patterns and leads away from realistic, non-egocentrically oriented, accurate news reporting. For more about this, see Tertiary Elaboration, p. 63.

Socialization of Thought and Social Speech

The shift from egocentric to communicative symbolizations that one observes in patients in late latency is a highlight in a contiguous and continuing series of related processes. Important among these other processes is the development of *social speech*, defined as the ability to shape one's words in a description so that meaning can be easily and clearly discerned by a listener.

Krauss and Glucksberg (1977) delineated the time of the shift from nonsocial speech to social speech. This was done using the following technique. Children of different ages were given a page of designs, which they were to study and communicate only through words to an isolated person holding a sheet of similar designs. The isolated person was required to find the design described among a disparate group of forms on the paper before him. It was found that even though adults could successfully communicate to children verbal descriptions of the shapes that they had in mind, children had great difficulty in verbally communicating shapes to each other, before the age of 12. Even 13- and 14-year-olds, though they had begun to advance their skills in using social speech, did not perform with adult competence. The shift to social speech only begins to gain momentum at 12 years of age.

It was felt by Krauss and Glucksberg that Piaget's (1945) concept of *childhood egocentrism* should be considered causally in this developmental shift to communicative capacity. However, they discovered that to a certain extent the communicative skill was present from very early on. The shift from egocentrism with the appearance of "reversibility" was not accompanied by greater ability in this area. "By the age of eight most children should be beyond the point where egocentrism is an important factor in their behavior, and yet 13 and 14 year olds did not perform with adult competence in our task" (p. 104). To explain the delay, they suggested that taking into account the knowledge and perspective of another person is necessary for an individual to be able to utilize communicative speech. A gradual shift from highly personalized to socialized thinking characterizes this maturational step, rather than an acute change with the coming of adolescence. As Krauss and

Glucksberg have pointed out, it is a process that extends over a period of years.

Socialized Thinking: An End Point with Multiple Precursors. Some signposts (Sarnoff 1976) on the way to the development of socialized thinking are

1. a shift in fantasy content that occurs with the appearance of the second cognitive organizing period of latency (7½ to 8½ years). Fantasy content goes from fantasic to humanoid elements.
2. a shift from inner- to reality-oriented perceptions as a fantasy source. "The shift from inner-oriented perceptions to reality-oriented perceptions as a source of fantasy content for the gratification of drives is a nearly universal phenomenon during the second cognitive organizing period of latency" (p. 129).
3. acquisition of verbal signifiers with shared social roots. "The capacity to learn in terms of verbal signifiers which have shared social roots and culturally validatable implications is the major cognitive step involved in fixing and codifying the shift of human attention from personalized fantastic responses to socially-oriented goals" (p. 120).

The most common clinical manifestations of this trend are the age-bound changes in the content of fear-fantasy imagery of the latency-age child. Anthony (1959), in a review of the literature on this subject, has described the imagery of the fear fantasies of children from 5 to 6 years of age as fantastic. From the age of 9 till 12 the imagery of fear fantasies is social. This, of course, relates to play, or ludic, symbols rather than those having to do with creativity, which is communicative.

One can see the intrusion of realistic and social factors into thought processes as part of an ongoing process that begins as early as 8 years of age. In the third cognitive organizing period of latency, whose product is adolescence, this process intensifies, and real objects become more important and communicative symbols replace evocative ones.

On the Cognitive Capacity to Fall in Love

Thus far we have demonstrated that psychoanalytic symbols function in at least two modes, one associated with the evocative group of symbols and the other, with the communicative group of symbols. "Group" is to a degree a misnomer here, for *any* symbol has the potential for serving in either mode.

Developmental level and defensive considerations determine which mode of function and which group assignment the symbol shall have. Groupings consist, respectively, of those symbols that emphasize the evocative pole of function and those that serve the communicative pole of function. There is a developmental shift in emphasis and frequency from use of the first to use of the second in early adolescence. The potential for this shift cognitively predates adolescence. In adolescence effective factors join to precipitate the ego structure that can support drive discharge in the context of communication with reality objects.

The shift to communicativeness is a process that transcends in area of influence, the symbolizing function. Its impact is felt on four levels:

1. Symbols become communicative.
2. More and more speech takes on communicative potentials.
3. Storytelling is modified to take into account the listener's verbal requirements for understanding.
4. The daily life needs and the instinctual requirements of a partner are incorporated into the thoughts, hopes, and plans of a person on a preconscious level (*the cognitive ability to fall in love*) and can influence thinking as though the two were one. This occurs when the observing object in the mind's eye comes to represent the loved one as the result of internalization. Narcissism is thus both served and set aside. Communicative skills then come to encompass one's adjustment and object relations.

What remains to be delineated are the causative factors that intensify and effectuate the shift to object orientation during late latency-early adolescence. In the rest of the chapter, we shall seek the factors that motivate an individual to utilize communicative speech when dealing with unconscious material in creativity and in therapeutic sessions (tertiary elaboration).

Tertiary Elaboration

Hoffer (1978), in discussing the work of Bernfeld, observed that the latter was aware of a change in the nature of fantasy formation during the transition from latency to adolescence. He coined the phrase "tertiary elaboration" to describe this phenomenon, which has been discussed a few times briefly above and is here given expanded treatment.

Tertiary elaboration refers to modifications of latent fantasy that take into account social demands and audience expectations in the area of symbol formation and storytelling. It may be present early on to some degree, but it achieves an effective level first during the transitional developmental phase associated with late latency–early adolescence.

Experimental psychologists and historians have studied the influence of society and the outside world as audience on symbolization and speech. Investigations have dealt with internal psychological factors in communication. These were factors that influence symbols and the writing of stories, as well as pressures to communicate demanded by audiences, and listeners, on the form and content of writing and speech.

Darnton (1975) has presented an excellent summary of the Pool-Schulman study (1959), which relates to these influences, since it describes the influence of the audience and attentiveness to the opinions of others on the content and style of writing. Darnton describes how

> Pool and Schulman got newspapermen to conjure up images of the public through a process of free association. They asked 33 reporters to name persons who came to mind as they were going over stories they had just completed. Some reporters named persons whom they liked and whom they expected to react warmly to stories containing good news. Others imagined hostile readers and took a certain pleasure in providing them with bad news. [p. 175]

An affective component was detected and designated as having possible influence on the accuracy of writing of reporters. This distortion factor was tested by supplying four groups of journalism students, consisting of thirty-three students each, with scrambled facts taken from stories that communicated both good news and bad news. Each student assembled the facts into his or her unique version of the story; each student then listed the people who had come to mind while writing. The students were interviewed to determine the degree of approval or criticism that might be attributed to the persons on their lists. Then the stories were checked for accuracy. The experimenters found that student writers who imaged critical persons reported bad news with more accuracy. Pool and Schulman concluded that accuracy was congruent with a reporter's fantasies about his public.

The influence of one's public becomes more important in late latency–early adolescence. This follows upon the internalization of objects associated with recruitment and metamorphosis (see Chapter 7, p. 140). The observing object in the mind's eye comes to represent the public in the absence of the object. As it becomes more impoitant, it influences the symbolizing function to select symbols on an aesthetic basis as the audience it represents becomes more a part of the internal self. Thus, in telling tales, the child is guided to elaborations that may please or entertain.

Tertiary elaboration shapes the reports and the stories one tells to fit and hold the interest of significant others. In dream psychology, the raw material of dreams often consists of disorganized fragments. The dreamer secondarily elaborates the fragments so that they make sense to him. In then telling the story to a listener, the elaborated fragments are bound with a matrix of sensibilities, details, and even a well-chosen conclusion which contains or excludes elements that would be pleasing, attractive, or opprobrious to the listener. Tertiary elaboration causes people reporting dreams to impart to them the theory-influenced expectations of the listener.

Summary

There is not just one form of psychoanalytic symbol; rather, there are many forms. Those that are most important in latency are evocative-mode symbols, whereas the forms most important in adolescence are communicative-mode symbols. The latter are the symbols involved in aesthetics, creativity, future planning, and finding objects of love.

Evocative-mode symbols have been known by many names. They are the ludic symbols of Piaget, the evocative symbols of certain paleoanthropologists, and the personalized symbols of those who study disorders of the symbolizing function in the schizophrenic process. Each of these symbolic forms can be differentiated, refined, and defined as a separate group with its shared characteristic.

The shared characteristic of evocative symbols is the selection of a symbolic signifier to represent unconscious content without regard for the communicative or aesthetic value that it has for an audience. Evocative symbols represent a victory for narcissism. The symbolic signifiers evoke—for the benefit of the egocentric aspects of the individual—inner feelings and experiences. In each case, already mastered fantasies and feelings are reexperienced at the expense of reality. The product of this repetition is momentary mastery through gratifying play based upon prior successful experiences.

Communicative symbols have, as their shared characteristic, inclusion of the needs of the audience when they are selected. Communicative symbols represent a victory for altruism, reality testing, and non-egocentric influences. The symbolic signifiers work for the benefit of object relations. Through communication and transformation, fantasies modified by changing their symbols and symbolic forms to match the will of the world enhance object relations. Contact with reality is achieved and past traumas can be deemphasized, reparatively mastered, and processed.

Nonegocentric influences are present from early on; egocentrism begins to wane shortly after birth. The influence of nonegocentric forces is at first slight, because there is very little articulation of the drives with reality-oriented libidinal love object peers. Their influence is most strongly felt in socialization experiences, such as toilet training, temper control, and the acquisition of nonidiosyncratic vocabulary. They primarily affect speech in early life. They cause the child to give up sensory–motor patterns of memory and to take on verbal patterns that coincide with the patterns of society. The motive forces are fear of punishment, fear of loss of love, and the reward of praise or love. Superego is very much influenced by these external factors as early as 5 or 6 years of age. In early latency, the affectomotor fantasy activity of the child and memory activity are brought under the sway of fantasies of a verbal sort, which provide the child with guidance in dealing with the society according to the society's demands for the shaping of the child's efforts. At about 9 or 10 years of age, when ethical individuation takes place, the child is further influenced by the outside world with a reshaping of his conscience by peer group pressures. The superego is shaped in part by external influences in latency. This shows the influence of non-egocentric forces earlier than pubertal adolescence.

Symbols, on the other hand, are affected late; indeed, the most impressive changes await puberty. The question must be raised, why the change to communicative symbols occurs in late latency–early adolescence? There must be another factor besides loss of egocentrism. The factor is probably not too far out of view, if we consider the following: In dealing with unconscious drive discharge, communicative speech, although possible early, is rejected by the child, who prefers to use ludic symbols in play. These are the tools through which gratification of drives through fantasy can occur. The shift in symbolic form to communicative symbol is influenced by the enhancement of reality testing, ludic demise (the loss of waking play symbols as drive discharge elements), and the awareness of communicative potential in providing real objects for drive discharge. There develop within the mind ideas that incorporate the needs of the loved one even when he or she is not present. For the creative person, an internalized representation of the audience for which the work was conceived is created. Whereas the latency-age child conceives of a word as a means of expressing his drives, the adolescent conceives of words as a communicative tool in seeking love objects, overseen by an internalized representation of the loved one. Narcissism is expressed and conquered all at once when the object to be pleased can be incorporated as part of the self.

In the conduct of psychotherapy, the nature of the behavior and communications of the child is influenced by the internalized image of the therapist. The choice of topics brought in by the patient and even the nature of the dreams reported conform to the internal image of the therapist that the child acquires as the result of creating a representation of the therapist in his mind's eye. Therapy techniques can, thus, alter the patient's adjustment without the therapist's realising it. A few words said or a positive response to a piece of information may be taken by the patient to be encouragement of form as well as content.

The next two chapters deal with a syndrome related to the adolescent brink (anorexia nervosa) and the narcissistic aspects of masturbation (the evolving expression of sexuality), and thus follow a longitudinal developmental pattern. More material on the matter of this chapter, with emphasis on enrichment of object relations in early adolescence associated with the development of the capacity to fall in love, will be found in Chapter 6.

Chapter 4

Derivatives of Latency in the Psychopathology of Anorexia Nervosa

There is a point during emergence from latency when a maturational process involving a burgeoning of physical secondary sexual characteristics, and a shift in primary love attachment from parents to peers is to be expected. In some young people, this expectation is interdicted by a cessation and regression in normal development; in effect, these young people make time stand still, or even turn back. Physical maturation slows; weight is lost; in girls menses ceases, and the figure recedes. Emotionally, involvement with the family intensifies, and involvement with friends becomes secondary. Usually, a strongly ambivalent quality invades peer ties. Peers are viewed as externalized rejecting and condemning superego figures. Therefore, the anger-laden passivity relationship to the mother is intensified for lack of peers to relate to and to trust.

The emotional configuration consists of a cessation of the process of removal (disengagement of drive-discharge functions from the parent) and a regression from the task of developing the capacity to relate sexually to a peer. The process described is *anorexia nervosa*. The cessation and regression in the normal developmental process is the result of a configuration of defenses that takes the place of adolescence. We are not dealing so much with a disease or a syndrome as with an alternative organization of the ego that is chosen over the often chaotic, but always challenging and sometimes frightening, variations available to the young teenager trying to find the best way to master the challenge of adolescent sexuality. Of the normally negotiated types of adjustment usually seen in adolescence, the ones most closely allied to anorexia nervosa are the withdrawn and the ascetic. In both, the child shies away from intense sexualized socialization; and in both, parents remain more important than peers in the area of close personal relationships. In all three adjustments (asceticism, withdrawal, anorexia nervosa), the pattern of reaction may be transient in the sexual adaptation of the child, in which case it gives way to a more mature experiencing of life. For many, though, the pattern may persist to become the basis upon which is built their future adjustment and character.

All three adjustments have in common disengagement from sexual encounters. The withdrawn has no contact with potential sexual partners; therefore, one so afflicted remains without skills for dealing with sexuality, nor has the opportunity to develop some. The ascetic confronts social situations and partners and learns personality skills to cope with sexual feelings through techniques of repression and denial. The anorectic changes bodily configuration to that of a younger child, seeking disqualification as an object of approach. For the anorectic, the primary mechanisms for dealing with sexuality entail withdrawing from peers and extinguishing, through starvation, the physical traits and configurations that announce sexuality and invite a sexual approach. The development of personality skills to deal with these is thus obviated.

Essentially, our purpose will be exploration of the characteristics of the phase of late latency–early adolescence, which persist in these youngsters and contribute elements to the disorders (such as anorexia), which make their first appearance during this phase (see Sarnoff 1976, Chapter 8). The other conditions that emerge at this time are depression with adult affect; adult-form paranoid schizophrenia; organized and repeated delinquent acts involving the property of others, and perversions without partners.

In my experience, female anorexia nervosa patients universally have a fantasy involving their psychic body image. The nonscaphoid abdomen is a sign of pregnancy. Manipulation of the true image of the body through starvation supports denial of sexuality from within at the same time that it fends off sexual approach by others. Both as a child psychiatrist doing consultation in a major hospital and as a practicing psychoanalyst, I have had the opportunity of seeing a wide spectrum of anorectics, ranging from those whose anorexia cleared after a few sessions of psychotherapy to others whose anorexia was intransigent and persisted through many years—and many therapists. In all cases, behavior and defenses were organized around specific fantasies involving body image, which are responded to by self-starvation.

The easily reachable, transient anorectic adjustment is associated with a discrete, thinly repressed, and well-organized body image fantasy in the context of a competent ego organization. The intransigent anorectic, on the other hand, has a bizarre, poorly organized body image fantasy, filled with contradictions. These, however, do not appear so to the child, since they exist in the context of an ego organization that shows impairment in reality testing, narcissistic deformations that caricature the expected deformations for the age, and the impress of the mother in both ego-ideal content and the interactions of object relations. All three of these elements carry the characteristics of latency ego states into the organization of the personality mobilized to confront the challenges of adolescence.

The reason for the imprint of latency on regressed adolescent adjustment is obvious: when the intensifications of sexuality that accompany puberty appear, the defenses of latency are near at hand, familiar, and made up of practiced skills. For those who are reticent to follow the direction of their drives to seek gratification in the world, the defenses of latency are available to help counter and stifle the drives through mediating their discharge with justification in fantasy, discharge of drive energies through regressed and sadistic, cruel interactions with parents who remain the center of interest in their lives, and a narcissistic deformation of object relations, which causes fantasies about people to seem more real than the people themselves.

When confronted with insights into these patterns, the intransigent anorectic readily agrees, but sees no reason to change her ways. The regression is conscious and felt to be justified; and as a result of support from the mother, it often provides secondary gains that entice the child to remain as she is.

The Transient Anorectic

The transient anorectic, on the other hand, finds insight a help. Much of her fantasy activity is repressed, leaving her bewildered at her state and unaware of her reasons for starving herself. The intransigent early adolescent anorectic is aware of what she is doing; her refusal to eat is a form of impulse disorder with an emphasis on overcontrol. The pathology of the transient anorectic is related to repression. In essence, she is food-phobic, with anxiety associated with eating and little understanding of what causes the fear.

Millie was such a child. She was 13 years old when I was called to see her in the hospital, to which she had been sent by her pediatrician for evaluation of her refusal to eat. She sat by her bed reading, and was wearing street clothes. She appeared to be of normal weight, and her development was that of early puberty. She told me that she had lost 15 pounds in the last few weeks; she had been much heavier before that. At 5′3″, her 110 pounds did not make her appear overly thin or in need of hospitalization from a life-threatening condition. However, Millie's pediatrician felt that the rate of weight loss was a cause for alarm. He had admitted her for a general work-up for the causes (organic or functional) of sudden weight loss. Uncovering no positive organic findings, he attributed her starvation diet and weight loss to anorexia nervosa, and thus called for a psychiatric consultation.

Millie's mother had called attention to the weight loss and the starvation diet. She was cooperative with the hospital, but not overly involved in the treatment. Many "get well" cards from friends were observed in Millie's room. The child was somewhat impatient with my presence, because she was expecting a visit from some of her friends.

In the course of the consultation, I asked a question which has been routine for me in dealing with anorectic youngsters: Dr. Mellita Sperling* had pointed out that a characteristic of all anorectic girls is a preoccupation with keeping the stomach flat. No matter how thin they are, the girls will intensify their self-starvation if the abdomen protrudes in any way. Behind this preoccupation is the fantasy that the protuberant abdomen is a sign of pregnancy. Starvation keeps the abdomen flat and hides from the world the sexual fantasies and preoccupations that gave rise to the psychic transmutation of a protuberant abdomen into a pregnant one. Therefore, I inquired whether she was worried about her stomach—does it bother her if it protrudes? She associated to my question with a recollection of her concern during a party at which she wore a tight dress that someone would think she was pregnant. I posited a relationship between her fear about

*Mellita Sperling, *Personal Communication* (1965).

eating and her concern lest her figure take on the configuration of a pregnant woman. "I think that's it," she said. "I probably could eat now." She did, and soon went home. There were only a few sessions, and these were related to her concern about how to behave with boys. I never saw her again. Her pediatrician reported nothing unusual for the rest of her adolescence.

The case of this child is remarkable in that she was brought to someone's attention. Transient anorectic adjustments to the sexual challenges of adolescence are more frequent than the number detected by physicians. The episodes are often masked as ordinary dieting. It is obvious in these cases that body-image-oriented fantasy made a decisive difference in choosing the particular avoidance technique for use in coping with the pubertal intensification of sexual drive energies. For all intents and purposes, I could detect no involvement, or even awareness, on the part of the mother of the true nature of Millie's condition. Loss of appetite and weight loss were the mother's reason for taking the child to the doctor for a work-up. Her cognition was normal for her age. She could apply abstract thinking to free standing ideas. She could grasp abstractions. She could remember them and apply her grasp to new situations in such a way that she could see them in a new light. As a result, she could differentiate the words of fantasy from the false reality that the words created when her situation was described for her. I am sure that these skills made it possible to set aside the latency style of functioning through fantasy that had reassumed dominance at the time of her anorexia.

The capacity to differentiate reality from fantasy, when confronted with the difference, necessitated the use of repression. Without repression to mask the fantasy from rational challenge, she could not have acted on the basis of an untenable hypothesis. In brief, she had a characterological *neurotic* cognitive style of ego organization. Thus, her condition was amenable to uncovering therapy, and consisted of a food phobia. When the irrational fantasy was stumbled upon and exposed by me, her rational faculties were brought to bear on it. Then, like ancient cities exposed to the light and air, it crumbled.

The Intransigent Anorectic

It was quite different with Myra. She was 16 years old and quite a beauty, if one could judge from pictures, her mother's descriptions, and the time or two that she gained weight. In latency she had been the ideal child for her mother. Her latency-age fantasy life had been rich. However, when she reached puberty, the cognitive changes that are part of maturation wrought havoc with the effectiveness of fantasy as a discharge pathway. The population of symbols of her persecutory fantasies ceased to be fantasy figures. In their place, other teenagers became her persecutory protagonists. Myra placed herself in the role of the persecuted. She could not make friends or go to parties. She feared that she would be considered dull or boring, or that she would be ignored. In actuality, she could not differentiate herself from the internalized "bad mother imago" of her childhood, and had projected this confusion into the thinking of her peers. This was intensified by the ambivalent relationship with her mother.

Myra's father had disengaged himself from the family and had devoted himself exclusively to his business at the first sign of a crisis. As the result of the loss of accessibility to others, her mother became her main—in fact, only—object tie. Although her mother often spoke of the burden of her constant contact with the girl, she did little to separate from her. She felt relief whenever her daughter was hospitalized, but never actively initiated separation. The closeness of the two intensified the child's ambivalence towards her mother. This, in turn, reinforced the negative aspects of the internalized maternal imago.

As a result, her misinterpretations of her peers' behavior were magnified. The more time she spent with her mother, the more she railed at the passivity she experienced as a pubertal child in contact with her mother. Constant attendance, and constant advice, by the mother stirred up rage in the child, but the negative feelings were projected onto peers. Thus, fighting with the mother resulted in an intensification of the bond with her.

Of course, much of this situation with her mother had been present before the age of 12. At that time, the relationship with the mother and her peers had been preserved by the ability to project the conflict into a fantasy, which was clinically manifest in the form of night fears.

That is the way a latency-age child manages to be "perfect." The depressive affect that accompanies such a situation is also dealt with within the personality. The affect of depression is rare when the mechanism of projection is actively involved in fantasy formations containing fantastic symbols. In that circumstance, anger or anxiety is the manifest affect. When real people are used to populate the fantasies, depression surfaces. Actualization through the fancied detection of feared situations in the reactions of peers justifies depressive affects.

At 12½ years, Myra experienced a marked manifest depression coupled with a feeling that she could not make friends and was disliked by her peers. Myra's parents decided to get psychotherapeutic help for her. Although the family had sufficient money, her father, who put little stock in psychotherapy, asked her pediatrician to make the lowest possible fee a prerequisite. They were referred to a Mr. M., whose office was many miles from their home. The office consisted of a desk and chairs set in the garage of his house. No attempt had been made to alter its appearance from that of a garage, and it was never cleaned. The mother mentioned cleaning her clothes after each visit. His abilities as a therapist were reported by the child to be as dilapidated as the setting. Mr. M. spent the time (18 months, two sessions a week) telling Myra about himself, and offered her rewards if she would go to parties. She tried. Her interpretations of the reactions of peers continued to have a quality of rejection.

In the meantime, Myra's figure matured and she began to attract the attention of young men. One day she decided that she was unliked because she was fat. She went on a diet. Her mother was delighted by her "fashion model" appearance. The child had mixed feelings about the whole situation. She liked her slimness; however, she did not like the feeling of hunger that went with starvation, the empty-space feeling inside her stomach, or the constipation and interference with bowel habits that accompanied it. Myra especially disliked giving up her favorite food, which was chocolate cookies. She hit upon a compromise. She would eat all she wanted of cookies and candies and then either spit out what was chewed or vomit what was swallowed.

In this way the impulse to eat could be responded to at will, while the feeling of emptiness within could be considered a product of her own design. Myra had a true disorganization and disorder in impulse control. She overcontrolled and undercontrolled her eating with little pattern or reason other than the urge to eat and the need to stay thin. Her mother considered the vomitus and the packages of spat-out food to be disgusting; but the girl considered her actions justified since, in her own mind, the chocolate tinge that pervaded it all made it look "just like shit," with the implication that the food had been digested. She began to lose weight rapidly. Her therapist declared the situation beyond his control. By this time she was 5′4″ and weighed 68 pounds. Her appearance was gaunt and skeletal. Her skin took on a yellowish cast. People who met her casually became fearful and withdrew, reinforcing her own fears.

There followed a series of hospitalizations, during which Myra was threatened with intravenous feeding. In response to these threats, she agreed to eat, and gained sufficiently to be able to go home. Her mother was quite fearful during this period; she appeared not to know what to do. Her response to the situation consisted of placating her daughter while begging for her cooperation. This was certainly a mixed message, and the girl followed her impulse of the moment. This is what appeared on the surface.

The problem occurred too close to late latency not to have implications in terms of the influence on behavior of the object relations of late latency. At that time, children (after 9 years of age) are beginning to look beyond their parents for superego contents. Peers and social influences, such as magazines, television, and films, provide children with notions that can be called upon to challenge parental guidance and fuel rebellion against passivity. As often as not, parents themselves, seeing the child's potential in terms of new levels of maturation, encourage development in areas, especially sexual, that they formerly forbade. In essence, the child finds herself in conflict with old parental imagoes, sometimes even with the current parent as an ally.

These are internal conflicts the resolution of which results in some of the more disquieting, though transient, psychopathological symptoms of late latency. Obsessional symptoms, paranoid reactions, hives, and gastrointestinal symptoms are common (for more on this, see Sarnoff 1976). The point is that, specifically at this age, internal conflicts between oneself and parental imagoes stir guilt, which may be dealt with through the use of body functions as primitive symbolic forms. Thus, the children withdraw from the conflict on a verbal level and occupy themselves with cathexes turned toward the self. In the process, the world is devalued and the form and functions of the body become more important than relations with others.

Even Myra's thoughts about her body changed as the process of turning inward of her attention progressed. She ceased to worry about weight as a deterrent to other's esteem, and began instead to seek the perfection of a personal ideal filtered through an immature and distorting cognition. All of this was conscious. She accepted without a qualm the contradictions between the reality of her thinness and her interpretation of what she saw in the mirror. Conscious contradiction formed a part of a new form of "rationalism" that she had coined for her own use (e.g., "No matter what you see in the mirror, I see the same thing and to me it is fat."). Myra was anxious and fearful when forced to eat. At one time she was enrolled in a program of voluntary hospitalization that placed little faith in a search for insight. Instead, there were rules about eating which emphasized discipline in eating and punished weight loss, which was measured on a scale and responded to with loss of privilege. She became quite anxious under this regimen and asked her mother to give her another chance with psychotherapy. That was when I first saw Myra; she was then 16.

She explained her rejection of the program on the basis of the fact that she felt fat if her abdomen protruded at all. She was so thin, that any food ingested, and at the time in the process of digestion, was perceivable as a distortion of her scaphoid abdomen. In her intuitive response, this little part seen as fat stood for a whole body that was fat and pregnant. Myra's cognition in the area of perception of her body was so distorted that all input was shaped to support her delusion. Since it was conscious and rationalized, interpretation could not avail her of new insight nor confrontation diminish her invariable response to all she heard or saw. She unquestionably loved the power she had over those who loved her or wanted to help her. Her power was the result of her personal, irrational, and unassailable logical system.

There was more than a touch of sadism exercised in Myra's refusal to yield to the logic of sound minds. She was the center of attraction in an adult world. The alternative, in her mind's eye, was to become a wallflower in a world of young teenagers. Narcissistic overcathexis of her own ideas, fantasies, and distorting cognition helped her to preserve her self-created world. In this way she was able to select a moment in her life and stop time at that moment. It was a moment when, as she recalled, she was praised for asexuality and was free of the roundings of the body and the menstrual period which led her towards adult sexuality. It was a moment when, as Wilson (1979) says, the anorectic has "the capacity to live in fantasy and to avoid reality." It was a moment from a time when all one had to do in order to learn was to memorize words, instead of having to understand, challenge, and catch the intrinsic essence of a process.

Myra had stopped time in latency. Wilson* in his extensive experience, has found that parents encourage this.

The parents, because of their character structure, admire their children most in the latency phase, and do not accept the aggressive and sexual changes of adolescence. The parents unconsciously like the latency figure and are repelled by the roundings of the female figure.

In addition, the parents engage in fighting with the children. The children respond in kind. This interferes with removal and the establishment of relationships with peers. There is a mutual interplay aimed at keeping the child forever young.

Myra's cognition interfered with interpretation. She could not learn from psychotherapeutic work in those areas involved in her complex. She had withdrawn from reality object ties. She learned by memorizing words and phrases by rote, so that her only exercise of logic consisted of twisting words to fit her needs rather than engaging in the search for new meanings. Her long thin arms and legs gave one the impression of a spider. Indeed, spiderlike, she had woven about herself a web of words through which she would not see, and it soon became her world. No matter how I tried to free her, she would not leave the safety of her web. It tangled close about her; reality receded, as the predator became prey to her own device. Her web of words served both as hiding place and prison. Although her loneliness was devastating, she reveled in her ability to outsmart others and to twist reality to suit her needs in a contest of wills, with herself the sole judge.

Within four months Myra had worked through her use of projection to fend off peers and had reestablished contact with old friends. She began to feel anxious in the treatment, and told her mother that she thought therapy put too much burden on her. She demanded to be allowed to drop out of therapy and return to the program that offered external controls. When her mother called to tell me what was afoot, she explained that she could not argue with her daughter. She feared the rage of the child should

---

*C. P. Wilson, *Personal Communication* (1979).

she defy her wishes. I met them four years later. They were shopping. Myra appeared to be essentially unchanged except that her affect was flatter.

Summary

We have delineated the person who develops anorexia during the period of emergence from latency. The residua of the latency state are present to be used by any child who wishes to turn from the sexual demands of puberty instead of exploring sexuality. Withdrawal and asceticism are other common examples of such a response. In essence, these people return to a world of fantasy in continued exercise of well-tried latency techniques of adjustment. For those who entangled their image of their bodies with fantasy, anorexia as a transient adjustment to sexuality becomes a means of causing the body, with the menstrual function, to regress to the form and function of the latency child. For those with neurotic character defenses, this condition is temporary. The fantasy (i.e., fat means pregnancy) is unconscious and can be dispelled when the unconscious fantasy is interpreted. At the other end of the spectrum are the intransigent anorectics. These children, too, wish to withdraw from sexuality through regression to fantasy and unraveling the process of puberty. Their heightened narcissistic ca-thexes of fantasy at the expense of reality, and their primitive cognition and understanding of causality allow them to establish a cognitive style that permits an indefinite continuation of this state. Since the illogic and contradictions are conscious and accepted by the child without challenge, the process of interpretation offers no new insight and, consequently, only slow progress in psychotherapy.

The occurrence of anorectic symptoms during the period of emergence from latency is a common event. Anorexia most often makes its appearance at this time. Skills exercised during the latency phase that make it possible to live without surrendering to reality, as well as the undemanding nature of the latency-age bodily configuration, make regression to the latency state a sanctuary from adolescent turmoil. Hypercathexis of fantasy as in latency and return to the latency-phase bodily configuration provide a potential agenda of responses which rivals asceticism and withdrawal as a technique for dealing with increased sexual and aggressive drives during puberty.

I have presented examples of the extremes of the spectrum of anorexia. The external characteristics of anorexia nervosa do not define a disease entity; rather, they are the products of a reaction pattern.

The underlying psychiatric diagnosis depends on the status and nature of ego functions, not the manifest symptom. The more pathological the cognitive impairments, the more likely is the child to become involved in an intransigent form of anorexia.

The more severe forms of anorexia involve intense aggressive interaction with parents. This encourages regression in physical form and interferes with removal. The emotionality and high noise level of the verbal interactions give the parents no time to convey the need for and encourage the development of more mature levels of abstraction and other logical processes. Failure to achieve some mastery of sexuality leaves the child without the personality skills acquired through gradual exposure. Thus, the longer anorexia lasts as a defensive configuration during emergence from latency, the more entrenched and necessary does the reaction become. For this reason, early psychotherapeutic intervention is indicated.

Part II
Early Adolescence

Chapter 5

Masturbation

Sexuality undergoes maturation and development that prepare the individual for adult life during early adolescence (most frequently from 12 to 16 years of age, but at times continuing until 17 or 18). In the successful adolescent, sexual energies shift from pleasurable discharge concentered all in self, through outlets using fantasy channels, to the use of genital organs specifically developed for the discharge of the drive. Biological maturation readies the genital organs. Culture and cognitive maturity define the limits and effectiveness of their use. Success is indicated by the extent to which a loved object is found and the degree to which fulfillment of the needs of the self and its drives also satisfies the needs of the object.

Physical Changes

To understand the cognitive maturation that provides the basis for the shift from fantasy to objects as the targets of sexual release, it is necessary to bring into focus the biological developmental events that create the organic background to propel, limit, and direct the psychological maturation of sexuality during adolescence. There appear at this point secondary sexual characteristics, enlargement and maturation of the genitalia, and increase in the sexual drives, to the point that the mechanisms of defense of latency cannot cope with them. In the years immediately preceding puberty (in boys, between 10 and 17 years of age) there is an approximately twentyfold increase in plasma testos-

terone (Faima 1972), with the most marked testosterone increases occurring between 12 and 14 (Faima). Correspondingly, in the serum of
most prepubertal girls, estradiol is undetectable (Faima). The cyclical
appearance of estradiol in the blood stream occurs at about 11 years of
age. At that time there appear the secondary sexual characteristics of
labial hair and subareolar breast buds, which precede menarche by
from one to three years. There is a period of several years, before sexual
maturation becomes apparent, during which preadolescent and early
adolescent children must deal on the emotional level with intensified
physiological stresses in the sexual area. The psychology of adolescence, including adolescent sexuality, commences prior to puberty, if
puberty is defined as the appearance of menarche and the first ejaculation.

The period of increased production of hormone in prepuberty is
accompanied by heightened sensitivity of target organs, increase in
body weight, and changes in the sensitivity of the hypothalamus to
hormone levels in the blood stream. The cognitive changes that support the capacity to fall in love (i.e., to articulate the expression of
one's sexual drives through fantasies, planning, situations, and conditions that take into account the needs of the partner) also begin to
mature in the prepubertal phase of late latency–early adolescence.
This fantasizing and/or planning function of the ego matures independently of the maturation of the hormonal releasing mechanisms of
the hypothalamus. This seems to indicate that the capacity to fall in
love is activated by the same maturational forces that cause increase in
the production of sexual hormones. It is not, however, a product of
gonadal hormonal function. Clinically, this can be seen in the fact that
eunuchs can love and that Kahlmann syndrome patients, when admin-
istered sex hormone, develop primary and secondary sexual characteristics but do not develop the capacity to fall in love.

The physical changes of early adolescence may therefore be taken
as a clue that changes in cognition are taking place. This has far-
reaching implications for therapists, who may expect child patients to
be ready to leave the playroom and to be receptive to more abstract
interpretations when early signs of puberty appear. There is a cognitive developmental continuum to be used for evaluating the developing adolescent. We must be aware that cognitive growth supports
personality maturation in adolescence. If there is a lag in development
(e.g., a persistence of omnipotentiality), it can be recognized in the
youngster who looks physically mature but behaves and thinks in the
manner of younger children. On the other hand, delay in the develop-

ment of abstract conceptual memory and abstract operational thinking are to be expected in one whose onset of puberty and growth spurt
begin at 17. Lags when detected must be coped with or countered.

Fantasies

With the beginnings of adolescence, relatively undisguised manifest
sexual fantasies derived from prelatency fantasy content appear. The
overtness of these fantasies is derived from alterations in cognition.
These alterations (ludic demise, march of symbols, passing of the
structure of latency, shift from evocative to communicative symbols)
mandate that there will be changes in emphasis, choice of symbols,
and the organization of defenses brought to bear on the latent content
of the fantasy. Memories of events, traumas, and fantasies of the
prelatency period are seen through adult "eyes." They are shaped into
influential memories, which propel children toward fantasy and behavior consonant with the cognitive capacities, cultural demands, and
the expectations of their peers. Issuing from the world of adolescence,
these fantasy products of the new cognition intrude on life to produce
neurotic distortions and behavior at their worst. At their best, they
color the creativity, sexuality, and dreams of adult life.

One must be careful in reconstructing germinal events of early
childhood from the associations of an adult patient. Many stages of
cognitive development are interposed between the early experience and
its recollection in the form of an adult derivative. Early on, the verbal
memory organization of latency can change the nature of the recall of
the affectomotor experiential memories of early childhood. What once
was reexperienced in sensory recall and feeling states can then be
condensed into words and presented as though the happenings are a
story. In latency, these stories are repressed by conversion through
symbols into a fantasy. They are reasserted and come out of repression
during early adolescence, when the power of the latency defense organizations ebbs. They are then served by new powers to distort. Reality
can be recruited to play out the reexperiencing of the recall.

At first, the tendency is to produce a direct representation (e.g.,
perversions without partners). Later, peers serve as symbols, or are
recruited to live out fantasies. In late adolescence and adult life, psychoanalytic dream-style symbols produce the fantasies that shape character. These fantasies, called core or masturbation fantasies, are the
source of the contents of fate neuroses and of the unconscious fantasies

that produce sensitivities and against which neurotic symptoms are a defense. The abstract conceptual memory organization introduces additional distortion to the recall of early experience which takes part in shaping the form of people's lives; this occurs during late latency–early adolescence. It reduces memories of experiences and word recalls to shortened abstracts. This memory function, when developed, can be applied to the recall of preexisting mental content just as it can be applied to observed phenomena. In the processing of mental content for retention in memory, the reductions required for abstract formation alter form and create similarities out of disparities. Condensations and reinforcements that use these similarities alter the validity of recalls. As a result, the interpretation of new experiences, in terms of memory, fantasy, and preconception, is open to distortions. Such distortions and their effects often cannot be corrected, either by determining the validity of the original experiences or by reconstruction of early trauma.

Although the physical changes of maturation (orgasm readiness, genital enlargement, etc.) make satisfactory sexuality possible and provide the sexual drive with an organ for discharge to be used independently of other functions, mature sexuality is incomplete without the social contexts (and the fantasies and planning that go into their production) that provide the settings and conditions for acceptable sexual encounters with love objects. Such mature sexuality first appears during adolescence in the form of *prospective fantasies*. These differ from those seen in latency in that their contents are reality-oriented. They are frankly sexual and they contain considerations for the needs of the loved object. The symbols in these fantasies are so close to reality that the thought process might better be called future planning than fantasy. However, their roots are in the unconscious drives and their symbols are used in the evocative mode, making their inclusion in the category of fantasy mandatory. Their claim to being considered future planning is based on the extent to which the real world is included as the source of symbolic representations. As such, they become stepping stones over which the child may tread with a sense of foreknowledge into the world of real objects.

Coordination with Other Chapters

Fantasy planning, with the pendant behavior to which it opens the door, is influenced by the cognitive changes in the developing adolescent, as well as by the degree of success in achieving these changes. The cognitive changes that occur at this age that contribute to this process include

1. the shift from evocative to communicative symbols in fantasy formation and creativity
2. the appearance of tertiary elaboration
3. the assumption of dominance by communicative speech

(For other aspects of these, see Chapter 3.)

4. the shift of the adaptive function of the mechanism of projection from persecutory nocturnal fantasies to sublimatory activity, exploration of social situations, and projective-introjective processes leading to modifications in the demands of the superego (see Sarnoff 1976, Chapter 8)
5. the impetus given to object-seeking and reality orientation by the organizing influence of the first ejaculation and menarche (see Chapter 1)
6. the final step in the use of symbols as objects that occurs in adolescence (This refers to a continuum from concrete symbolizations of childhood through a number of steps to the use of objects in reality through the acting out of fantasies in life situations, as symbols of primary objects. See Sarnoff 1976, Chapter 4.

These cognitive changes are developed in temporal congruity with sexual maturation. They influence sexual behavior and related fantasy formation in adolescence. (See also Chapter 9.)

Adolescent Masturbation

In the sexual sphere, the work of adolescence consists of the undoing of latency constraints, disengagement from latency fantasy as an organ for sexual discharge, and the integration of thought, action, drive, and object into an acceptable pattern for discharge using a new primary organ. One of the basic steps in this process is the rapprochement of sexual fantasy and genital masturbation so that both occur in concert.

The function of masturbation in adolescence is twofold. First, it is a technique for the discharge of sexual tension. Second, masturbation plays a vital role in providing outlet for fantasy and an arena in which an individual can work through getting used to and acquainted with sexual feelings before essaying sexual experience with real objects. Masturbation may continue until heterosexual relations are established, or overt masturbation, especially in girls, may be a brief episode.

Developmental Aspects

In an individual who has reached the point at which orgastic responses are available and individual couple dating has become a possibility, the capacity to masturbate becomes important. A person who has experienced masturbation, and is comfortable with it and with the feelings it stimulates, can use it as a means of expressing the love relationship with the sexual partner. Indeed, mutual masturbation is a frequent technique of sexual relationship in adolescence, because it is something previously experienced and something with which the children are familiar. In addition, it serves to give expression to sexual drives without stirring the fears of pregnancy or conflicts about virginity, which are age-appropriate during adolescence.

In adolescence there is no such thing as pathological masturbation. However, a view of masturbation as the all-good misses the point of the role of masturbation, which is a complex process, with a development, natural history, and resolution peculiar to each individual. As such, within masturbatory activity that is considered normal in itself there are elements that may be considered to lead in the direction of health and those that contribute psychopathogenic elements to the developing personality. Masturbation is a normal phase in the development of the personality. Irregularities in the course of the development of masturbation or the style and content of its fantasies, the techniques of masturbation, and the degree to which masturbation is conscious provide points of departure that could contribute to future psychological difficulties. One need only reflect on those cases in which obsessional techniques for the control of masturbation later become the lifelong character style of the individual (A. Freud 1949) to realize the truth of this statement. It should be emphasized that masturbation itself is not pathological, but that maturational and developmental lags, fantasies, and ego styles that are focused during the period of masturbation are elements that presage and set the stage for future difficulties.

At birth, the mouth, the ear, and the genital region are settled upon by the exploring hand of the newborn child. Frequently thereafter, the child can be seen to rub the genitals, especially when attention is called to the area of heightened sensation during diaper changing time. By 3 years of age, rubbing of the genitals can be seen as a spontaneous activity sought out by the child. Frequently, a specific mood state ushers in the rubbing—for instance, on occasions of disappointment with the mother. By 5, masturbatory rubbing is sought as a means of obtaining pleasure. A 4½-year-old called to her mother, "Mommy, it feels good in my tummy when I put my finger in my vagina." This presents first-hand evidence of the erotic component in prelatency masturbation. Masturbation tends toward masked forms with latency, and begins to reappear at about age 8. In many children, however, masked forms continue to dominate. The presence of masturbation in children so young is well known to physicians, nurses, and teachers, but is not so well known to parents. The cause of this is that the former group see so many children that they come to observe overt masturbators frequently. Parents, however, often crush the masturbatory urges of a child and force the child to seek masked forms of masturbation.

A woman told me that she uses psychology to control the masturbation of her 5-year-old grandson. "I know how much that part means to them," she said, "so I get him to stop it by telling him that if he does that, it will fall off." Other favorite threats have to do with masturbation causing brain softening and insanity, or the warning that it will cause weakness.

The Masked Masturbator

These threats, coming at the time that masturbation is accompanied by oedipal fantasies, create castration anxiety in the child. They hurry the coming of latency. Parental admonitions and attitudes begin to convey the idea that things having to do with the genitals are dangerous, dirty, and guilt-laden. Concurrently, powerful latent fantasy content and intense feelings frighten the child. As a result, the urge to find pleasure through one's own body seeks secret ways to find expression. In the prelatency child, riding on the parent's leg or rubbing against the body of the parent was acceptable, but in latency, masturbation tends toward hidden forms. When a child masks masturbation, he or she is hiding the meaning of the activity from himself or herself. In this way conscious guilt is circumvented. An adult untutored in such matters will be kept in the dark about what is going on. Although masked masturbation occurs in prelatency, open masturbation is more the rule. With the onset of latency, the influence of the newly strengthened superego turns the period of 6 to 13 years into the "Golden Age" of masked masturbation. Such activities as horseback riding, swinging the thighs together, compression of the thighs, and excited jumping during fantasy play give rise to a heightened pleasurable awareness of the genitals. In one case, a boy dressed in his mother's clothes and achieved a tingling sensation in his legs.

Return of Open Masturbation

During late latency–early adolescence, masturbation becomes open and overt in the mind of the masturbator. The nature and the extent of occurrence of masked masturbation is diminished by two factors during this phase. One is the intensification of the drives with puberty; the other is the appearance of physiological orgasm readiness and the progress of organ sensitivity that accompanies it. Physiological orgasm readiness refers to the fact that from a certain time during late latency and early adolescence, girls can produce a climax to a rhythmic masturbatory practice, a warm feeling in the genitals, vaginal contractions, and an excitement with an accelerating rhythm that spreads through most of the body. In like manner, during this period boys develop the capacity to produce a crescendo of excitement accompanied by contractions in the prostate and seminal vesicles with the ejaculation of seminal fluid as the outcome of a rhythmic masturbatory practice.

The March of Sensitivity

The *march of sensitivity* refers to the changing pattern of organ sensitivity that relates to the development of physiological orgasm readiness. In boys, stimulation of the scrotum (testicular masturbation) brings on a soothing response, with drive gratification as a result of friction. Stimulation of the penis brings on excitement, which is gratifying, but leaves the child excited and stimulated without a satisfactory outlet. Many boys who get into these states act aggressively and excitedly. After the onset of physiological orgasm readiness, the child can relieve the tension by orgasm and ejaculation. With the onset of orgasm readiness, boys experience a shift from stimulation of the testicles to stimulation of the penis. In girls at the start of this period, labial stimulation is soothing, very much like the corollary testicular masturbation in boys. However, the exciting nature of response to stimulation of the mucous membrane of the clitoris and vulva is not present at the onset.

One child of 12 reported to me that from about the age of 8˙she rubbed the anterior surface of her thighs when thinking of her mother when she was excited. At age 11, she observed her older sister masturbate with orgasm; the sister claimed orgasm readiness at age 8. The younger child tried to imitate her sister's activity, but found pleasure only in stroking the labia majora. Conscious and excitement-oriented stimulation of the vagina and vulval mucous membrane did not elicit an excitement response. Until she was 12, she actively engaged in labial masturbation with direct contact with the skin while fantasizing before going to sleep at night and while listening to records during the day. At 12, she noticed that she had developed an exciting response to the stimulation of the vulvar and vaginal mucous membrane, as well as a heightened sensation in the clitoris. She substituted this form of masturbation during the day, but avoided vaginal masturbation at night because it made her excited in bed and then she couldn't go to sleep. Nocturnal masturbation using stimulation of the mucous membrane did not start until the following year, when she developed the capacity to have orgasms.

Masked Masturbation During Early Adolescence

Masked masturbation continues beyond the latency years. The nature of the techniques used to mask masturbation changes along with the nature of sexual potentials and organ maturation. Before the shift in sensitivity to the primary copulative structures, masturbation was an activity aimed at achieving drive gratification through soothing friction with no specific end point. Therefore, gratification could be achieved through stroking the genitals or by rhythmic activity that in some ways conveyed stimulation to the genitals. With the onset of orgasmic capability, casual stimulation is insufficient to produce gratification and satisfy the newly heightened capacity to develop and discharge excitement. Almost any rhythmic activity could be a masked masturbation prior to the development of physiological orgasm capability. A far more restricted group of activities can be used for masked masturbation after the development of physiological orgasm readiness. This is especially so in boys, since there is identifiable physical evidence of masturbation in the form of the ejaculate. In girls, thigh pressure, or "riding" a pillow or a towel can produce orgastic responses. If one were to ask the girl if she masturbates, she would deny

it, saying that she never touches herself "there." The use of a great deal
of toilet paper while wiping oneself can also be effective in producing
sexual stimulation. Boys will rub against pillows, or view the whole
process as something external to themselves.

> One youngster of 17 told me that he did not masturbate. He did,
> however, have ejaculations that occurred when his penis was
> erect and in contact with the bed sheet. When he saw that he had
> developed an erection, he would move and think exciting
> thoughts about girls "to help the process along." He obviously
> masked to himself his role in the masturbatory procedures by
> isolating himself from the activity.

Orgasm Inhibition Versus Abortive Masturbation

Another technique of masked masturbation in boys is abortive masturbation. As in most situations of masked masturbation, this would be
recognizable to anyone else as orgasm-oriented (true) masturbation;
however, the individual hides his activity from himself by creating his
own definition. In this activity, the child stimulates himself to the
point of contractions but prevents actual ejaculation. This conscious
activity should be differentiated from unconscious avoidance of orgasm (orgasm inhibition rather than abortive masturbation), which
occurs in both boys and girls. This latter is a failure to reach orgasm in
someone who had been consciously trying to achieve it through masturbation or intercourse, but could not because of the nature of intrud-
ing fantasies.

> A boy of 13 tried to masturbate often and fiercely. At times he
> developed sores from the masturbation. Repeatedly he would lose
> all of his excitement just before orgasm. This was always accom-
> panied by the change in the identity of the girl he was thinking
> about from a pin-up girl in a magazine to a mental image of his
> mother or sister. He felt great guilt about the appearance of his
> mother in these fantasies. This affect was translated into his or-
> gasm inhibition.

This case highlights another important point: some people capable of physiological orgastic responses may not be psychologically
ready. In spite of physical growth, social forces represented internally
by guilt and the contents of the superego can respond to the growth of
sexuality and the fantasies linked to it, derived from the id, by forcing

suppression and limitation of the activity. Some can have orgasm through masturbation but not through intercourse. Others need special conditions for the production of an orgasm. In adolescence this is not seen as pathological, but if this is not resolved in adolescence it can persist as adult perversions, impotence, and frigidity. The individual who can masturbate in adolescence without impediment or difficulty, and with heterosexual fantasies, has a better prognosis than the adolescent who cannot bear to accept the fact of his or her own sexuality, or has need of homosexual fantasies, or needs to use an article of clothing to rub against.

Nocturnal Emissions

Excitement leading to orgasm in adolescents who have physiological orgastic capabilities may come from sources other than direct stimulation of the genitals. In rare cases, there is an orgasm during the excitement of taking an examination. More commonly, orgasm can be stimulated through the fantasy-forming function of the ego. The most widespread such phenomenon is the nocturnal emission. In this, the individual is asleep and dreaming. The dream contains sexual fantasy elements, such as having sexual intercourse. In some cases it precedes intromission, and is thus a dream representation of premature ejaculation.

The first appearance of nocturnal emission ("wet dream") is taken by many as a sign of the beginning of a capacity for ejaculation and orgasm in boys. This is of course a mental representation of the event. Orgastic dreams also occur in girls. The absence of concrete representations to mark the event, that is, the boy's ejaculate, causes this event not to take on the same importance that it does for boys. Instead, the event that represents maturity to the mind of the observer of children is the appearance of the first menstrual period.

Masturbation and Object Relations

Through masturbation, the adolescent finds one of the avenues by which one can attempt to resolve the core fantasies that were left unresolved at the end of latency. In this context, *resolve* means to use a fantasy repeatedly until it loses its meaning in its displaced form. This is then followed by a less displaced fantasy. Eventually, the person can express the latent fantasy more directly, release it from repression, and decide whether or not he wishes to keep it. An example would be a fantasy of intercourse with a woman with large breasts. Eventually a cunnilingus fantasy may come to the surface as the more direct expression of the oral heterosexual wishes expressed in the fantasy of the woman with large breasts. Should the cunnilingus fantasy appear in a person as a result of a softening of the superego through achieving the psychoanalytic ideal that nothing within oneself which is human need be considered foreign, the formerly repressed and symbolized fantasy can be accepted as part of the self and of precoital play without a sense of guilt or embarrassment. The fantasy comes to be accepted by the person, who now has a less severe superego than he did when he first inhibited and repressed the impulse. In intercourse, the resolution of fantasy in this way introduces the addition of unsuggested techniques of lovemaking in experienced, long-term sexual partners.

In some adolescents, the process of undoing fantasy displacements is too threatening, and masturbation may cease, with a flight from masturbation and sexuality or a flight into pseudo-sexuality (e.g., sexual experience without meaningful participation) as a defensive measure. Individuals who do not get to know and accept their sexuality better through masturbation do not resolve the core fantasies during adolescence. They enter adult life with a pathogenetic immaturity that remains a potential source of pathological adjustment into adult life. The strength of the fantasies, their nature, and the defenses of the ego that are available dictate whether or not masturbation during adolescence can provide an arena in which the individual may work through, become accustomed to, and get acquainted with his own sexuality prior to assaying sexual experience with real objects.

The Impact of Masturbation Fantasies on Life Adjustments

The degree to which manifestations of latent fantasy permeate the life of an individual varies from person to person. There are those in whom self-defeating core fantasies permeate all of life, so that they become incapable in all spheres of endeavor. In others, only the relationship with the spouse will bear the earmarks of the core fantasy. In adolescence, it is not unusual for the permeation by derivatives of a core fantasy, such as those oriented toward self-deprecation, to be far more intense than it will be in adult life. The resolution of this situation usually occurs with the ego integration that occurs about 18 years of age. At that time, there is better goal orientation, better capacity to give up present pleasures to prevent future pain, and diminution of the unmodified manifestations of drive-expressive behavior. Should the resolution not occur, then the individual enters adulthood with life dominated by impulsive fantasy. Pervasive, all-encompassing, drive-oriented (evocative) behavior in adolescence offers a poor prognosis for the future. One cannot expect, nor does one see, full integration in such people by the age of 18. So much has been lost in learning, social skills, and educational achievement (i.e., good grades) that the future of the child is handicapped in competition with others.

A youngster who could not achieve orgasm because of the appearance of his mother in his masturbation fantasies had a core fantasy related to desire for his mother and fear of his father that pervaded all areas of his life. He became a thief (displacing his wish to steal from his mother), and dared not compete with his father, so that he could not dare to achieve in school.

Without outside help, such a totally fantasy-pervaded individual would have a poor future.

Pathological Aspects of Adolescent Masturbation

So far we have discussed the normal uses of masturbation in adolescence: the discharge of tension, an outlet for fantasy, and an area for growth. Now we shall dwell on some uses of masturbation that are related in themselves to pathology.

As described, masturbation is a sexual outlet for the lonely. Feeling, affect, and excitement accompany the appearance of people in fantasies. A person is not alone, and that which is lost is returned in the fantasy. On a deeper level, the comfort that comes from masturbation in boys is related to the reassurance they get that no matter how inadequate they may have been shown to be, their penis is still intact—they are not injured or castrated. In this regard, masturbation becomes a technique for the symbolic countering of injuries to narcissism.

Stekel (1911), a psychoanalyst of years past, felt that masturbation served a useful purpose in that it served as an outlet for otherwise inexpressible fantasy wishes.

In this regard, a man who wished to kill his father had the act deflected by the following fantasy: His father's head was to be chopped off. When the blood gushed out, the man had his orgasm.

It seems likely from current knowledge that masturbation fantasies are but one of many pathways for the expression of one's core fantasies. It is more the function of displacement rather than the type of derivative (i.e., masturbation fantasy, dream, conscious fantasy, living out in a displaced manner) that protects the individual from expressing directly a core fantasy with negative implications.

Masturbation as a Comfort and a Life-Style

In individuals who have difficulties in establishing contact with members of the opposite sex—such as those who fear rejection, or fear injury during intercourse—masturbation provides the possibility of a self-contained sexual world in which anything is possible; and this is usually far more than the person could have accepted of himself in society, and certainly exceeds what society would be willing to accept in him. The self-contained sexual world of the masturbator is a world without fear of loss of the loved one, or domination by that person, or concern about injury, or the need to search beyond oneself for a responsive lover. To the narcissistic person who does not want to give of himself, it serves as an ideal expression of his love relationship. In short, for the anxious, the frightened, the prideful, masturbation serves as a refuge from the demands of adult life. For these, masturbation is a technique by which to avoid mature sexuality. As such, it can continue as the primary sexual outlet throughout life.

Masturbation can serve as a comfort for the depressed. Remember the action of the young child when mother was angry or going away: he began to rub himself for comfort. The adolescent finds a soothing response to testicular masturbation. In periods of depression and sadness, masturbation increases and, at that time, serves as a comfort. If one remembers that masturbation is accompanied by fantasies and that fantasies contain people, one can realize why masturbation affords comfort.

Summary

Because masturbation fantasies contain people—and masturbation helps a person to tolerate fantasies through repetition, and affects through experience—they form the basis for the most important role of masturbation as an elementary tool used in the work of adolescence. Adolescent masturbation serves as a bridge from evocation and fantasy to communicative relationships with the world of reality. The aspect of adolescent masturbation that relates to its role as one of the bridges to the object world will be pursued in the following chapter.

Chapter 6

Bridges to the Object World

Step by step, moment by moment, sexuality during late latency–early adolescence pursues a predestined course, from an evocative, narcissistic, fantasy symbol-oriented discharge organization to one with predominantly communicative, altruistic, reality-oriented discharge function. It is necessary for the personality of the child to make a series of changes, primarily cognitive, in order to negotiate this shift. At first the changes are internal. For instance, drive energies begin to intensify under the pressure of increased secretion of sexual hormones and the form of representations to be used as symbols more and more takes on the shape of humankind. Playthings give way to real things. Symbols are chosen less and less for their ability to evoke a private world of memories and feelings, and increasingly for their ability to serve as communicative links with the real and object world. The father of the past comes to serve less as a guide, while the reality of future potentials organizes, guides, and reshapes fantasy until it becomes future planning. All these changes reflect maturational modifications within the ego. Internal changes in the strength of drives and in cognition reshape the potential forms of sexual discharge of the child in late latency–early adolescence. They activate and energize the child's ability to find gratification in reality. They do not provide the loved one.

The work of growing up and finding a partner in late latency–early adolescence could be likened to the tasks of an explorer traveling to a new land. Much preparation is necessary before his ships can cross the unknown sea. Some image of the new land must be formed. Upon this, planning can be made and provisions stocked. Then, once embarked, the new land must still be found; and even then, the secrets and the reality of the new land must be incorporated to change the explorer's image of the land if it is to be won or colonized. So it goes with the child. Daydreams shape impressions and fantasies about potential real objects of love. These reassuring images make incursions into reality seem possible and safe. Fantasied familiarity enables approaches to the unknown. Then new realities make known the true nature of the person to whom the child is now bound by object ties that are slow to dissolve. At that point, the child must reshape his or her behavior to conform to the needs of the real object in order to hold it and seem to win it.

The function of internal changes in the strength of drives and in cognition may be likened to that of the supporting pier on one side of a bridge. To stretch a span to reality from the pier requires the dynamic influence of three processes that make it possible to engage the loved one in the real world. These parts of the bridge to the object world consist of

1. masturbation as a means of mastering intense affect and trial action,
2. projection of reassuring images, and
3. maturation of the observing object in the mind's eye.

Masturbation as a Bridge to the Object World

Though there was emphasis in the preceding chapter on the use of masturbation as a kind of holding action (i.e., a way in which drives can be turned from the object world toward the self for gratification), there is an aspect of masturbation that adds a plank to the bridge to the object world. The realignment of masturbatory fantasy and the act of masturbation that occurs during late latency–early adolescence serves this important purpose. Through masturbation, the maturing organism learns to test, experience, bear, and finally enjoy the welling sensations of orgasm before he is called upon to experience them after having established a relationship with an object in reality. The content of the concurrent masturbation fantasies in turn provides patterns for the search for a life partner. Passive fantasy invites aggressive partners. Therapeutic interventions can help at this age to reshape a future of which the masturbation fantasy is a warning harbinger. Laufer (1968) emphasizes the role of conscious early adolescent masturbation fantasies as a tool to be used by the developing person to experience, in "trial action[,] . . . adult sexual behavior" (p. 115). In addition, it provides the therapy with topics and wishes that would be unavailable otherwise.

Affects

Disguised sexuality tends to decrease during adolescence. As a result, masturbation becomes more overt. Orgastic feelings, which accompany masturbatory acts and fantasies, are sometimes overwhelming and create fears in the child of the intense affects to be expected with sexual intercourse. This widens rather than bridges the gap between the drive and the potential loved one. The intense physical response requires "getting used to." Masturbation aids in this reorientation. Solely in charge of the activation of his feelings, the masturbating child can master and get used to intense orgastic feelings at a rate that is adjustable to the individual tolerance. Children should not be pressed to embark on sexual activities with others until this task has been mastered.

Fantasies

Age-appropriate increase in overt sexual activity is both an outcome of an increase in sexual drive and the product of a decrease in the influence of latency defenses. Distortion decreases and reality orientation of manifest fantasy increases in the child. A retreat to the use of evocative fantasy as a means of discharge for sexual drive is blocked as the result of maturation. Overt fear-inducing masturbatory fantasies become potentially threatening and a cause for retreat when they seem to describe the nature of reality. Cognitive maturation both pushes the child toward reality objects and opens the door to anxiety and fear about growing up as the result of the articulation of fear fantasies with reality. The child therapist must be careful in exploring such fantasies that panic reactions are not induced by encouraging object-finding through the analysis of fear (masturbatory) fantasies that inhibit social growth. Here one proceeds with care. For example, a 14-year-old girl with a masturbation fantasy that revolved around being raped was caused to retreat from dating situations by her fear of the aggressiveness that she read into sexual situations.

Even when an object has been found and a love relationship established, planning and acting in the area of sexual drive discharge are still very much fantasy-dominated in early adolescence. However, at this time the fantasy has normally begun to be modified by aware-ness of the needs of the partner. In pathological states of falling in love (sexual thralldom), primitive fantasy components persist, or the needs of the partner must be excluded or very special partners with congru-ent fantasy-dominated sexuality sought. Libidinal cathexes are then said to be directed more toward one's inner fantasies than toward loved objects. This state of pathological narcissism, which often extends into adult life (fixation), parallels the distribution of cathexes of libidinal energies seen in the secondary narcissism of late latency. Fixations at this stage of the developmental continuum contribute to pathological sexual adjustments in adult life.

Projection as a Bridge to the Object World

Projection is a mechanism of defense that is most often associated with pathological states. Prohibited urges and wishes generated within the self are projected onto others. Even an acceptable urge—such as anger—when it exceeds the tolerance of a person, may be assigned (projected) to someone else. This produces distortions of perceived reality. The role of projection in the production of impaired reality testing tends to give projection a bad name. In actuality, projection is a complex form of displacement. Displacement in every phase of devel-opment distorts the relationship between the self and differentiated objects. When love objects are first sought, the initial bridge to the object world is established through the reassuring belief that the new object can be forced into the mold of the past as though it were an extension of the self rather than something with an existence of its own. A sense of control of the object is created. Even though the wish that is projected onto the new object as a generalized identity is hostile and generates fear, it is not as much to be feared as the possibly benign reality of the new person. (The devil that one knows is less to be feared than the angel who comes as a stranger.) Projection of a familiar fantasy permits the establishment of a bridge to the object world.

Shift in Projection

During late latency–early adolescence, there occurs a change in projec-tion. There is also a definitive change in its uses. The change in projection is seen in a shift in its basic component defenses. There is a shift from projection associated with repression, which is supported in achieving a decathexis of original content by the formation of masking symbols, toward projection associated with denial, which is supported in achieving disavowal of original content by the use of displacement of the origin of urges and wishes to real objects. Even though real objects are utilized in the latter situation, they still serve as symbols as long as they are used to serve evocative ends. Real objects once introduced into fantasy projections provide a pathway for the shift from an evocative mode to a communicative mode. This makes possible the modification of one's world view through the introduction of reality. With this in mind, the child therapist can strengthen reality testing by actively exploring the difference between the child's fears of the nature of people and reality experiences. Even without such interventions, there is, according to Pumpian-Mindlin (1965), an ". . . 'acting out' of the omnipotential phantasies in reality, thereby submitting them to testing. Gradually, as they are tested against reality, the diffuse omnipotential energies are channelized to modify the omnipotential fantasies in accord with the demands of reality" (p. 9). Consequently, there is a modification of masturbatory demands to conform to reality.

This shift is supported by a number of phase-related developmental phenomena, the most important of which is the passing from prominence of the typical ego structure of latency (Sarnoff 1987a). Residues of the structure of latency persist in daydreaming, future planning, and sublimations, but the use of symbols and fantasy structures diminishes. Direct involvement of drives with objects, instead of involvement with fantasy representations, now takes place. This may be seen clinically in a patient's shift from fear of attack by robbers to fear of being forced into sexual acts by peers. There is a spontaneous thrust in the direction of communicative symbols, speech, and language to carry relationships into the province of reality.

There is a similarity of psychic events in late latency–early adolescence to psychic events in the separation–individuation phase of infancy. In both, there is an experience of separation from the mother, with increasing individuation manifested in the child's increasing executive functions. Problems of passivity coupled with fear and eagerness for the fusion that is implied in passivity are present in both phases. Most striking is the fact that in both phases there is awareness of changes in the body. In the adolescent there is massive growth and the development of secondary sexual characteristics. In the infant the sense of bodily change is related to the developmental–maturational growth of cognitive functions, with a concomitant constantly modifying perception of body form. The parallel between the two periods sets the stage for a regression in the adolescent that permits the utilization of defenses, i.e., denial and displacement, appropriate to the earlier period.

Changes in the Content of Projection

During late latency and early adolescence there is a change in emphasis in the content of projections, with a shift from projection of id impulses to projection of superego introjects. Through projection, the superego is externalized. Peers or respected teachers appear to the child to be the sources of ego-ideal imagery. This is a step in removal. It is a manifestation of the urge to rebel against the parent, and is also a derivative of the thrust toward a communicative involvement with the world, which dominates the age period. At first this imagery consists primarily of parental commands and respected prior ethical and cultural conditions projected onto teachers and peers. Thus, the initial content of the externalized ego ideal is based on the child's prior experiences; but peers or teachers have ideas of their own. These are added to the external ego ideal, creating a new ego ideal, which is imbued with characteristics of the ego ideal of the new object. Reinternalization of the ego ideal is an ongoing process. The projection–reinternalization involved is a dynamic series of events. Projection is part of the process of preadolescent ethical and personal individuation, which encourages projection of preconceptions onto newly perceived objects in their separateness in an attempt to make them familiar. Reinternalization is a manifestation of introjection. It is fueled by introjective defenses used to deal with aloneness, partings, and separations. The same individuation, removal, and socialization that encourage the externalization of the ego ideal trigger reinternalization as a compensation for loss.

As a result of the fusion of the projected ego ideal and new cultural, peer-based content, a new ego ideal is synthesized. With reinternalization, modifications of the internalized superego occur. In this way the self-observing functions of the superego take on new guidelines. That is, an observing object comes to be developed in the mind's eye, which guides and provides an unconscious sensitivity to the needs of readers, lovers, audiences, or society. The process is closely related to recruitment and metamorphosis, in which the child recruits others to play a role in their own fantasy and, once the person has come close, adds the reality experiences imposed by the presence and needs of new people to the body of memory data through which the world will be interpreted and from which the conditions and elements of future planning will be derived.

Changes in the use of the mechanism of projection can be expected during late latency. It is used more intently and for purposes different from those that produce evocative pathology, such as fear fantasies, paranoia, and phobias. Intensification of projection, often manifested in these syndromes, can be seen at or just preceding puberty. Eight-year-olds with adultiform paranoid schizophrenia and premature puberty are an example of this. Acute paranoid reactions during ethical individuation also illustrate this.

The cognitive shift of late latency–early adolescence toward the communicative mode affects projection as it affects symbols, and projection becomes a useful mechanism which serves socialization, altruism, and the ability to fall in love through its participation in the process of projection–reinternalization. These normal changes in the use of projection during late latency–early adolescence provide a healthy alternative to the negative prognoses made as a result of the presence of persecutory fantasies during latency. Failure during late latency–early adolescence to achieve a communicative mode for projection produces grandiose (narcissistic) states and paranoia, which begin to be identified at this time.

The change to the communicative mode in the use of projection is seen in the shift from the primary role of the defense from fantasy and symptom formation to an important role in (1) testing fantasy against reality, (2) sublimation and creativity, and (3) opening up the superego to contemporary cultural influences and the development of the observing object in the mind.

Fantasy as a Bridge to the Object World

The development of healthy object ties in adolescence is the product of a multitude of forces. Foremost among these forces is the influence of the communicative mode. Through tertiary elaboration, which is strongly influenced by the observing object in the mind's eye, the communicative mode reshapes the fantasy content of expectations of reality object contact to fit that which is generally expected by the world beyond the self. In this way the needs and wishes of the child part company with demanding personal fantasies. The child's needs and wishes are brought into line with the world's demands and those wishes which in reality one might have some hope of fulfilling.

Communicative symbols are used for fantasy formation as a means of effecting this task.

In early adolescence, fantasy models of contact derived most of their content from evocations of drives, previous repressed affects, unprocessed or unmastered traumatic experiences, and fantasy distortions. The transmutation of id forces and unconscious contents into latent fantasy is an important example of the contribution of the evocative mode to creativity and object ties. The transmutation of latent fantasy into socially acceptable planning and behavior through tertiary elaboration is an important example of the contribution of the communicative mode to creativity and acceptable functioning in the object world.

Creativity in the form of fantasy formation plays an important part in defining the subject's role in object relations. Through the formation of a fantasy, a highly personalized trial action is devised. Evocative symbols are the means through which personalization is effected. Their communicative component brings a dimly seen world beyond the self into a province whose boundaries enclose influences of the unconscious and the id. Through their role in fantasy formation, evocative symbols participate in the communicative acts of adolescents. Around personalized trial action, excursions can be planned into *a world beyond the self*, a world beyond primary objects.

One part of the work of adolescence is to establish a pattern of people and behavior around oneself that will permit a reality-oriented area in which the sexual and aggressive drives, identities, and ambitions can be realized. During late latency–early adolescence there is a transition phase in which these parts of the life arena are tried, tested, and deserted and—sometimes—regressed from. With healthy resolutions the adolescent eventually finds his place in this world.

If at first there is not at this time a regular, reliable, sustained outlet for drives, a shift toward self-gratification, evocative symbols, and evocative-mode fantasies threatens. It is the work of the therapist to counter such regressions through confrontation and reality testing.

Drives have force, and will claim their way. If objects and reality do not provide gratification, there will be a shift to a reassertion of the latency-age use of fantasy as a drive (sexual) outlet. The ego is tempted away from reality toward gratification in self and in fantasy. This is countered by the process of puberty, which brings the first ejaculation or menarche, ludic demise, and the function that walks as their shadow—the ability to use objects in reality as symbols in the formation of fantasies for active and passive drive discharge. In this way, regression to fantasy does not mean a return to latency evocations of past moods. Instead, it provides an arena for trial action and planning that, using communicative-mode symbols, will ready the child to seek again real people. Puberty provides the maturation of an organ that seeks a partner for sexual drive discharge and so establishes the need for an object in reality. Should the real object not wish to cooperate in a permissive context, the reticent real object can be loved in an accepting though limited context in planning fantasy that takes the real object's needs into account. As a result the evocative mode becomes less influential. To aid the process, the child psychotherapist should encourage fantasy more and more akin to future planning.

Symbols with immediate links to the real world are invested with a strong potential communicative mode. This use of reality guarantees some freedom of the ego from the influence of the id. This is a form of repression. Such a recruitment of elements in reality to serve to hold the attention of consciousness at the expense of latent fantasy and inner drives is called countercathexis. As a result of the heightened ability during late latency–early adolescence to use reality as countercathexis, evocations and their derivatives play a role during adolescence that is less than primary. The child therapist should encourage repression of evocations through the enhancement of reality hypercathexes.

From a vocabulary of symbols derived from the surrounding world are chosen the words and symbols used by tertiary elaboration. Unconscious fantasy is transmuted in this way by tertiary elaboration to become a bridge to the object world. It becomes the armature around which conscious behavior and motivation will be shaped by the influence of reality. This process makes its greatest developmental strides during late latency–early adolescence. This fact is the theoretical underpinning of a number of aspects of psychotherapy during this period. For instance, free association tends to take the patient's thoughts to descriptions of a multitude of distinct relationships between peers.

The high school student speaks of the girls and boys he observes or the movies he has seen, and not, apparently, of himself. His choice of couples and stories is a key to his involvement in life. Why is it that he observes while others are involved?

The therapist must be alert to common themes that reflect the subtly hidden evocative contribution to the choice of the people, situations, or events of which the patient chooses to speak. Since the world of the late latency–early adolescent child is in its beginning, the goal of therapy is less emphatically on changing the present than on changing the future. A mind in transition is malleable. Therapeutic intervention can be directed to analyzing sources of evocative areas within a given symbol derived from past experiences. These cause distortions in future planning.

A youth exposed to ridicule as a child had fantasies of being teased for small size by a sexual partner.

A girl whose father called her frazzle nose was afraid to go to a party for fear she would be rejected for "ugliness."

A boy from a foster home was afraid that he would be asked by a girl on a date to get her a radio. He had no idea that one could refuse the request of a girl in this situation.

A boy whose father and older brothers continually spoke of their sexual prowess feared that he would not know what to do, and would be unfavorably compared, if a girl demanded sexual intercourse on their first date.

The selection of countercathexes can be encouraged by the therapist to take a direction most apt to provide preparation for communicative and constructive function in adult life. Cathexis of inner fantasy at the expense of reality can be discouraged through confrontations that enhance reality testing.

The Audience: The World

A most important factor involved in the formation of the personality, trial action fantasy, creative process, and the personal contribution to the shape of life in the years of adolescence and beyond is the audience. During psychotherapy, the therapist is the audience. In school, it is the teacher and peers. In loving, it is the lover.

As removal progresses, the influence of parents yields to that of the world. In essence, sources of symbols in the world beyond the self, which had been summoned to populate fantasy evocations for use in drive discharge, cease to be passive vessels that carry the drives. Instead, now they provide, in part, a source for the fantasy. They insinuate their own identities and needs. The communicative poles of such "borrowed" symbols reshape fantasy to a new mold. The object hunger of the maturing child pulls him toward change. Unwilling to take life's first steps alone, the child develops new shapes of fantasy and character in order to win the audience that is his world. Whether the product is the self as a work of art, or is a more conventional artifact, the child pays attention to the communicative aspects of the self or product. The form of the product takes shape from the influences of the borrowed symbols. The aggressive child who takes on the characteristics of a mythic hero in his fantasies channels his character to fit the patterns of the hero. Projection of wishes onto a new object, borrowed to play out a role in a fantasy, extends the boundary of the child to include the new object. Aspects of the object become a part of the self. If the real object so chosen is then to be wooed, won, and held, it becomes a part of the expectant and powerfully influencing audience. The fantasy must be changed to suit the needs of the loved one.

The shape and direction taken by the communicative mode in the use of symbols within fantasies that express drives connected with being in love are guided by the lover through the observing object in the mind's eye. The act of borrowing symbols to serve evocative needs is often accompanied by such an epigenetic internalization. This leaves a mark on the tastes and choices of the child that transcends the moment and leads into the future. Influence is present even when an act of creation occurs when the child is alone, and the prospective audience or lover is absent in reality. The audience, the observing object—which shapes the aesthetic aspect of the creative act—and the details of love exist for the child in that circumstance in the *mind alone*. The internalized, remembered audience continues to shape creativity and hopes.

The will of the internalized, remembered audience augments the internalized "contents of the superego demands." Here are the sources, stored within the self, that shape the influences of tertiary elaboration; here are the sources of the words and customs that make it possible to enter the strange land of the world beyond the self with a sense of familiarity and ease.

The Observing Object in the Mind's Eye

The observing object, which influences spontaneous creativity and behavior from adolescence into adulthood, first appears in infancy. It is important in the control of demeanor and behavior from early on. It contributes, for instance, to superego formation in early childhood.

During the latency age period, it influences symbolic form. Common tales provide symbols. These symbols draw the play of the latency child into the passive and rote use of socially determined nonverbal symbols and signs, and mythic images. These may be characters and symbols from stories, myths, *Märchen*, fairy tales and T.V. cartoons. When in early latency affectomotor memory is replaced with verbal concept memory, stories read to children or overheard or seen on television become the carriers of the affectomotor experience. Children whose minds are limited in their outward expression to symbols common to a dominating current culture—said to be ensnared by cultural capture—play out their fantasies using Shera, Batman, or Superman to express *themselves*.

Fantasies of future planning find their footing in reality through the symbols of the real that have been introduced in early latency. For a child in early latency the need to find new carriers for their complexes and memories weights apparently neutral symbols of a culture with the qualities of the evocative mood. This means that secret implications can be carried into reality situations.

Reality symbols carrying memories that have been lost to the infantile amnesia are the characteristic representations from which are selected the evocative symbols used in latency-age fantasy activity. Not every symbol presented to the child by parents, peers, and teachers is retained and used for fantasy. Certain ones are chosen, above all others, to be the personal symbols that identify the child. Because fantasy at this age does not require the inclusion of an object in reality, the selection of symbols is dominated by the content implications of the evocative pole of the symbol. The observing object formed from those who provided the symbols will therefore be weak, since the child is more apt to be influenced by inner callings.

For the latency-age child, the pertinent aspects of chosen elements have a highly personalized appeal; they reflect experiences, feelings, and repressed affectomotor memory elements which cannot be shared with others. Even the mythic elements, which bind memory elements into repression at the same time that they sweep the verbal skills of the child into channels of expression that reflect cultural capture, are selected with little emphasis on communicative value. Companions and observers cannot crack this cryptic code of the unconscious. This serves well the purpose of fantasy in the latency years, since the purpose is to preserve mood and memory from being shared through the use of the evocative mode in selecting symbols. The observing object in the mind's eye has little demand to make in the world of creativity and the seeking of love objects during the latency years.

The shift to the communicative pole, the harnessing of fantasy to drive with discharge considering the needs of an object, changes the situation and orientation of the early adolescent child. At this stage, fantasy content is influenced by needs to entertain, communicate, and be coherent. These are part of the cognitive transformations of late latency. The need to pursue communicative speech becomes so strong that even in the absence of an audience, phrasing and symbol selection are dominated by it. With the strengthening of the need to use reality, the observing object in the mind's eye becomes stronger too. With the strengthening of awareness that will lead to planning that is acceptable to the world and the setting aside of personal evocations, the child is readied to cross a bridge into the object world.

The Observing Object in the Mind's Eye Transcends Late Latency–Early Adolescence

The observing object is a consistent element among the internalized structures of the personality. In this chapter we are concentrating on its activation to influence symbol formation and communicative speech in early adolescence. This should not, however, be taken to indicate a devaluation of its importance in early childhood and latency or its influence in adult life. The following clinical vignettes, which reflect the role of the observing object in the mind's eye during adolescence and adulthood, illustrate the more general nature of the psychological structure.

A patient's masturbatory activity from age 12 to 16 was accompanied by the thought that there was a television camera watching her, through which her father was able to watch her. When she moved to a new city, she began to keep a diary of her experiences and thoughts. The diary was written with me as the observing object. This continued her therapy even when I was no longer present. She continued certain resistances, keeping out of the writing material that she had kept out of therapy.

In another case, a woman in her 40s was preoccupied with her obituary. She repeatedly compared her obituary with the obituaries of men and looked forward to the day when analysis would free her from the emotional restrictions that kept her from being able to achieve more than the chores of a housewife, so that she would have an obituary that would be comparable to that of a man. In effect, she lived her life with the observing object in her mind's eye being the great unseen audience consisting of people who read the obituaries of those who have just died and judge their lives accordingly.

A man in his mid-fifties, who had excellent writing skills and was a Chaucerian scholar, suffered a writing block. He was unable to do creative writing because of his fear that the aggressive nature of the people who read what he had to write would lead to destructive reactions on their part.

The observing object in the mind's eye takes on special importance when the cognitive transformations of late latency–early adolescence place emphasis on communication and the needs of the audience in selecting symbols. The observing object becomes the focal point in the shaping of adolescent fantasy. With the beginning of adolescence, transmission of unconscious content is increasingly channeled into verbal conduits consisting of communicative symbols. There is a distinct change in the preferred symbolic forms to be used in creativity and in free association. Aesthetic and communicative considerations are taken into account in the selection of symbols through which latent fantasies are to be expressed. Even in the absence of a literal audience, the observing object persists and influences the symbolizing function to select symbols with high aesthetic and communicative potential.

From the standpoint of clinical manifestations, the introduction of aesthetic considerations pushes symbols toward adult mature forms with verbal emphasis. In the shift from latency to adolescence, this is characterized by a change of the nature of the symbolic forms used in spontaneous fantasy formation as the evocative, personal-experience, and/or rote symbols of latency retreat before the communicative, aesthetically determined symbols of adolescence.

The Therapist as Observing Object

The shift to communicative symbols *requires* that the symbolizer have in the mind's eye an observing object for guidance in the shaping of symbols. The observing object in late latency–early adolescence becomes the internal manifestation of the shift of cathexis to extrafamilial objects that accompanies the child's emergence from latency. This influences the symbolizing function and the symbolic forms it produces. It causes the nature of the symbol to shift from evocation, which relates to the inner world, to communication, which relates to the observing object. Often, in this time of flux, the only consistent entity is the therapist. Whether or not he or she so wishes, the therapist's ways, words, and values shape the child's image of the world's expectations. A great deal of personal influence, often therapeutic, is unknowingly brought to bear during therapy sessions.

Inhibiting Aspects of the Observing Object

In adolescence, the effects of the observing object in the mind's eye are more far-reaching than the investment of symbols with communicative power. In using the observing object in the mind's eye for reaching toward real objects for drive discharge, the adolescent frequently clothes peers and authorities with attitudes and reactions derived from the internalized observing object. If the attitudes of this object are harsh and critical, the world becomes a place to be feared; new situations, performances, and activities may be avoided. Therapeutic techniques must be aimed at the exploration of reality, and analysis to find a source of the emphasis on the projections of condemning and controlling aspects of the internalized observing object. This negative influence of the internalized observing object occurs to some extent in every adolescent. The process is often at the root of mood swings associated with limitations of social activities. When this feature of the internalized observing object can be disentangled from reality, there occurs a decrease in the energy needed for the child's mastering of imagined humiliations.

The Role of the Observing Object in the Mind's Eye in the Shift from Evocative to Communicative Symbols

As noted earlier, scientists have investigated the influence on symbol formation of outside factors retained as memory elements and the way reporting news is formulated (see p. 64). Research has defined social factors in the psychology of communication (e.g., symbols, the writing of stories, and the effect of communicative needs on speech).

The observing object in the mind's eye represents the public in its absence. Even when alone, the child experiences the influence of society that contributed to the formation of his thought in the form of the observing object, which becomes more important and influences the symbolizing function to select symbols on an aesthetic (i.e., communicative) basis when the audience it represents becomes more important to the child. This occurs when the child acquires the capacity, through the setting aside of narcissism, to have sufficient need of the audience that he or she will shape communication to win its negative or positive attention. In the case of fantasy planning that involves drive gratification, the attention sought through the use of pleasing symbols and contexts is love.

The Communicative Symbol Comes of Age

The communicative symbol dominates art and therapy from the beginning of adolescence. It is in turn dominated by society. This form of symbol takes into account the real world and the needs of the audience in the selection of the signifier, i.e., communicative symbols are shaped by choices based upon consensual recognition of meaning. Therefore, they play a significant part in communicative work, art, and writing.

The shift in symbol from those that function in the evocative mode to those that function in the communicative mode is strongly furthered by the internalized representation of the audience for which the work is conceived. Thus, the latency-age child conceives of the word as a means of expressing his drives, whereas the adolescent conceives of the word as a communication to an internalized representation. This change in emphasis marks the characteristics acquired during adolescence by the observing object in the mind's eye.

Limiting Drive Gratification for
the Survival of the Group

"The transmission of traditions has provided man with the means of maintaining the identity and integrity of the group (the smallest unit capable of survival) (Sarnoff 1976, p. 379). A man is often powerless alone where a group can survive. The creativity of individuals which modifies reality provides both an evolutionary strength and a danger." There is evolutionary strength in man's evolutionary potential for adaptive survival, which depends on the sustained capacity for development of alternative potentials. Creativity is part of this; however, in order to survive in the group, this creative potential must sometimes be stifled. Therefore, the potential for the communicative, creative establishment of new, potentially group-dissolving patterns has to be suppressed if the old groups are to survive and function. Oneiric symbols provide a pathway for the occult exercise of the expression of individual wishes, and thus they serve a necessary function in the evolution of man. They preserve a skill. They provide an evolutionary adjustment which permits man to maintain flexibility while continuing to be bound by mythically organized group solidarity. At the point that creativity is needed, the ability for original thought is channeled into communicative forms of symbolization, providing new ways of perceiving the environment and organizing the world in the mental life of the individual. Once this new way of organizing the world has proved adaptive, the entire group patterns itself (establishes a guardian observing object in the mind's eye) within this new set; and creativity once again becomes channeled into oneiric symbolic exercises, with its originality deflected from reality, to preserve the group's survival potential. It thus appears that the development of play and dream symbols is influenced by social pressures.

Summary

For those who work with adolescents it is important to know that there is a natural maturational and developmental stage during which the capacity to fall in love emerges. The changes occur normally, and it therefore should not be attributed to therapeutic maneuvers. Therapy can only *enable* where development has been stayed by pathological factors. It is also important to realize that at times this normal step is not taken. Failure to develop the *capacity* to fall in love has very serious diagnostic and prognostic clinical implications. For instance, the child who does not move to communicative symbols, but continues to work within the area of highly personalized, egocentric (autistic) symbols, has failed to move toward an object relatedness. Communicative symbols with shared and conventional meanings become the basic vocabulary of compromise, group planning and shared hopes populated by shared realities.

The successful shift to communicative symbols, communicative speech, and tertiary elaboration is necessary if the needs of society are to become operative in the formulations of a person as he creates future planning. They are the piers of a bridge to the object world. They form the operating ego activities and functions that permit the observing object in the mind's eye to influence behavior. When communicative symbols, communicative speech, and tertiary elaboration serve an observing object in the mind's eye that represents a *libidinal* object, the symbolizing subject will produce fantasies and planning while taking into account the loved one, on a preconscious level, quite voluntarily. When the loved one can be permitted to join the observing object in the mind's eye, two things happen: one is never again quite alone, and one's thoughts and actions are born out of an inner awareness of the loved one's needs. This is the state of being in love. The mature state is not inborn. Rather, it is a product of maturation and development during late latency–early adolescence.

The development of the capacity to fall in love interposes delay in gratification. This development depends upon the maturation of communicative symbols, communicative speech, and tertiary elaboration. Impairments in the capacity to fall in love reflect defects in these component ego skills. Diagnostic assessments in adolescence should mark these skills for evaluation in the case of selfish and narcissistic patients.

Chapter 7

The Object World Responds

The work of adolescence consists of a continuous reshaping of the personality in response to two ongoing changes. The first is the maturation of internal forces and mechanisms; and the second, are social imperatives and the responses of the object world to obvious changes in the maturation of the child.

Internal maturation is a true example of anatomy as destiny. The superb athlete who does not have his growth spurt until 18 years of age loses out on years of seasoning in a chosen sport. Height and facial features, which take their final form in adolescence, dictate important aspects of self image. Delay in sexual maturation results in a loss of place in the line of social development. The internal pressures and changes of youth are the same in all cultures and all people. They are relatively fixed in their age relationship to the adolescent time period. Foremost among the elements of internal maturation are

1. puberty,
2. rapid growth,
3. menarche,
4. first ejaculation,
5. maturation of sensitivity and neurophysiological pathways leading to the developmental capacity for
    orgastic masturbation,
    adultiform orgasms,
    sexual intercourse, and
    falling in love.

6. seeking undisguised drive gratification with objects outside the immediate family
   [The urge to date (seek love objects) shifts from a parental demand to an internal need.]
7. development of true abstract thinking (abstract operational thinking with an abstract conceptual memory organization).

External pressures and social imperatives vary in their nature and time of application. Rare is the external pressure that has not influenced some group in the world before or after adolescence. Social pressures are facultative; they are never obligate factors in the shaping of the personality during adolescence. Even within the same society, attitudes toward dependence and sexual freedom may vary from generation to generation. The response of the child to social pressures and acceptance of biological givens are the areas of malleability in which the therapist can expect movement in the course of treatment. In fact, by strengthening the impact of the future, increasing self-reflective awareness, and reinforcing adaptive aspects of superego demands, psychotherapy during late latency through early adolescence becomes itself an external pressure that serves social imperatives. Psychotherapeutic strategies lean heavily on knowledge that differentiates between what is internal, biological, and immutable and what is external and subject to change. The biology of the maturation of youth limits therapeutic ambition to a role of helping to shape personality while undoing pathological development. External pressures of the object world shape, limit, and entice all at once, giving rise to the eventual character seen at the younger edge of adulthood.

Foremost among the elements of external influence on development in the adolescent in the classical family in Western society are expectations for

1. some functioning independent from parents;
2. age-appropriate progression academically;
3. self-reliance;
4. ability to take on and complete independent tasks;
5. carriage, clothing, and manner appropriate to sexual roles assignment;
6. work experience;
7. community service;
8. sustained friendships;
9. active social life;
10. leadership qualities
11. ability to take criticism;

12. social consciousness;
13. proficiency in hobbies and sports;
14. dating and an interest in the opposite sex;
15. signs of progress in sexual performance; and
16. physical growth and maturation according to a preconceived family expectation and timetable.

Although these may seem like modest demands to an adult who has successfully negotiated and then forgotten the terrors of adolescence, they can be experienced as severe stresses to the child who is starting from the beginning and finds that not only are external demands changing as he grows, but his inner structure is a constantly changing, quixotic quicksilver, causing continuous alteration in his stance and equipment. External pressure for sexual performance is stressful for the person just entering puberty. More stress is added when the philosophy of asceticism that may have been created to deal with social wants is threatened after a few months by burgeoning internal sexual pressures. Similarly, a boy of small stature becomes distressed when confronted with the mixed message, "You'll be tall someday."

A boy who was just under 5 feet tall when 11 years old was overheard by his father crying himself to sleep to the phrase "I don't want to be a midget."

A child who has not yet resolved conflicts over sexual identity may find external social pressures in support of heterosexual functioning extremely vexing. At first the list of external demands is seen through the eyes of adolescent omnipotence (projection) as requiring 100 percent performances. Tolerance by the world and acceptance of stratification by the child permit external demands to be seen as less threatening. The child can then soften his superego and develop tolerance for himself. This chapter will be devoted to a discussion of the way in which these problems of adolescence are resolved as the work of adolescence progresses, with reflections on questions and problems, often encountered in psychotherapy, that confuse and stymie the child.

The March of Adolescent Dating Patterns

Social pressures may enforce the demands of "elements of external influence" on adolescence at any age. They are not in a fixed association with any particular numerical age.

The relationship between the sexes may be taken as an example: There is not a sudden leap from the estrangement between the sexes of the latency years to the full-blown romantic involvements of late adolescence. Instead, the child traverses a set of patterned relationships of gradually increasing complexity. The foremost steps in the progression are group activities, group dating, multiple-couple dating, single-couple dating, and cohabitation.

Although the developmental march through this series of relationships is obviously dependent upon biological maturation to define its outer boundaries, social pressures in the form of mores and moralities may cause a shrinking of the time span required to negotiate the course and a shift in the timing of a component to an earlier or later age. For instance, the sexual permissiveness that has evolved over the 1960s and 1970s has produced a marked series of changes in the timing of the march of adolescent dating patterns. In the early 1960s, there was a rising incidence of a very early age of onset of "going steady" and sexual intercourse (as young as age 12). This pattern did not persist, although early intercourse (age 13 for boys, age 16 for girls) is now (1986) acceptable for college-bound youngsters who are emotionally ready. A reverse pattern had developed during the early 1980s, with a slowing of the march of the dating relationship pattern. This resulted in a delay of the first sexual relationship to late adolescence. The mechanism by which this was accomplished was an extension of the years occupied by group and multiple-couple dating. The effect was to provide an intrusive social milieu that militated against a unique relationship between two people, within which a meaningful, though impermanent, sexual relationship might be established.

There is a basic pattern to the march of dating relationships. There is, however, so much individual variation that the pattern cannot be used to predict, from age alone, where on the march a person is. (The ages included in the following paragraphs are thus only guides.) Rather, one can use the pattern to predict where the person is going and what the next step will be in his or her career. One can also surmise quite well from this information the problems and conflicts that are to be confronted in psychotherapy.

Group Activities

The move toward mature sexuality in adolescence is characterized by a relatively slow pace. At the onset of late latency–early adolescence, there are residua of the latency-age social structure, in which peers of the same sex were formed into groups. Heterosexual interest is roused more from parental expectations than from internal changes. Simply, the first heterosexual contacts occur when parents bring the two groups together under the same roof. The first contact between the sexes then takes place at parties organized by parents, at which the boys talk about sports and the like while the girls talk about movie stars, while self-segregated according to sex and clustered on opposite sides of the room. From time to time, this pattern is broken up by kissing games or dancing, during which physical contact is created between two people who have hardly any relationship with one another. The transitory nature of the relationships may be illustrated by the nature of the game "spin the bottle." Here the participants do not even know whom they will be kissing after their next chance to spin. A bottle is spun and whomever it points at when it comes to rest is the sexual partner of the moment. This form of introduction to kissing bypasses the need to get to know someone and the problem of overcoming fear of rejection. A partner and a kiss are provided. The child begins to experience sexually stimulating body contact with someone other than close family members. The external calls forth the internal.

Group Dating

Parent-designed group parties for children aged 10 to 13 have a parallel in less structured activity initiated by the children, that is, group dating. This includes such activities as going to parks, movies, and bowling involving groups of boys and girls. The two groups are together. There is no specific pairing off, although some more advanced youngsters begin to team up as couples. Group dates enable youngsters to begin pairing off in a situation in which moment by moment the degree of involvement can be adjusted to suit the changing needs of the child for comfort and closeness, as well as a means of retreat if the budding relationship becomes too intense. By and large, on group dates a boy is more closely allied to the other boys than to any girl in the group. In boys' groups there is typically some negative reaction to the formation of couples. "She's your wife" is a pejorative phrase in describing too close a relationship as late as 17 years of age.

Usually, both persons are the same age. The girls are more mature physically, and more interested in forming couples. Often, they discuss the situation with girlfriends (at the expense of homework assignments). The interested boy is fascinated by the girl, but reconstitutes the old gang when she is not present and foremost. This is a reflection of the persistence into adolescence of latency-age male bonding.

In one such dating situation, a group of 15-year-old boys were out with a group of 13-year-old girls. Though some couple interaction took place, the high point of the evening for the boys was the moment when they were able to get the girls to go home by bus alone, thus saving the boys the expense of a taxi. There was awareness in the boys of a sexual goal in dating, but they weren't yet ready to pursue it.

Multiple-Couple Dating

Gradually group dating evolves toward a social life involving a group of couples. Such multiple-couple dating is referred to as double or triple dating. The emphasis shifts from the joining of two single-sex affinity groups, with some erotic interaction on a couple basis, to a group of couples each consisting of one girl and one boy. The group of couples is together throughout the date. The couples do not leave each other alone. A sexual goal is definite, and sexual activity is explicit. Sexual play and petting may occur in this situation, but are limited by the group superego. The presence of other people enhances the exhibitionistic, self-proving aspect of dating. It also gives a sense of security to the participants in that they are assured that they will not go beyond preset limits. Limitations on how far one may become involved in sexual activity are enforced by the limiting presence of others. There is provided an opportunity to become involved in sexual activity with safeguards that the situation will not get out of hand.

Homoerotic bonding involved in group dating may not be fully resolved at the time that the children begin to date as couples in groups. In these situations the coupling is only a superficial characteristic. In actuality, the boys' and girls' groups are participating in sexuality the way they might have in bowling or the like. In these situations, two couples may be in bed, engaged in heavy petting and sex play, when at a signal they switch partners. This variant on couple dating provides a possibility for the continuation of group activity.

The main purpose of multiple-couple dating, as alluded to before, is to provide the possibility of establishing sexual physical contact with an individual who is chosen to be a partner on the basis of a meaningful, ongoing relationship. The relationship is nurtured in a context in which protection is provided from going beyond one's readiness to experience sexuality by the presence of a trusted friend, who can be relied upon to support protests should things go too far. Such a situation protects the adolescent from going "too far" on two counts: first, it protects the individual from the demands of a predatory partner; and second, it protects the individual from the demands of the predatory self. It is a means of drive inhibition.

A young woman accepted a date from a young man whom she hardly knew on the proviso that he would get a friend for her friend. They were in their late teens. Her friend was a prim, proper young lady living at a women's residence hotel. At the end of the date the four went to one of the young men's apartments. The first young woman teasingly suggested that they play strip poker. There was some kissing and petting involved. When her girlfriend slipped into the bedroom and began having intercourse with her date and her own partner began to make unmistakable advances, she had no alternative but to throw her raincoat over her half-clad body and run out of the apartment. She had expected her girlfriend to serve as a brake to the activity set in motion by her teasing. When this multiple-couple dating use of the other person as defense failed, she had to escape.

Single-Couple Dating

Once a person has reached the point of no longer needing to draw strength from the presence of familiar same-sex peers on dates, it becomes possible to become involved in couple dating. Assurance that one can handle one's own and one's partner's sexual propensities enables single-couple dating, with sexual activity, to begin in earnest.

Some youngsters experience a period of individual dating in which they avoid any situation (such as being alone) in which there is a possibility of sexual activity. As maturity progresses, single-couple dating becomes the rule.

The shift from group to individual-couple dating runs parallel to the shift from uncertainty and ignorance to sophistication and knowledge. A youngster with no experience of couple dating often lacks courtesy and finesse in dealing with the opposite sex. When first approaching sexual activity during parties and group dating, there are many doubts and uncertainties. Social graces and behavior are unknown. The areas that really concern the children are unteachable by parents. Questions that arise are answered by research or myth. There is a search to learn as much as possible about sex and anatomy and the opposite sex, what is right and what is wrong.

Girls are concerned about what to say when they are approached, how to stand, what kind of clothes to wear. Should one kiss a boy on the first date? Can one become pregnant from kissing? Why do they want to touch my breasts? Boys are concerned about what to say when approaching a girl in order to avoid rejection. They are concerned about what they should do if the girl insists that they have intercourse on the first date. At 12 and 13 this is highly unlikely, but this fact is no reassurance to the boy whose fear so thinly masks his desires. Boys may be concerned about what to do if a girl requests a very expensive purchase while they are out on the date. The boy is aware of how little economic power he has, and wonders that he dares address himself to dating, which is a field of endeavour in which such champions as his fiscally sound father have displayed their abilities.

The boy tends to shy away from the girls at parties, and to group with the boys for another reason besides familiarity with male companionship: There is terror in many boys that involvement with girls at a party will result in the development of an erection, with the attendant appearance of the telltale distortion of the clothing that characterizes this physiological state. The matter is taken so seriously by 12- and 13-year-olds that it is often the sole content of conversations.

> A group of boys were discussing the problem. One recommended putting one's hands in one's pockets and pushing out to cover the protuberance. (It is amazing how many youngsters, tense-faced and sweating, one can see doing this during the course of one party.) Another recommended remaining seated until flaccidity returns. "What happens if the parent tells you to come get some cake while you have a boner?" rejoined a second boy. "I had that happen once," said another. "What did you do?" asked the others. "I said, 'Look! I'm a dog!' and ran over to her on my hands and knees."

Adolescence is not an easy time of life.

Remarkably, there is not much worry about the occurrence of erections during social dancing; perhaps the nearness of the girl covers it. There are concerns as to whether the girl can feel it, and if she likes it or is offended by it. This is a manifestation of the guilt and self-consciousness experienced by boys in relation to their sexuality. The typical early adolescent position for kissing is either sitting or standing with the bodies far apart. This avoids the problem of erections, felt by the girl. When self-consciousness and guilt over sexual feelings are overcome to the point that fear of contact with the erection is diminished, closer standing and juxtaposition of the genitals as a sexual activity in petting become possible.

Such are the events, feelings, and experiences in the life of the late latency–early adolescent patient in psychotherapy which occur in daily life, while in sessions one is answering questions about experiences and worries with "Everything is fine. Nothing new has happened." It is difficult for the therapist to have retained in memory his or her own experience of adolescence besides having knowledge of trends that are the sum of the variegated adolescent defensive structures and experiences of many children. Therefore, this book contains chapters that deal specifically with therapy as well as with the extraordinary and ever-changing horizons of the region called adolescence.

Pedagogy in the Psychotherapy Situation

Education is obviously needed in matters of sexuality for late latency–early adolescent children. Unfortunately, they do not seek it when needed. Schools aim teaching at age groups rather than levels of development, ignoring the fact that children learn about sex, and use the knowledge, when they are ready for it. Any of the stages or situations described here can be reached at 13, or at 20. The age spectrum for a given degree of need for information is broad. There is no specific age at which sex education can be most usefully taught to a group, but for the individual, that is not the case. Some source of information should be available when needed, and in the form of a knowledgeable adult. Because of the specific nature of the material covered and the nearness to the situation involved, the child therapist often finds himself in the position of supplying information or correcting misinformation that has been the basis of fears or of avoidance of maturing life situations. Some of the areas frequently brought up in psychotherapy follow.

It is not particularly remarkable that so much concern is directed toward erections. They are palpable, visible signs of sexuality, and they are not always under the control of the child. Young children may develop the myth that they are robots controlled by alien forces. They offer erections as evidence of the effect of these forces. Erections are the area of sex education that attracts the least emphasis. In fact, I know of only one book (Kuhn 1948) with a section on sex education that explains the physiology and purpose of erections adequately.

One 6-year-old who had been carefully tutored by her mother in all the particulars of sex asked me, "I know what happens, but how does the man get that loose thing into the lady?"

The question of what is right to do comes up repeatedly. Morality is not the province of the therapist. Mores are areas to be observed and not influenced. Subtle variations of attitudes of patients are influenced by neurotic factors, such as inhibitions and strong superego attitudes. There is no interpretation of right or wrong in the therapist's interventions, only exploration of the origins of attitudes that impede the way to happiness or drain energy in useless digressions into guilt. Frequently, the therapist is confronted with paradoxical situations that draw patients in and then threaten to overwhelm them. Modern social demands, coupled with relaxed restrictions on sexual mores, encourage the social trappings of dating and communication between the sexes. At the same time there is provided a brake in the form of a morality that contains a persistence of childhood sexual prohibitions and the religious view that sex is something wrong for girls outside of marriage. In recent years there has been a tendency to soften this attitude, although I have met young men who seem to forget their espousal of sexual equality when marriage time comes along, and begin to seek the more chaste and selective females.

What is a child to think when he is told that sex is "good" and is then confronted with a street corner culture that thrives on the sale of prurience? If he himself has sexual thoughts, how does he know if he represents the good or is a member of the street culture? A good sign of the degree to which the child judges himself to be part of a degraded tradition is found in the difficulty with which a child can talk about sex with a therapist, in comparison with the freedom experienced by an adult. The child in late latency–early adolescence usually has not caught up with the liberated sexual morality of our time.

The cultural context of late latency–early adolescence tends to equate sex with dirtiness and to attach guilt to sexual actions. To some extent this is part of the legacy of the Judeo-Christian heritage. Therapists should be carful to define the strength of the religious identity of the patient and beware the possibility that they are preaching their personal belief in the guise of clearing the way for healthy functioning through freeing the patient from inhibitions. Lack of clarification by adults of the role of sex in life results in considerable slowing-up of the process of acclimation to the expression of the physiology of drives that are in themselves overwhelmingly strong and require adjusting to on their own. Guidance, the permission conveyed by silence during psychotherapy, and encouragement of more advanced peers create some leeway. Guilt is rarely overcome during adolescence. It is usually diminished in favor of drive expression, when attachment to an individual softens the tie to the parents. This is of importance dynamically. Conscience and superego are actually internalizations of the parents and their demands. An individual carries his or her parents' admonitions with her. When people care for someone else enough to forget parents, they forget parental admonitions. In some cases girls are unable to conceive of a gradual establishment of a relationship with a boy, and the gradual increase of sexual involvement. These children may enter into sexual relations precipitously, without orgasm and without entering into a meaningful relationship.

A girl of 18 was not able to accept her sexuality consciously. She therefore avoided gradual involvement. On dates she would go into dream states during which she would participate in sexual relations. She claimed little memory afterwards for what had happened. In this way she bypassed her superego. Repeated pregnancies forced her to seek an understanding of herself and to accept her own sexuality so that she could avoid future pregnancies.

Once a person has been able to date in individual couple relationships and has been able to loosen up the legacy of childhood guilt sufficiently to take part physically in sexual activities, there remains the problem of coming to terms with one's own overwhelming feelings of excitement. Only through experience and becoming accustomed to the feelings, or by analyzing the reasons one cannot bear intense feelings, can sexual inhibition be overcome. This was frequently heard from young women of past generations who, in speaking of the early days of marriage, said that one could not overcome many years of fear in one night.

With each new sexual activity that comes to mind or is suggested by the partner, there is a period of fear and inhibition closely allied to feelings of guilt. It is intensified by the aura of excitement that attaches itself to each new step. New activities and new sexual partners stir up a heightening of excitement or of fear and inhibition, depending on the fantasies and response patterns of the individual. In pursuit of these excitements, some people constantly seek new mates in order to experience again the excitement of "first times." In others there is frigidity or impotence due to the fact that the individual relates to a new person according to personal fantasy. These people can only become sexually capable and comfortable after they know the reality of the other person to the degree that the fears and fantasies that they had attached originally are dispelled. Thus, a man who fears that women will hurt him or compare him unfavorably with other men is loath to start a new relationship until he knows the person as a kind, supporting individual. In like manner, each new sexual step stirs up inhibiting excitement, which is overcome through experiencing and learning that there is no danger of ego disintegration or punishment for "moral wrongs."

When the fantasies that stir the inhibitions are too strong, the sexual feelings remain isolated or repressed even during the activity. In fact, this is the condition under which the activity can be permitted. Under these circumstances it is possible that the feelings can be brought into consciousness and enjoyed. When this cannot be accomplished, psychotherapeutic help may be of value.

In moving toward sexual maturity, the adolescent therefore experiences through gradual acclimatization and education the following: the capacity to relate to an individual of the opposite sex; sufficient sexual knowledge so that he or she understands what is going on; a softening of the superego that permits participation in sexual activities; decathexis of the parents as sexual objects, so that full attention may be directed toward a peer; disentanglement of sexual acts from fantasy, so that they can be enjoyed without the inhibiting reflections on unrelated meanings and fantasy implications that frighten the 14-year-old, and acclimatization to activities that stir up feelings threatening and inhibiting to the child who has not yet developed the insulating cloak of foreknowledge and experience that offers reassurance.

Fantasy and the Object World in Early Adolescence

To understand the adolescent experience of coming to terms with the object world, we must make a place for daydreams and an understanding of their role in the mental life of the early-teenage child.

We have described adolescence as a time of maturation, change, progress, turmoil, and chaos. The description is accurate, but insufficiently detailed to help us with psychotherapeutic strategies—for that, we must turn to the dynamics of fantasy during early adolescence. Fantasy and daydreams provide a bridge, born of drives and infantile needs, that conveys object-modifying, self-centered demands to an object world equipped with designs of its own.

Fantasy as the Expression of Inner Needs

Fantasies are ever present as conduits that bring the influence of unconscious contents to bear on awareness, interpretation of events, and those who occupy the object world. They are present in the system preconscious throughout the prelatency, latency, and adolescent years. The three phases have the same unconscious latent fantasy content, yet each phase has differentiating characteristics. The sources of these differences are to be found in the ego. The configuration of ego functions that serves them during a given phase is specific for that phase.

In prelatency, the tendency was to have little distortion in the creation of the manifest fantasy out of the latent one. Fantasy was constructed of symbols that utilized parents and siblings as the objects for the discharge of drives and the mastery of past trauma.

In latency, we saw the submergence of the fantasy. When circumstances stirred fantasy, its manifest expression was populated with substitute feelings and substitute objects. These served as symbols representing the latent content of the fantasy. Latency is the age of symbols.

In adolescence, fantasies assert themselves in a content that is less distorted in form than in fantasies of latency. This is an echo of the fantasy formation of the prelatency years. There is the tendency to say that prelatency fantasies disappear during latency, only to reappear during early adolescence. This axiom is true with respect to the surface appearance of events, but falls short of describing the inner vicissitudes of fantasy in the child. In actuality, the latent fantasies retain their force and form during the latency years. Their manifest appearance submits to distortion through the interposition of masking symbols. This makes it appear that the interests of children have wandered to playthings, toys, and phantasmagoria. This is a thin veneer that lightly muffles the drives and passions which on a latent level are sustained throughout childhood. When the latent fantasy becomes more recognizable in early adolescence, it becomes so through articulation of the core fantasy with reality, using as defining symbols real objects other than the parents.

The parents and sibs have been displaced by the incest barrier. A weak point develops as a result of the use of real people to represent parents. There is a proneness for development of recognition breakthroughs of the parent within the reality symbol used for masking. Primary objects (parents) are the latent contents of the fantasies that the early adolescent is trying to live out through use and manipulation of reality. When the child spies the parent beneath the skin of the object pursued, the anxiety that forced the repression of the original fantasy surfaces.

Such anxiety accompanies the sexual fantasies of adolescence, because the roles of the parents in the fantasies are so near the surface.

This contributes to the slow acceptance of sexuality and accounts for the awkwardness in approaching sexual matters in adolescence. Fantasies of a sexual nature arouse affect when, during adolescence, they first begin to be expressed consciously. There may be breakthroughs of affect or there may be breakthroughs of underlying identity. In the latter case, parents appear in manifest, active roles as objects in these fantasies. A common example of this is the appearance of the image of the mother in place of a fantasized girl during an orgastic climax during masturbation. It is enough to make a boy give up masturbating—for a while. This is an example of the reestablishment of the old prelatency configuration of manifest symbols in fantasy. "When I grow up, I'm going to marry you Daddy" is common for the prelatency child, unheard of for the latency-age child, and available but unacceptable for the adolescent.

In the emergent core fantasies of early adolescence, parents are not acceptable objects. Substitutes must be found in conscious fantasy, as in masturbation, or in reality, as in living out the fantasy with a peer. The attempt to articulate the drives and fantasies with substitutes while the parents are still very much present and stirring up feelings threatens to make of simple relationships with peers the focus of the resolution of painful and unresolved conflicts with the parents.

Seeking drive gratification through the living out of fantasy is exemplified by the youngster who had to fantasy that he was a baby being powdered and diapered in order to bring himself to orgasm while masturbating.

A woman had to fantasize that she was being raped by a series of men while being beaten in order to achieve orgasm in intercourse.

A woman had to live out the fantasy that intercourse is a fight by fighting with her husband prior to intercourse.

Another example of a fantasy lived out would be the experience of a young woman who could only have orgasm if she were seen by a man with whom she had recently had intercourse when she was meeting another man with whom she was soon to have intercourse.

A third example of living out a fantasy is that of the young woman who felt she was fulfilling her wish to be equal to men by being promiscuous. In her mind, men are by nature promiscuous.

It is obvious from these examples that the expression of one's sexual drives through fantasies must result in difficulties of adjustment in adolescence and adulthood. For this reason, the decathexis of the fantasy and the finding of an outlet for drives within the structure of reality defined by a culture is a healthy resolution of the problem. Rarely is this achieved before late adolescence or adulthood. Fantasy structures are too strongly imbedded to be extirpated without some work toward their resolution.

The shift of interest and the drive from the parent to the peer as symbol, which occurs as part of a lived-out fantasy is usually referred to as removal (Katan 1937). This takes two forms. The first, and by far the healthier, form occurs when the adolescent discards the fantasy because he no longer needs or uses it for seeking sexual gratification. The second form of removal refers to the circumstance in which the parent–child relationship of prelatency forms the pattern for the relationship that occurs with a selected peer who becomes the boyfriend or girlfriend. It is in the context of such relationships that the *living out of fantasies* just described can take place. In such a relationship there is a total involvement in a love or pal relationship with a peer. The fears, sensitivities, and patterns that constitute the relationship are identical with the prelatency fantasies involving the parents.

The young boy who was the apple of mother's eye during the day, and a discarded lover when father came home in the evening, in adolescence becomes preoccupied with jealousy about what the lady of his choice is doing when he is not with her.

Preconscious fantasy may either color new relationships formed by the adolescent or, in the case of individuals not yet able to establish sexually oriented object relationships, the fantasies determine the necessary mental content for successful masturbation.

No matter how skillfully the adolescent masks the identity of the parent with a substitute object, there is always the possibility that there will be a breakthrough into consciousness of the parent as the real object.

One youngster of 15 was unable to masturbate because the movie star he fantasized about turned into his mother whenever his excitement began to mount.

To strengthen the defense so as to prevent or avoid such situations, adolescents shift to objects less likely to be confused with the parent. Individuals who are not related, or are in different professions, are chosen as protagonists of private fantasies and fantasies in action. Fascination with individuals of other races or religions occurs. Often this results in much friction between parents and children and in effect serves to widen a protective gap, filled with hostility, between them. The negative feelings thus engendered in themselves help to protect the child from a breakthrough of oedipal feelings.

> A young woman of Orthodox Jewish background began to date a young man of Italian extraction when she was 16. They married when she was 21. Just before the marriage, the groom, in order to do something that he felt would improve his relationship with his new family, went with his future father-in-law to undergo a circumcision. This was done as a surprise for the bride. She reported that she had experienced intense anxiety when she learned of the operation on her future spouse. The onset of a street phobia could be dated from the time of the circumcision of the husband.

Adolescents in need of a defense against their oedipal feelings select partners with characteristics other than those of their parents. Often these resolutions of adolescence are carried over into adult life. Such a resolution may be unstable, and its continuation may remain an ever-present psychopathogenic factor in the life of the individual.

When a child enters adolescence while living in the home of adults who are not his or her biological parents a special situation exists. The incest barrier is not as strong. Some of these children (e.g., foster children) may need to develop stronger defenses to deal with the surfacing of incestuous feelings. Others develop conscious fantasies involving the foster parents with less of the kind of anxiety that keeps such thoughts out of consciousness and forces them to be masked in natural children. The predictable end of the relationship at age 18 makes direct fantasies more tolerable, for the end is always in sight. For this reason there is not the reinforcement of the hostility that occurs between parent and child during adolescence. It is typical for a biological mother–daughter unit to exhibit mocking, belittling, and open battling between mother and daughter. In foster care mother–daughter units this is rare. The rare cases of open hostility in such units often presage the development of a psychotic process in the child.

Impulsions

The drives and fantasies that shape the lives of adolescents are the same as were present in latency. The loss of latency-age symbolic function (ludic demise) causes a move toward the use of reality-oriented objects as the symbolic bridge between the fantasy and the world. Social awareness and reality testing shift the emphasis in drive manifestation to real-world representations. As a result, a degree of sophistication characterizes the fantasy-informed relationships of the individual to the world.

Impulsions take the form of intrusive thoughts that impel one to an action that tends to be rejected in the ordinary thinking of the adolescent.

A boy of 16 had difficulty in concentrating during discussions with his friends because of intrusive thoughts about sucking their penises.

A 13-year-old responded with mixed bewilderment and bemusement at the impulsion to jump in front of a subway train.

"Jump on the tracks," his mind said as he waited somewhat bemused by the tricks his mind played on him while he waited for the train.

Another 13-year-old boy was bothered by an urge to kill his father.

A girl of 17 could not enjoy a date in which her mind was occupied with a driven need to touch her date's genitals.

"Suck him, sock him" were the thoughts that alternated in the mind of the honor student as he waited for the principal to finish his introduction.

The child therapist's role in dealing with impulsions is to point out that these are only thoughts, and are at odds with the true wishes and character of the child. They can be used to illustrate the existence of the unconscious. Tolerance for them implies mastery of the psychotherapeutic goal to "let nothing that is human be foreign." One must be careful in pursuing the latter course to avoid emphasizing the frightening nature of repressed material and instead, emphasize the value of understanding oneself in gaining self-mastery both within and in contact with the world.

What causes impulsions? At times, the need to discharge is sufficiently great to demand an expression of drive that is unrefined instinct. Thereby an impulsion is created. Impulsions are breakthroughs of the contents of the system unconscious. An impulsion is created when a barely modified core fantasy is forced into conscious word, thought, or action. The demand manifested is clear. There is no doubt concerning what is wanted. This differs from a compulsion, in which the core fantasy is modified and masked before it comes into consciousness, and in which doubt is a constant feature.

Impulsions often are mobilized by regressive defensive moves in the face of the new stresses of reality that adolescence brings. In early adolescence, when the threat of the newness of the sexual feelings and the danger of rejection by potential peer group partners is high, a simple solution is hit on by the child. "Why not get Mother to do it for me?" This seems an obvious breakthrough of the oedipal wish. The thought is rarely acted on. It is a manifestation of a regression to the oral-dependent level, when the mother took care of all needs and healed all the things that hurt with a kiss.

Impulsions are frequent in adolescence. They are rare in adults. The same fantasies occurring in prelatency children do not give rise to fears that they would be acted upon. Prelatency children have greater tolerance for their own raw fantasies. Latency-age children mask them and even blunt affects through fantasy formation. Such urges do not impinge on their consciousness, nor is there danger that they could come to pass. In adolescence urges can become realities. The objects are available, and masking symbols that could blur meaning are reserved for dreaming and, in later adolescence, neurotic symptoms. Impulsions stir a constant fear of loss of control.

Impulsions may in later life contribute to the manifest character structure of the idividual in the form of fantasy conditions for sexual gratification.

> With the onset of adolescence, a mild-mannered 12-year-old girl developed constant impulsions to scream at people and tell them not to do something. The "something" could be any action that a peer casually engaged in. The impulsion contained not only words but also the urge to hover menacingly over the other person. She saw her mother as "bossy." The impulsion had taken root from her mother's perceived behavior. In addition, she expressed a fear of sexual intercourse, dating, and joining a camp-

ing club. Analysis of the fear revealed an underlying fear fantasy that to belong to the club, she would have to submit to forced sexual intercourse with all of the boys in the club.

This is an example of a bridge between adolescent psychology and adult pathology. The impulsion to be actively hostile and bossy, through reversal into the opposite, creates the ground for the later development of a characterological manifestation of the same fantasy. The steps are:

1. Active impulsion to boss,
2. Reversal into passivity of the impulsion with fear that she will be bossed,
3. Actively seeking to be passively dealt with through subjugation by men as a condition for sexual intercourse.

The presence of such impulsions and of distressing character patterns with neurotic overtones creates for adolescents some of the most trying moments of their lives. They wonder if they are mentally ill or perverted. They feel disgust for themselves. Often the impulsions have contents that will later be limited to acting out during precoital play in marriage. This is no comfort to the 12-year-old who knows nothing of these matters and, in fact, may be under the impression that his parents have never even had "normal" sexual relations. The fact that these thoughts are part of the human condition and not foreign at all—as well as the fact that he can control the urges, get help in understanding them, and even act on them in appropriate circumstances—gives no comfort to the child who has insufficient breadth of experience to be able to differentiate, or to figure out which impulsion to handle in which way.

Passivity in Early Adolescence

During prelatency and latency, the force with which the drives seek gratification remains about the same. There is no decrease in drive energies with the onset of latency. Rather, there is a strengthening of the ego, which produces an external calm; this may be interpreted incorrectly as a diminution of drive energies. Each developmental period has its own mechanisms for dealing with the force of the drives. In prelatency, the parents are there to help the child contain his excitements and aggressions. They serve to set limits. In latency, the structure of latency with its safety valve of fantasy serves to hold the drives in check. During adolescence, the drives increase in force after puberty. At the same time, parents and society find themselves with less control over the expression of sexual excitements as peer influences and new social institutions make themselves felt. Resistance to passivity intensifies defiance and concomitantly reinforces gestures and sexual statements of independence.

The early adolescent thus faces the first steps toward adult independence with a coupled upsurge of drive and diminution of external control. He is suddenly confronted with the problem of tolerating, experiencing, and eventually enjoying that part of his physiological makeup that consists of sexual excitements. Many hurry to catch up with what is newly allowed.

> This situation is exemplified by the early adolescent boy who is told about masturbation by his peers and is encouraged by the tolerant attitude and privacy provided by his parents to experiment. Even though the fantasy content may be sufficiently under control to permit orgasm, the child may be unable to surrender himself and lose control to the degree necessary for orgastic experience.

> A girl of 18 who had had frequent intercourse with her boyfriend insisted upon an abrupt interruption of the sexual act because she could not tolerate the mounting excitement that accompanied the initial stages of what would have been her first orgasm.

In these situations we could describe the experience as fear of ego disintegration in the face of mounting drive pressures experienced as sexual excitement.

A similar situation occurs with the aggressive drive. Going "ape," "flipping out," "blowing your cool," and "flipping your wig," are slang expressions that attempt to describe the states of blind rage to which adolescents are subject and against which they defend with overcompliance, retreat into passivity, and warnings to others not to stir them up.

Of all the core fantasies, which express conflicts not seen in manifest form consistently since the prelatency period, the one most often involved in the problems of early adolescence is that of passive fear. This fantasy is characterized by the belief of children that adults wish to exercise too much control over them. Its earliest manifestation was the "terrible twos." This is the period of defiance of authority involved in resistance to toilet training during the third year of life (anal phase). It appears again during the fourth to fifth year of life (phallic phase), when surrender to passivity enters into some resolutions of the Oedipus complex. The prelatency boy who accepts passivity gives up the wish for the mother and surrenders to the father, succumbing to symbolic castration at his hands in order to receive his love and care. The very regression of the 6-year-old child away from unchanneled oedipal wishes, which invite retaliation, toward well-defended, anal-sadistic wishes that imbue the world with calm is a manifestation of a resolution of passivity. Latency states are the primary resolution of passivity during the latency age period. During adolescence, passivity again becomes a problem when the defenses that support latency are outgrown, worn out, and easily undone.

Defiances of authority in early adolescence may be seen as undefended resurgences of early conflicts about passivity. As such, the passivity fear fantasy of adolescence with its attendant defiance represents a defense against a negative resolution of the Oedipus complex in the boy.

In the girl, it is related to fantasies involving feelings of weakness. The girl has the attitude that she is weak and helpless, and blames this on her female identity. Were she born a boy she would be strong. She deals with this by wishing that she could have someone to care for her and to be strong where she is weak.

Where inner feelings of weakness threaten the child, they are defended against by defiance of the parents, whose control is wished for by the child on a deeper level. (Behind the fear comes the wish.) This reaction to passive wishes fuels the defiant posture of early adolescence.

The selection of a passive resolution for the Oedipus complex is intensified in those children who have a low capacity to express aggression directly. In both the boy and the girl, these wishes, which constitute an admission of weakness and a desire to be cared for, are strengthened in individuals whose capacity to show aggression in the period of toilet training had been muted.

Characterologically, early adolescents who are engaged in major defiance of passivity are active and effective primarily in giving the impression of rebelliousness. Usually they are blunted in the effective expression of aggression and in the ability to do useful work. They present no real danger to anyone. Still, they are known for their sadistic jibes, attempts to dominate conversations, and tendency to be overcritical.

Adolescence is a time of striving for independence. We have traced at least two moving factors in this matter:

First, reality and the real world have become more important, and so the child is not as involved with the parents as previously. Cognitive maturation in late latency–early adolescence permits greater psychic and emotional mobility, just as the capacity to walk and crawl heightened the capacity for physical mobility at the end of the first year.

Second, fantasy interpretations of the world intervene in the management of life. In latency fantasy provided a road of escape, whereas in adolescence fantasy provides the first guidebook to future planning. Recurrence of oedipal fantasy, coupled with the incest barrier, promotes the seeking of love objects independent of the home. Defense against potential situations that would activate passive fear fantasies strengthens independence. The striving for independence that is fostered by these factors runs contrary to the dependency needs of the child. The child resolves the conflict by projecting his need to be cared for to his parents. In his mind's eye, they seem to demand that he accept their control and guidance (a condition in part supported by fact). The child sees willful control as the parents' goal rather than their expressed wish to give helpful guidance through the shoals of inexperience. The child shifts his attention away from the deeper wish to be cared for and dominated by his parents. He distorts the situation so that it appears that he does not want care. It is the therapist's task to untwist the child's distortions.

To a certain extent it is true that parents want to help their children avoid the errors and discomforts that they themselves experienced in life; therefore, they try to guide the child. There are, however, situations in which the parents are culpable; then the reality must be disentangled from fantasy for the child. Since it is usually the moods of the parents that are brought to bear on the child, the therapist is well advised to suggest that the therapy be aimed at the establishment of a means for protecting the child's future from the influence of the parent's moods. This makes for a particularly acceptable way of verbalizing an approach to a rather sensitive topic. Children will often begin verbalizing, as well as feeling, great aggression toward their parents when the passive fears of children and the active hopes and strivings of parents coincide. It is important that the therapist explain that the process of therapy mobilizes such feelings in order to make them available for understanding and insight, not as a means of fueling revolt. Otherwise the situation may get out of control.

In other contexts, essentially depressed parents cannot bear to lose their children to adolescent independence. These people exercise large amounts of coercion. Whatever the strength of the reality, the child's own fears of being dominated intensify the reaction of the child. Some of the most violent parent–child explosions are produced in the area of this conflict. Therefore, the psychotherapist must be ever on the alert for passivity problems that interfere with removal and are manifested in aggressive outbursts.

In order to erase all signs of parental domination, the child may spread rebellion beyond mere fighting and words to an effacement of identifications with the parent. For example, the child of a conservative may become involved with liberal causes. There appears to be a breakdown in identification with the parent as a source of a template for the ego ideal during adolescence. It is no error, however, for the parents to attempt to communicate to the child the attitudes and goals that they consider to be important. In later years, when the individual seeks guidelines for living and incorporation of the parents into the makeup of a mature personality, the touchstones of parental guidance given in adolescence will become useful templates for adulthood.

Adolescent identifications and character may exhibit wide divergence from parental patterns. Often the parent cannot understand the child, and the child is impatient with the parent. The adolescent lives in a world incomprehensible to the parent, for it is a strange world, not only not of the parent's making, but not that for which the parent had hoped to prepare the child. Fads, strange clothes, exotic hairdos, and excited music are the accoutrements of this period of parent–child estrangement. Hero worship sends the son of a scholar into a preoccupation with baseball. After all, baseball heroes do not give orders. Scoutmasters, teachers, and coaches become the pattern setters for the child who is uncomfortable with parental guidance. In children who reject all adult domination, cliques of peers provide the patterns. These are apt to be the situations in which the greatest straying from culturally acceptable modes occurs. Totally new moralities are established in these peer groups. These in effect establish short-lived, totally dominating subcultures, which provide cultural sanction for the acting out of fantasy derivatives.

A girl who fantasized that she could be the "equal of a man" if she were "promiscuous like a man" was encouraged, through the attitudes of a promiscuous peer group, toward acting in a manner that contradicted strict parental and religious admonitions.

There is mutual interaction in such cases. The group encourages, but the girl seeks out the group. There is mutual encouragement through the interaction of a drive-dominated teenager and a condoning or example-setting peer group.

Sensitization by Fantasy

Domination by fantasy takes place in two ways. First, there is the active search for means to express the fantasy. In the adolescent, core fantasy, as we have described, dominates masturbatory thought content and influences behavior with peers. Making up exciting sexual fantasies during masturbation is an example of active expression of fantasy. Recruiting of peers to play out one's fantasies is not uncommon. An example would be a youngster who feels a repeated urge to start a fight with her boyfriend as a condition for successful sexual activity.

More subtle, but just as important, is the second means of fantasy expression: expression through sensitivity. In these situations the child patient says, "Why do these things happen to me?" There is complaint about life situations that strangely occur again and again. Problems with life situations are attributed to real events that they had no part in shaping. They appear to be the unwilling victims of fate. One might be taken in by this, unless one realizes that not everyone would notice these events or group them in the manner of this type of child patient. Unconscious fantasy primes the child to have special sensitivity for certain configurations and types of events. Thus, the child with a fear of passivity bristles at every suggestion by the parent; the promiscuous boy or girl recognizes sexual possibilities in situations which hold no such connotations for an individual not so alerted, and the paranoid finds persecutors behind every bush.

Sensitivity to situations enhances the expression of drives by means of taking advantage of or transmuting reality. One may perceive a continuum, which runs from wholly fantasy-dominated masturbation to reality-dominated situations that play into the needs of the psyche prepared and sensitized by fantasy.

Recruitment and Metamorphosis

The response of the object world to recruitment by the beckoning call of fantasy and the enticements of its tentacles is not always acquiescence. Fantasy may be more than a source of distortion of reality; rather, it can become a bridge to the object world. The shy adolescent who goes to a party reassured that he or she can predict cruel behavior in others can sally forth with the assurance of having some kind of control of the world they enter. Their power lies in the magic of prediction. The predictions they make are evocatively symbolized representations of their own inner fears. This is an example of defensive omnipotence. Should the object world not conform to the fantasy, the child who can put aside omnipotence can replace his evocative symbol with a reality that makes the world a less fearful place for future plans and relationships. Congenial peers can replace fears with brighter expectations. Each new relationship can bring a corrective experience to the malleable child. This can result in a change of personality and approaches to the object world in adolescence. As the foregone conclusions of the beginner are replaced by the experiences of the sophisticate, room is made for the realities and the needs of others to enter into the future planning and preparations of the child. Corrective relationships in series produce a metamorphosis in the early adolescent. It is the role of the child therapist to point out discordances between feared expectations and fortunate realities, to encourage testing fantasies against reality, and to undermine the defensive omnipotent regression that would halt the process.

"Et In Arcadia Ego"—Death

Along with so many other affect-charged aspects of the human condition, death is transmuted during latency into a symbol element to be used in play ("Bang, bang, you're dead."), while death itself is denied or processed into an affect-binding fantasy (as in the motion picture "Forbidden Games"). With the weakening of the defensive strength of the waking symbolizing function in late latency–early adolescence, troubling thoughts of death come alive for the child. The idea that was dealt with by the structure of latency must now be dealt with directly. The early adolescent world is tainted with preoccupations about life and the end of life. Teenage poems, such as William Cullen Bryant's (1903) "Thanatopsis," deal with death, death's mastery, and poetic metaphors of dying. Direct contact with dying is rare in this age group. When a fellow teenager dies, the effect is massive. Tears, monuments, poems spring up as if creativity could erase doom. The reinforcement of the sense of one's mortality and vulnerability intensifies fears, triggers depression, and intensifies the impact of the impending separations from the family that jobs and colleges away from home imply.

These losses on the distant horizon are brought into close, sharp focus by death, either real or as a concept. Separations are seen as little deaths. Often prelatency children are told of someone who has died, "He went away, and won't come back." Adolescent views of death take coloration from these explanations. The early adolescent is, therefore, left bewildered about what death is. One of the tasks of adolescence is to solve this riddle as part of the mastery of separation. It is also part of the growth which with each passing day brings both maturity and a lessening of life left. The child therapist would do well not to neglect this important topic, especially in view of the near-certainty of separations and losses of peers, parents, and pets. Part of the mastery of separation and growth is a preoccupation with and working through of death.

Transient Homosexuality in Early Adolescence

Homoeroticism is a frequent occurrence in adolescence. When sexuality emerges from the defenses of latency, there is a tendency to search for sexual objects near at hand. In addition, narcissism makes those who resemble oneself more understandable and attractive. Same-sex groupings, which are a legacy from the accepted socialization patterns of the latency years, encourage homoerotic explorations through convenience and propinquity. Displays of closeness are common from early on. Therefore, adult supervision finds nothing amiss in such ties, while visible heterosexuality—as represented by coupling in young teenagers—undergoes the suppression dealt out to implied sexuality in general.

> An 11-year-old girl came into her session a little late. "I think you'll like the story I have to tell you," she said. "I was on top of my girl friend. We were making believe we were having sex. She got a little frightened and asked if what we were doing wasn't wrong. I told her, 'Think how wrong it would be if I were a boy.'"

Transient adolescent homoeroticism may take the form of intense pal relationships, crushes on a teacher, overt sexual activity, or fantasies and impulsions about homosexual acts. In most cases these are transient phenomena. For some, this state will be permanent. There are prognostic indicators that can be used as guides to finding those for whom this will be a permanent orientation. These indicators can be found in accompanying personality symptomatology. There is a tendency toward aloneness, with an inability to become one of the group in spite of active attempts to be accepted. There are depressive periods; irritability with outbursts of aggression; effeminacy in boys; intense masculinity, or a history of failure to play with dolls in girls; interest in the theatre (especially in performing), and the total absence of spontaneous, conscious fantasies involving sexuality with partners of the opposite sex. Only the last characteristic is definitive. The others are clues which should alert responsible adults to the possibility of a potential problem.

There are two types of the transient form of homosexuality in adolescence:

The first is characterized by its early age of occurrence (12–14) and the absence of prior sexual experience. It is illustrated by the following case.

A child was sent away to a boarding school far from home. The removal of his intense involvement with his parents had just begun before he went away. The separation accelerated the process. The boys at the school shared sexual information and confidences. Heightened drive and the availability of pals led to episodes of experimentation involving mutual masturbation. All homosexual activity stopped by the time he was 15. He did not consider the activity to be "perverse" at the time. In his late teens, he began to be concerned with the possibility that he had a perversion. He sought help and reassurance at that time. This availed him little. This then precipitated a heterosexual affair in which he proved to himself his sexual capacities. He later married and had many children.

Girls are permitted more leeway than boys in these matters. Two girls who spend the afternoon weighing each other's breasts may have less inkling that there is sexual stimulation involved than do two boys handling each other's penises. In situations in which female virginity is valued, there is a tendency for these relationships to be extended.

Two factors are involved in the development of this type of early adolescent homosexual involvement.

First, at the time removal begins, the closest peer group members are of the same sex. It is only later that heterosexual objects become available. Therefore, the children first begin to act on sexual urges with peers of the same sex. In adults, the situational absence of suitable opposite-sex partners can similarly produce homosexual behavior. In group settings involving children without parents (normal-child caring institutions) strict regulations regarding involvements and contacts with the opposite sex intensify and prolong the period of transient adolescent homosexual activity.

Second, very early adolescents tend to be quite narcissistic. They admire what is like themselves and despise what is different. Boys dislike girls, and vice versa. The tie and attraction is to a person who looks like them. This is called a narcissistic object choice.

The second type of transient adolescent homosexual activity occurs later (after age 15). The person has usually had some heterosexual experience or has thought of attempting some. Whatever the reality situation may be, the precipitant of the situation is related to concern about heterosexual relations. There is fear of rejection, fear of failure, or fear of damage to the penis or vagina during the sexual act. The person recoils from heterosexuality as the result of imagined, feared, or implied danger inherent in the activity.

Notice the resemblance of this to the prelatency oedipal situation, in which the child withdrew from heterosexuality because of the danger of attack from the parent of the same sex. Heterosexuality and danger were equated in prelatency. The equation resurfaces in early adolescence. The heterosexual fear fantasy of adolescence is derived from this earlier fantasy.

In the adolescent, the way to heterosexuality is blocked by fear. The drives remain. They will need to find outlet. A homosexual object is chosen. Why? A strong contributing factor is to be found in the predisposing life patterns of early childhood. Let us return to the prelatency child.

The Boy. The boy starts life in a passive, receptive relationship to his mother. When he begins to develop phallic penetrative strivings toward the mother, fear of the father causes the boy to give up the mother as object. He turns to the father and seeks to protect himself from the father by offering himself to the father as a passive, receptive, nonthreatening partner. (We say he accepts castration and offers himself for penetration. Many manifest homosexuals act on this fantasy in their sexual activity, using the rectum as the receptive organ). A homosexual object is chosen as a way of handling a problem in a way that parallels its handling in early childhood. Conflicts arising from the problem of the initiation of adolescent heterosexuality are thus resolved by techniques based on a paradigm with origins in the resolution of prelatency conflict. This is an ego regression. The shift to a passive receptive attitude after the achievement of a phallic penetrative attitude is a libidinal regression. The shift of object from mother to father is a nonregressive, but parallel, move.

The following case illustrates the clinical appearance of such a situation. The fantasy nature of the homoerotic activity does not lessen its impact on the child who has the fantasy. The therapist would do well to recognize that such thoughts are unnerving for an adolescent and deserve attention both for the reassurance required and for the signal of trouble in sociosexual growth in heterosexual areas that is implied.

An 18-year-old boy began to make sexual advances toward his girlfriend. When she subsequently declined a date, he became somewhat morose and began to think about becoming a homosexual and fantasized kissing his best friend.

At times, the passive receptive attitude is manifested in the form of the fantasy of oral receptivity. In these cases, the father's danger is minimized by turning him into a nurturing mother who takes care of the boy. This is clinically manifested in fellatio fantasies in which the mouth serves as the receptive organ. In manifest homosexual activity, there are homosexuals who suck at a penis with the unconscious fantasy that it is the mother's breast.

The Girl. In the girl, the situation is complicated by the fact that there are two possible regressions that can participate in the development of the transient homoerotism of adolescence. This parallels the more complicated prelatency relationships of the girl and her parents.

In prelatency the girl begins with a passive receptive attitude toward the mother. This is followed by a progressive shift to an active, phallic, penetrative attitude toward the parents. So far, the relationships parallel those of the growing boy. Next, the girl, to the extent that she finds mother wanting, concentrates her phallic penetrative fantasy attentions on the father (parallel shift). Recognizing the limits of this fantasy for herself, she soon shifts from phallic penetrative attitudes to passive receptive attitudes with respect to the father (a regressive shift, but normal for the girl). When the situation becomes dangerous because the jealous ire (at times imagined?) of the parent of the same sex becomes a source of fear and danger, the girl, like the boy, seeks protection in regression. Because the pregenital maturational schema has more steps in the girl than in the boy, the girl can regress to two different positions.

The first form of regression that underlies transient homoerotism in early-adolescent girls is a regression to the level of a passive, receptive, infantile relationship to the mother. This relationship is expressed in the passive wish to be cared for and loved. It is important to recognize that in adolescence, regressions to passivity stir up defenses. Passivity may also be manifested in the defended form of active caring for someone else (passive turned to active—reversal into the opposite).

Actively rejected and disappointed in love, a girl picked up a kitten from the streets and took it home and fed it.

At times the girl attempts to turn the man into the mother. In such a situation, should the girl be ill, she may decline genital sexuality in favor of having the man nurse her. An example of homoerotic manifestation of such fantasy interpretations of relationships is the following case.

A girl had developed rich orgastic relationship with a young man. She was in her late teens. During the relationship, he attempted to squeeze a pimple on her back. "Don't!" she exclaimed, "I save those for Madelaine." Some questioning revealed that during the periods of disagreement with her boyfriend, she would live with, and sleep with, her girlfriend. She saved certain physical manipulations of her body such as squeezing and backscratching for her girlfriend.

The second form of regression that underlies transient homoerotism in early adolescent girls is a regression to the level of a phallic penetrative fantasy in relation to the mother.

A 12-year-old girl waited up all night for her father to come home from a trip. When he arrived home early the next morning, he brought no gift. She was frustrated. She did not show any anger to the father beyond what is manifested in showing little interest in him. She became very much involved with her mother, and ordered her around and demanded that she obey her. She reported the fantasy of saving her mother from a stranger who was going to stick a knife in the mother.

It is rare to find these relationships acted out in a manifest sexual form during adolescence. Usually, the manifestation is displaced and recognizable through the attendant fantasy, or by games in which the girl takes the part of a boy.

Summary

The response of the object world has a strong influence on the final shape of the personality. It is the source of the socialization and reality influences that put their stamp on the ultimate form. From the standpoint of late latency–early adolescence, the interactions of drives, talents, and needs, which make up the adolescent thrust, and the responses of the object world follow a predictable pattern, which results in a predictable and acceptable product. Disorders in the development are a form of psychopathology in this age period. They stand quite apart from the formal emotional disorders, such as psychoses, neuroses, and adult character disorders. In relation to wayward development during late latency–early adolescence, the child therapists have a unique function: They are required, in addition to the ordinary therapeutic tasks of lifting repressions and strengthening reality, to monitor and guide the synthesis of the forces of inner growth and the responses of the object world toward an appropriate adult personality. This role of the therapist in the life of the late latency–early adolescent will be dealt with in Part III.

Part III
Psychotherapy

Chapter 8

Assessment

The diagnostic assessment of emotionally disturbed children in late latency–early adolescence (9 to 15 years old) requires that the clinician acquire special techniques and background knowledge. The reader is referred to Chambers (1985), Goodman and Sours (1967), Herjanic and Campbell (1970), Puig-Antic and Chambers (1983), Rutter and Graham (1968), and Werkman (1965). In assessment of children in this age period, the focus is on areas different from those commonly dealt with when assessing the mental health of younger children or adults. Early-adolescent development is not marked by the expected homogeneity of development of the latency-age child, or the stability of adulthood. Early adolescents move toward maturity through a multitude of disparate paths. Any one of these could lead to a healthy adult adjustment or to chaos. At times, even an unruffled early adolescence can signify a rigorous defense against progress in drive expression, which pleases parents while leaving the child unprepared to deal with peer sexual partners in late adolescence and adulthood. Subtle indicators, such as persistent omnipotence, and a history of accidents of fate, such as the setting of initial sexual experiences, may be of greater importance in determining the developmental outcome of a child than do superficially chaotic patterns of adjustment, which may be short lived though overwhelming at the time of a clinical interview. Therefore, relevant therapies are often better aimed at the following functions than to the immediate correction of current behavior.

1. Strengthening reality testing
2. Strengthening self-reflective awareness

3. Expression of aggression that has been turned inward (depression) as a characterological response to anger
4. Understanding the future implications of present behavior
5. Disentanglement from the seductiveness of the symbol- and fantasy-dominated omnipotent adjustment of latency (the structure of latency)
6. Improving tolerance to passivity
7. Diminishing narcissistic vulnerability and omnipotent responses

Late latency–early adolescence is characterized by cognitive and psychological features which would be confusing at best and represent marked pathology at worst if found in a later adolescent or adult. Among the factors that sometimes create difficulty in the assessment of the adolescent are the protean nature of the ego structure in late latency–early adolescence; disrespect for the investigative aspect of the therapeutic process (this disrespect results in voluntary mutism, withholding of data, lying, tricks with words, and drug use during sessions); variations in the timing of onset of puberty and the onset of cognitive steps, so that one is required at times to judge a 17-year-old by the standards of development appropriate for a child of 13.

Assessing Adjustment to Sexuality during Early Adolescence

With so much to create anxiety in the child, it is no wonder that early adolescence is a period of great emotional stress. Many new experiences and events, which are totally real and will become a vital part of adult functioning, pour in on the adolescent. Sexual drive development is one of the strongest contributors to early adolescent stress.

Gradually, through trial and error, acclimatization, advice from others, and help from more experienced partners, the adolescent finds his way to an adult and mature attitude toward his drives and the demands they make. During the period between the onset of intense demands on the child and their resolution, the child uses the defenses of adolescence to keep his drives under control and provide himself with some comfort. Adolescence does not have such a well-defined and well-organized ego structure as has latency. Rather, the defenses selected are characteristic of the individual, and are highly variable. All have the capacity to provide momentary relief during periods of stress. All can offer a point of fixation from which persistent later behavior with pathological coloring can be derived. In themselves they are not pathological. Their persistence, not their presence, is the pathological indicator in assessing the child in late latency–early adolescence.

The many patterns of defense and adaptation to the burgeoning demands of the sexual drive can be resolved into seven groups. Five will be discussed presently. Drug addiction is described elsewhere in the chapter; transient adolescent homosexuality was discussed in Chapter 7.

The Ascetic

The ascetic adolescent (A. Freud 1958) responds to growing drives by eschewing them. Although he remains well in contact with his peers, he does not participate in the expressions of excitement, sexuality, and aggression that they do. He may attend parties, but will be found talking to the boys rather than pursuing the girls. Sports, abstruse knowledge, or schoolwork makes up the content of his conversations with them. If kissing games are played, the ascetic boy or girl may be distinguished from the others by such comments to the partner as "let's not and say we did." Drinking, smoking, gambling, and mastur-bation are excluded, too. Very early in adolescence, asceticism is a common technique for holding off the drives until the child is ready to deal with them. It diminishes in degree and in number of adherents as the older age groups are reached.

It is not rare for an individual to remain ascetic for a lifetime. Asceticism is rarely considered by the general population to be a form of psychopathology. Superficial relationships with people appear good, and there is a heightened capacity for creative and constructive, socially acceptable behavior. The individuals are well-controlled, well-organized, and contributing members of society. Ascetics as adults can find many social institutions that encourage and reward asceticism. There is a niche of respectability for the person who does not resolve the sexual and drive discharge problems of adolescence if that person chooses asceticism as the lifetime resolution of the problem. The old-maid school teacher, the maiden aunt, membership in abstinent reli-gious organizations (e.g., Shakers) are examples of social institutions of bygone days that made it possible for an ascetic to fit into the adult world.

There is a good deal of resemblance between latency and ascetic adolescence. The capacity for work, peer relationships, strong super-ego, and the capacity for creativity are found in both. The tendency to resolve upsurges of drive with escape into fantasy is also present.

Fantasy formation becomes involved in sublimation to a greater extent and becomes more adaptive in the ascetic adolescent and adult. Thus, writing of poems, painting, and aesthetics become a part of the creativity of the individual.

In those who join ascetic groups, there may be participation in group activities in denial of body needs; abstinence with kinship to sado-masochistic torture situations (hairshirts and self-flagellation) has been described. During the Middle Ages, the denial of the body and its needs by members of such a group became so extreme that a portion of a book (*Malleus Maleficarum* [Kramer and Sprenger 1489]) was devoted to a proof that the deity did not defecate.

It is possible to consider ascetic adolescence a continuation of latency, but it would be better to recognize that the defenses of latency are being used in a potentially pathological manner to deal with the problems of early adolescence. Whereas the latency-age child is doing what is expected of him, the ascetic adolescent is set apart from the others by failure to come to terms with and utilize the full potential of his body and mind.

Withdrawal

In the entire animal kingdom, one of the techniques most frequently used to deal with the new, the unknown and strange, the frightening, and the anxiety provoking is to run and hide. The ostrich supposedly hides its head in the sand; the opossum plays dead; the rat avoids new things. To paraphrase the old adage, "He who runs, lives." *Withdrawal* as a defensive technique in adolescence refers to the complete disengagement of the individual from any person, thing, thought, or situation that would result in the stirring up of inner drives. The withdrawing youngster avoids parties and such. Thus the internalized aspects of the superego need not be overly strong, since the person never puts himself into situations in which control would be necessary. There are few friends, no dating. Fantasy must be minimized or devoted to vastly displaced and innocuous-appearing thoughts having to do with dependency. These people are loners, uncertain of themselves, who rarely create, although they are always planning something.

A comparison with the ascetic might be of value in helping us to delineate the withdrawn adolescent. The ascetic makes contact with the world. He engages others in discussions to prove that his approach is right. He recognizes the drives. He feels holier than his peers, for he controls his feelings. He refrains from the exciting actions of others on conscious principle. The withdrawn child avoids contact with the drives. He does not recognize them. Since he avoids all stimulating situations, his failure to be aware of the drives is a reflection of the reality he has created for himself. The Judeo-Christian ethic has high praise for asceticism, which is historically a response to the temple prostitution of Biblical times. There is no such praise for withdrawal. The withdrawn person who continues this technique beyond adolescence into adulthood finds himself alone and unsought.

The social world of adolescence serves as a test area in which drives can be dealt with and techniques of social intercourse learned. Failure to come to terms with biological reality, the drives, and this social world produces a misanthropic adult who is unsure of himself and unable to participate effectively in the sexual comforts and activities of adult life. Such an individual is described as *schizoid*. Withdrawal in adolescence is not pathological per se, since there is always the chance that situations, friends, and maturational factors will tip the balance in favor of another resolution. However, withdrawn adolescents are the ones most in need of help and least likely to be able to resolve the problem without outside guidance. Whereas the ascetic is trying to figure things out and is involved negatively, the withdrawn child is not involved at all. He is not even slightly engaged in an attempt to resolve his problems. The tragedy in these cases is that they are considered by parents to be "good children." They do not stay out late. They do not get into trouble. They get average marks. Therefore, no one leads them to help. The instinctual drives are strong in adolescence. The withdrawn child deals with them by withdrawal from stimuli and through masked masturbation. A calm world for the child and an apparent low level of sexual pressure should be taken by a clinical assessor as a danger signal that one should evaluate the child for excessive narcissism and immaturity. Withdrawn and ascetic adolescents have in common a disassociation from participation in the sexual and aggressive, exciting activities of adolescence, and so we have placed them together in spite of certain differences.

Affect Avoidance

Affect avoidance describes the act of participation in sexual activities without emotional involvement. Most individuals enter the adolescent period with an inability to sustain the excitements attendant upon the expression of their drives. We have already discussed those who dissociate themselves from social manifestations of drives (the ascetic and the withdrawn). We now turn to those who participate, but derive no enjoyment or gratification because, though the flesh is willing, the psyche is incapable. Inhibitions and defenses block pleasure, or shift the cathectic energies into symptoms, such as phobias or hysterical amnesia. It is not unusual to hear such a person say "I can kiss, but I just don't feel excited." They are not more capable of mature drive gratification than the ascetic. Social pressures command that there be sexual activity. They participate to please others, to be able to say they have done "it."

Since these youngsters are participating, they have repeated opportunities to develop social graces and to attempt to resolve their inhibitions. Those who fail develop into adult neurotics. Unlike the adult withdrawn individual or the adult ascetic, they are superficially indistinguishable from normally oriented adults. Studies of symptoms and behavior patterns reveal them rather easily. They are in conflict as adolescents. They know that something is wrong. These children often seek psychiatric help. Unlike the withdrawn and ascetic individuals, whose behavior is syntonic, these people are dissatisfied with themselves.

It should be kept in mind that there is great variability between individuals. In extreme cases, neuroses begin with adolescence and—although it cannot be predicted from the start—continue into adult life. There is no capacity to involve a real object in unconscious fantasy that is defended against with the neurotic symptom. The fantasy is bound by the symptom. Intercourse will be possible, but internal inhibitions will make it less satisfactory than it could have been, and symptoms will take up the energies that should have been involved in the enhancement of the sexual act. Individuals who are unfamiliar with this fact criticize the psychoanalytic explanation of the contribution of sexuality to the formation of neuroses on the basis of the fact that the individual can participate in sexual intercourse. In less severe cases, the individual participates and finds gratifications, and so can relinquish the need to sustain the neurotic symptom. Conversely, there are individuals who are moving along satisfactorily and are precipitated into neurotic patterns of adjustment by events during sexual participation with emotional involvement which stir up affects which are so strong that it is difficult for the child to deal with them. This is an example of how the setting of initial sexual experiences can have more importance in determining the developmental outcome of a child than (unexpectedly) transient superficially chaotic patterns of adjustment.

A 14-year-old boy who had been involved in a kissing relationship with a girl, with minimal excitation for himself, ceased further pursuit of the girl after he witnessed the masturbation and ejaculation of a friend. As in all these matters, it was not the ejaculation, but what it meant to the boy, that counted. In this case, he experienced an intense feeling of nausea. Analysis revealed that behind this was a desire to suck the penis of the other boy and to swallow his semen. In the next four years the boy developed a neurotic pattern manifested in superficial socialization, neurotic constipation, anal masturbation, and a moderate degree of asceticism.

A girl of 15 partook of sexual play with boys whom she knew only casually. On one occasion she and a boy were in a face-to-face position with juxtaposition of genitals. She was fully clothed. His penis was exposed. He ejaculated on her dress. She became panicky. Here the ejaculate had a highly personal meaning. Her mother had died in childbirth. To her, the ejaculate meant pregnancy, and pregnancy meant death. From that day on, she disengaged herself from all sexual activity.

Social participation without emotional involvement is manifested in varying ways. It is not unusual to see young people who date, and involve themselves in kissing games and the other superficial trappings of incipient heterosexuality, but when alone with a person of opposite sex become sexual abstainers. This pattern is more common in girls than in boys. Furthermore, there are promiscuous girls who derive no gratification from the sexual act. They involve themselves in sexual relations, but do not participate emotionally. The defense of isolation is used to block a genuine emotional response; a genuine response would be overwhelming.

In girls, social participation without emotional involvement may take the form of promiscuity without orgasm; among boys, the adolescent Don Juan—the boy who recites to all who will listen tales of his conquests—comes close to this. He is interested in a sexuality through which he can manifest his masculinity to the world and at the same time hide his uncertainties from himself. He is not interested in gratifications from sexuality, but in proving himself a man to other men.

Alternate Outlets in Defense of Virginity

Alternate outlets in defense of virginity describes an expression of the sexual drive in which the early adolescent child, either out of fear or as a result of inhibition, seeks to establish alternate outlets for the libidinal drives as a goal instead of sexual intercourse. The most common substitute techniques are mutual masturbation and juxtaposition of the genitals. Occasionally fellatio occurs. It would be naive to formulate an understanding of this activity solely on the basis of social elements already mentioned and to ignore psychodynamic factors. Conscious seeking of substitute outlets is rarely seen. From a psychodynamic standpoint, the clinical assessor should take a signal from detecting such intentions. It implies that the search for participation in sexual intercourse or the fantasy about it is inhibited. This is often the result of a near-surface fantasy which, if stirred up by situations or other manifest fantasies, would be anxiety-provoking. Such a fantasy might contain a confusion between the partner and the father on the part of a girl. Another possibility is the fear that sexual intercourse is "what the grown-ups do," which would result in anger on the part of the parent whose place the child is taking in fantasy.

The situation is similar to that experienced during the oedipal period. At that time, we may recall, the child was confronted with threatening problems. Oedipal feelings and sexuality (genital fantasies) were resolved through regression to the anal-sadistic level. That was the starting point for latency. The course of events during adolescence is similar. Regression to pre-oedipal fantasy may also take place. Regressing from interpersonal sexuality, the child may begin to overeat to answer oral needs, or may develop a preoccupation with scatology. In interpersonal situations, sexual activity may be limited to oral sexual acts, or the entire relationship may be overshadowed by a motif of anal sadism in which sadomasochistic interactions become the acceptable area of interaction for the couple.

It is important to differentiate between common substitute techniques (e.g., mutual masturbation and juxtaposition of the genitals) as exploratory techniques being used by youngsters as a step in a constantly broadening armamentarium of sexual techniques, and the situation in which they are maintained as the ultimate technique over a long period of time. The latter is a case of a regression in which a less mature technique is substituted for a more mature one when the more mature technique is too threatening.

Age-Appropriate Gradual Involvement (Object Relationship with Gradually Expanding Heterosexual Activity)

Up to this point we have dealt with techniques used to hold the individual together and give him or her time to resolve the challenges of late latency–early adolescence, foremost among which are renewed fantasies, stronger drives, and social demands. Now we turn to a group of techniques used in resolving these problems. Nowhere else is the difference between adolescence and latency so clearly to be discerned. In latency, the emphasis is not on the resolution of problems, but on holding the line through a characteristic pattern of defenses, that is, the structure of latency. In adolescence, the emphasis is on working through the problems, while holding the line through a polyglot defensive structure, which is often transient, evanescent, and changeable.

One of the main sources of difficulty in regard to sexuality is the tendency of the child to confuse the characteristics of all drives (hunger, sex, and aggression) in such a way that they are seen as alike. The typical way of dealing with the aggressive drive creates confusion in the response to the sexual drive in early adolescence. In our culture, the resolution of problems related to aggressiveness is routine. The child who is frightened or passive when it comes to fighting or shopping or new experiences, is encouraged by the parent through precept and example to be more assertive and to go after things. However, the capacity to unleash to the fullest the expression of *rage* is not encouraged. In regard to aggression, the latency standard is taken as the model for adulthood and adolescence. Therefore, the normal child has been prepared by experience to deal with aggression in an acceptable manner when adolescence begins. With the sexual drive, the situation is the reverse. The adult is expected to be assertive and go after things, and the adolescent is expected to work toward this. Contrary to the characteristics of the aggressive drive, the sexual drive calls forth a need to be able to surrender with abandon to the excitements of the sexual drive. The unlimited potential for escalating rage that marks the aggressive drive, which the child is taught to hold in check, becomes the characteristic of the sexual drive in the mind of the child. As a result, the adolescent often confuses the two drives and fails to realize that sexual excitement is self-limiting. Orgasm does not go on forever; aggression, in contrast, can mount continuously. Only by experience or reassurance can this confusion be dispelled.

At the beginning of adolescence, both aggression and sexuality are under rigid inhibition and control. Aggression must remain so, with little loosening up. Sexuality must be permitted to unfold and reach full expression. Through gradual physical progress and exploration in interpersonal contacts, trial action through fantasy, discussions with others, including therapists, and masturbatory practice to master the affects of orgasm, the early adolescent prepares for intercourse.

Zones of Assessment for Normalcy

As in the case of the latency-age child, the assessment of the child in late latency–early adolescence requires that two zones of function be considered: socially defined behavioral normalcy, and biologically defined maturational normalcy.

Socially Defined Behavioral Normalcy

In industrial cultures, adult pursuits emphasize regard for abstract knowledge, reading, and the expansion of products, customs, and interests into the world and lives of their neighbors. The child in late latency–early adolescence faces the task of changing from calm learner to purveyor and user of these skills. The identifying abstract elements of the culture which have been absorbed in the latency years are now to be applied in making one's way in the world. The child begins to remove his drives and fantasies from his family and, turning to the real world, effects insertion and integration of his unique self into the main culture. Adult adjustments with sexual partners and aggressive realignment of the environment are now just within reach. Fantasy becomes ever less the organ for discharge and mastery. Instead, the world itself stands ready to be used, and the early adolescent must try, test, and practice using his weapons and skills in the realignment and rearrangement of reality to fit his needs. The key to the successful attainment of maturity in this respect is the ability to understand quickly when the world will not or cannot bend.

In evaluating the child from this point of view, the assessor should investigate the ability of the child to set his own preconceptions and fantasies aside when confronted with the limits the world places on him. The role of parents in guaranteeing survival should also be examined. Many times a child seems to be doing very well, and it is found that parents are buying the world to fit the child's fantasies and thus protecting the child from the impact of reality. Another impairment to growth is the tendency of parents to respond to the anguish and clamor of the child rather than to the child's logic. In these situations, the child's omnipotence is encouraged. This ill prepares the child to go it alone in life.

Biologically Defined Maturational Normalcy: Phase-Specific Considerations

Symbols in Late Latency–Early Adolescence. The symbolizing function during late latency–early adolescence is characterized by shifting forms. Ludic demise removes the child from the arena of expressive play through toys. Real objects replace fantasy figures as symbolic representations of unconscious referents. When symbols are used, there is greater potential to employ them in a communicative rather than an evocative mode. As a result, speech and language become more communicative. This leads the evaluator to expect that along with the apparent verbal maturity of the child, there will be an adultiform use of words and speech to convey truth. In clinical settings one expects to believe what one is told. This is one of the pitfalls of interviewing adolescents. The shadow of latency play falls on their use of words. If the child has come for treatment through his own will, the likelihood is that one can trust the words. One should keep in mind, though, that in cases in which the child comes grudgingly or against his will, there may be disrespect for the investigative process and disdain for the assessor. These last may produce an unwillingness to talk ("I'll go but I won't talk to him"). Withholding often occurs. I remember that once in one week I was told by three girls that they had had no sexual experience. Each was pregnant at the time, and knew it. Such tricks with words reflect a tendency in early teenagers to insist that their words be taken as truth, and a belief that if they can make words dance, people will believe that the world of reality is changing. This is a manifestation of grandiosity and poor reality testing.

Readiness in Comprehending Environmental Phenomena. The cathexis of the object world, which is one of the prime developmental events of late latency–early adolescence, depends upon the ability to make a consistent and accurate interpretation of that which is perceived. This level of interpretation is achieved through the development of the abstract conceptual memory organization. The *abstract conceptual memory organization* consists of the ability to interpret events in terms of their intrinsic substance, coupled with the retention of knowledge so acquired in memory through reduction to abstractions. The abstract reductions are represented by words whose relationship to the abstraction must be learned. At times, they are wordless. By the age of 12, the abstract conceptual memory organization should have acquired a body of abstractions concerning environmental observations that can be used to interpret proverbs and other verbal abstractions. At this point, the child is prepared to interpret and make conclusions when dealing with a multitude of verbal sources. Indeed, at this point interpretations and opinions can be formed about things that have not been seen, and never could have been seen (for instance, images of distant stars borne by ancient light which give clues to the origins of the contemporary universe, or times in the distant past, which when recalled to memory give clues to the content of the unconscious and to those motivations that silently give rise to the events of private contemporary worlds). This provides a great intellectual potential. At the same time, this efficient style of memory and thought gives rise to a potential handhold for mental pathology. When perceptions are reduced to abstractions, details must be lost. In detecting similarities, a certain amount of experience and talent is required in order that abstract reductions that seem identical, but have been reduced from disparate observations, not be taken for the same thing.

During late latency–early adolescence, when this process is beginning to approach the level that it can be applied to reality, communication is quite vulnerable to disorders within the process. Ordinarily, the errors of false similarity are corrected by memory of the original percepts that the abstract concept is meant to represent. An automatic deabstraction occurs, and this permits accurate interpretation of new percepts. This need only occur once. In people who have never experienced the percept, education schools the mind to make the proper connections. There are those whose grandiosity is such that they create equalities out of similarities and refuse to bother with the origins of the abstract reductions, often in the service of a false belief. During adolescence this usually grows out of a lack of experience and education, or an omnipotent position held so as not to admit to being wrong. The therapist must beware such omnipotence, since it may be a sign of schizophrenia. Persistence of such belief in identities based on similarities of abstract reductions is the basis for predicate identifications, a form of thought disorder.

Zones of Assessment for Pathology

In late latency–early adolescence, the child is beginning to be independent of his parents. In many areas, especially in regard to sexual play, he is somewhat autonomous. The presence of "secret" areas of function often brings the child for therapy at his own request. Quite often, though, concerns about passivity and about the therapist as a spy for the parents cause the early adolescent to be a mostly reluctant participant.

The capacity to create higher-order abstractions to be utilized while making interpretations in psychotherapy becomes functional in adolescence. With the development of these skills, conversations with children produce verbal insights that have a chance of being remembered. Assessment should take the development of these skills into account, since they will help in determining the efficacy of psychotherapy or the need to add to the psychotherapeutic task the requirement that skills in abstraction be introduced. Because attempts to provide logical answers and lines of association may stir up affects in the cognitively immature, ego building sometimes must come before interpretation and insight.

As the child grows older, the nature of the assessment process shifts from a primary dependence upon parents for facts to use of the interview with the child as a major source of information.

Drug Use during Early Adolescence

After silence of the negativistic adolescent, one of the prime forms of resistance is the use of drugs just prior to a consultation for the assessment of the child. The drug is usually marijuana. The youngsters actually believe that its use cannot be detected, but the experienced therapist has a good chance of detecting it. The characteristics of acute drug use are concrete thinking, bloodshot eyes, and easy giggling. When left to free-associate, they create lists instead of pursuing logical progressions of thought. The therapist senses that time is passing at a different rate for them than it is for himself. Typically, their answers to questions follow a different cadence from the rhythm at which they are asked. Of course there is the telltale odor, which if present (usually in the waiting room) gives the secret away. More chronic use of marijuana is reflected in any or all of the following: development of loss of motivation and falling-off of school grades; a change of friends to those with antisocial leanings; loss of self-reflective awareness; inability to recognize the danger in the drug; a history of immature sexual development (in those with very early onset of addiction, the drugs are used to relieve sexual tensions, obviating the need to overcome the hurdles in the way of sexuality common in early-adolescent experience), and persistent and sustained separation reactions in a child with formerly normal progress.

A history of an isolated hallucinatory psychotic episode followed by the intensification of preexisting neurotic concerns should suggest marijuana abuse. The promise of a state of comfort offered by drugs in the face of disquieting affects is an equivalent of the lost world of defensive fantasy that had been made available by the structure of latency.

Assessment of Adolescent Psychopathology

The assessment of adolescent psychopathology involves the following avenues of approach:

1. Parent interview
2. Clinical interview with the child
3. Educational testing
4. Reports from schools
5. Reports of previous therapists and other professionals
6. Medical examination reports

The assessment of adolescent psychopathology requires that the following zones of pathology be considered and, where indicated, investigated:

A. Social maladjustment
   1. Separation problems
   2. Affect starvation
   3. Drug use
   4. Physical or sexual abuse
   5. Sibling rivalry
   6. Lack of socialization
   7. Ethical individuation conflicts
B. Organicity
   1. Cognitive problems (central processing disorders)
      a. Learning disabilities
      b. Cognitive social discordance
      c. Retardation versus isolated innate flaw
   2. Mental retardation
   3. Hyperactivity (with attention deficit)
   4. Epileptic disorder
      a. Petit mal
      b. Epileptic explosive personality traits
      c. Fugues
      d. Temporal lobe epilepsy
   5. *Pavor*
      a. *Nocturnus*
      b. *Diurnus*
   6. Confusional states
      a. Postconcussive
      b. Tumor
      c. Hemorrhage
      d. Granulomatous meningitis
      e. Other emotional illnesses associated with physical conditions
C. Mental disease entities
   1. Schizophrenia (disorders of relatedness and the sense of testing of reality)

    a. Residual childhood
       Autism
       Symbiotic psychosis
       Persistent schizophreniform psychosis of late childhood
       Prepubescent
       Associated with cognitive impairment
    b. Adult schizophrenia of early onset
       Hebephrenia
       Undifferentiated
       Paranoid type associated with premature puberty
       Paranoia
       Asparger syndrome
  2. Depressions (affect disorders)
    a. Reactive
    b. Endogenous
    c. Bipolar
  3. Neuroses (consistent symptom patterns, with anxiety)
    a. Phobia
    b. Hysteria
    c. Obsessive–Compulsive
D. Psychosomatic disorders
  1. Anorexia nervosa
  2. Ulcerative colitis
  3. Anesthesias
E. Transient disorders associated with sexual adjustment problems of early adolescence
  1. Asceticism
  2. Withdrawal
  3. Affect avoidance
  4. Alternate outlets in defense of virginity
  5. Age-appropriate gradual involvement
  6. Drug abuse
  7. Homosexuality
F. Adolescent derivatives of masochism
  1. Masochistic braggadocio
  2. Masochistic perversions
  3. Adolescent shyness
  4. Incipient masochistic character traits

Interviewing the Parent

A great deal of the information needed by the examiner in the search for clues to the contribution of the child's psyche to his current problems is to be found in historical patterns of growth matched to the child's developmental history. To acquire this information, one turns to the significant adults in the child's life. Personal histories of parents and other family members are needed for the establishment of a family history of mental illness. The interview with the parent provides information that helps in the child's interview. It aids one in formulating the problems to explore and the questions to ask during the interview with the child. Often, the diagnosis or problem can be identified quickly when the interview with the parents has helped to focus attention on the appropriate portion of the differential diagnosis.

It is not required that parents be seen to make a diagnosis. Early adolescents have patterns of signs and symptoms in their behaviors and personalities which can be discovered, named, and treated by a psychotherapist.

Parents should be seen early in the assessment if at all. Because the confidentiality required by the material might make it impossible to see the parents without the child being present, an interview with them before the child is seen is essential. Otherwise, very personal data may be unavailable.

Clinical Interview:
Direct Examination of the Child

Many early adolescents have asked for help. Others, especially those who are involved in antisocial activity, would rather not see a therapist. These people are particularly difficult to interview. They tend to lie and to obstruct. If possible, the interview should take the form of getting to know one another. Rare is the angry, defiant early adolescent who is willing to tell very private troubles to a complete stranger to whom he or she has been introduced by an angry parent in a punishing mood. Still the situation is easier than with a young latency-age child. In the case of the early adolescent, the child speaks somewhat the same language as the therapist. It is of value for an interviewer to be familiar with teenage idols and movie and music trends. This will save much time otherwise devoted to asking questions about teenage culture.

For the early adolescent, the request to draw a person is a good starter. It provides a nonverbal access to the psychology of the child. I have found that drawings suggest interview topics and questions. Some therapists (DiLeo 1970, 1973, Fein 1976, Machover 1958) have reported being able to assess level of cognitive development, body image, sexual identity, organicity, mood, intelligence, presence of hallucinations, superego formation, reality testing, and fantasy through figure drawings.

The initial interview is shaped by the examiner's personal technique. Aggressive questioning tends to put children off. One should start with neutral areas such as school facts, sports, television, and movies; show the child that talking can be fun. Often ludic demise is recent and poorly sustained. For this reason, it should be possible for the child to turn to toys after a moment of silence. Try to remember the material the child was dealing with before the silence, for it may be a key to the areas of stress that cause his regressions. It often indicates internalized relationships (such as punisher/victim fantasies) that are sources of repeated neurotic patterns of behavior.

As with the assessment of the latency-age child, it is necessary to differentiate between information concerning direct representations of happenings that traumatized the child and fantasies, which represent a distorted internalization of past experience. The former usually gives rise to reactive behavioral difficulties in the places of the trauma, either at home or in school. The internalized fantasy goes everywhere the child goes and contributes strongly to fantasy-derived misbehavior. Internalized fantasy is one of the factors that produce psychopathological signs and symptoms. Although depression is sometimes a reflection of ongoing family troubles requiring parent counseling, and is seen as the province of the family therapist, internalized conflicts usually require a psychoanalytically oriented, dynamic approach and are the province of the child therapist or analyst.

In addition, the move into early adolescence is accompanied by maturational steps that produce clinical changes in object relations, overtness of private masturbatory activity, and the experience of uncomfortable affects. Each of these requires a change in the content of the clinical interview as compared with the interview of the latency-age child. Relationships with opposite-sex peers are pursued to determine where along the march of adolescent dating patterns the child is functioning. The pattern of adjustment to the sexual drive can also be explored. An important factor is the evaluation of the strength of narcissistic vulnerability and responsive grandiosity in establishing adjustments in these areas during late latency–early adolescence. This gives the child an idea of the possibility of giving up idiosyncratic reactions, such as asceticism, withdrawal, and substitutive sexual acts—tinged with disdain and a sense of superiority—with the arrival of maturity.

Even though the child now masturbates overtly, the action is still private. Pursuit of information about masturbatory activities and fantasies should be conducted with delicacy to avoid reactions that could interfere with the development of a therapeutic relationship. After the patient is secure in a therapeutic relationship, it is possible to ask how the child comforts himself when lonely or emotionally uncomfortable. Within the context of a free and comfortable answer to that question, one has the best chance to obtain information about masturbatory practices. Because the structure of latency is harnessed to the task of future planning at this age, the latency-age faculty of extinguishing uncomfortable affects in a flood of fantasy is no longer available. Depressive affects are more apt to be conscious and techniques for dealing with them very much on the mind of the child. For this reason, suicide becomes more frequent at this age. For a like reason, suicidal potential should be evaluated in each child with depressive mood changes. The potential is more intense when one or both parents are dead, when there are strong symbiotic elements and removal has been faulty, and when the child speaks of stopping the discomfort with a potentially dangerous activity, such as taking sleeping pills.

In conducting the diagnostic interview with a child in late latency–early adolescence, it is difficult to avoid a nonstructured session. The best the interviewer can do is to ask questions that follow ideas suggested by the patient which can be guided to cover the following areas:

1. Appearance and behavior, orientation and relatedness
2. Thought content and primary fantasies and fantasy structures (including whether internalized, and if productive of regressions)
3. Organization of cognition, thought, and memory
4. Affect and mood (including wish to hurt self, if present)
5. Impulse control in session
6. Major interests and reported relatedness to friends
7. Future planning and life ambitions
8. Capacity to stand apart and look at self
9. Degree of ludic demise
10. Narcissistic vulnerability and degree of omnipotent response
11. Nature of the symbolizing function (communicative versus evocative mode?)
12. Superego development (content of observing object in the mind's eye)
13. Suicidal ideation

14. Minor neurological findings
15. Status of the central processing system

Educational Testing

Educational testing is useful when there are learning problems. Such testing can demonstrate and delineate central processing disorders and related learning disabilities. These are often the hidden source of low self-esteem and poor academic performance. Through such testing, cognitive problems can be quantified and prescriptive teaching used to gear the child's education to his needs.

Outside Data

Increasingly as he or she grows, the person's life in late latency–early adolescence moves into areas far removed from home and semistructured situations. The permissiveness of the noncaring world brings out symptoms, and also many strengths. Schools, previous therapists, and other professionals, especially the child's pediatrician, can often give an objective, long-term view of the child's family and problems that would not be available within the time limitations of the average assessment.

Summary

Assessment in late latency–early adolescence has been presented from the standpoint of the specific features of maturation and development that change and add to the basic interview as it was designed for work with the latency-age child. The move into early adolescence is accompanied by maturational changes that influence the development of object relations; overtness of private masturbatory activity; relationships with opposite-sex peers; initiation of the pursuit of adolescent dating patterns; adjustment to the burgeoning of the sexual drive, coupled with the loss of latency-age defenses; strengthening of narcissistic vulnerability and responsive grandiosity; new directions in symbol usage (ludic demise and the appearance of communicative speech, tertiary elaboration, and emphasis on the communicative pole in symbol formation), and new exposure to uncomfortable affects in the face of the effective loss of present affect control accompanying the reorganization of the structure of latency to serve the task of future planning at this age.

There is so much that is new, typical of late latency–early adolescence, and unavailable to those who would try to understand what characteristics mark that special age from reconstructions of events and symptoms removed in time and place. Remarkably, late latency–early adolescence, a very font of future personality activity, is mostly transient. It soon passes into adolescence and then adulthood, when bridges bring the object world into position to welcome, and attend the metamorphosis of the early-adolescent child into an adult.

Chapter 9

Psychotherapeutic Strategies

Adolescent psychotherapy patients differ from latency-age patients in that ludic symbols play no important part in their associations. This rather obvious difference dictates that play therapy is inappropriate for the adolescent age group.

As participants in psychotherapy, however, the difference between the early adolescent and the older adolescent is more subtle. The cognitively mature adolescent who willingly seeks therapy, who is verbal, and who is psychologically minded is likely to benefit from the free association-based interpretive process that works well in the form of psychoanalytically oriented psychotherapy for adults. Unfortunately, few early adolescents fit into this category.

For the most part, it is required that the psychotherapeutic strategy applied to early adolescents be adjusted to take into account certain characteristics of the early-adolescent life-stage. These include, in part, developmentally mandated requirements (e.g., immature thinking processes—thought disorders) and socially defined immaturities (e.g., lack of comprehension of the role of educated professionals in providing expert help in areas of need). Therefore, this chapter is devoted to those psychotherapeutic strategies and techniques derived from information about the psychology of psychotherapy, discussed previously in this book, which set the psychotherapeutic treatment of the early adolescent apart from the treatment protocols used for children of latency age and adults.

Initiating Therapy

More often than not, the early adolescent is brought to treatment against his will. Even if brought to therapy willingly, the idea of therapy—what is required, what should be done in therapy, what the act of therapy requires, and whether secrets can be told—is a source of bewilderment to the child. Furthermore, the symbol-surfaced mirror of fantasy play is unavailable to reflect, in the early sessions, the inner world of the troubled child. There are available to the therapist only speech and symbolic acts. Should the child refuse to speak, refuse to direct his thoughts to his trouble areas, or be unable to do so, progress will be very slow.

To motivate the unmotivated child one must interview, in the first sessions, with the aim in mind of discovering a discomfort the relief of which could become the goal of the therapy for the child while the therapist pursues the larger goals of extending insight and enabling progression. The object of the search should be easily recognized by both therapist and patient as a valid psychotherapeutic goal.

At 14, the slightly overweight redheaded girl proclaimed in her very first interview that her life was a shambles because of her parents. "They don't let me do anything. They interfere with my life." She had been taken to see two therapists prior to this appointment by her parents. She had refused loudly to return to one and had run from the office of another because she did not like the questions she had been asked.

"The only reason I'm here today is that my parents say they won't take me to Florida for Christmas and won't buy me a car when I'm 18 if I don't come here," she said. "There is nothing wrong with me. I don't need a damned psychiatrist. You've got an hour. I'll answer your questions. NOTHING wrong!— Shoot," she shouted.

As her story unfolded it became clear that she needed extra freedom and late hours in order to pursue drugs and sex, and that her school work was suffering. She related as poorly to peers as she did to her parents. Her approach was to shout and demand, to lie and expect to be believed and forgiven as easily as one could expect to remove soil from the hand by washing. Obviously her life was out of control. For her, words were things and people were things, and people and words could be interchanged. Everyone and everything could be moved about as the agents and objects of her will, like the symbols and situations of a fantasy.

Even she could see that there was a problem in her functioning. Sometimes it didn't work. She didn't blame herself. She blamed the world for the selfishness that resulted in her failures.

When the session ended, she looked at me defiantly and barked, "O.K. I've told you about me. Can you find anything wrong with me?"

"Yes," I said, "I think so. You can't control your parents. They can't control you. Your life is out of control. You don't know how to control people." I had selected from all the problems that I saw in her the deficit in the ego function of *the ability to influence people*. I chose it because of her felt need to control, which was manifest in her behavior toward me. It was the one criticism that could be ego-syntonic.

She seemed stopped in her tracks. "You could help me with that?—When is the next session?" she said in response to my assent.

The early-adolescent child has a poor concept of the contextual relationship between current behavior and the future. This a part of the object–ground differentiation thought disorder, which is a maturational way station. This contributes to the fact that early-adolescent children can see no need for therapy. The impact of today's disorders of behavior on the quality of life in their mid-20s is beyond their spontaneous ken.

A lad of 15, darkly handsome, anxious, and defiant proclaimed at our first meeting that there was nothing wrong with him. His school work suffered as the result of long hours out after curfew. He often came home confused, with bloodshot eyes, listing as he walked, and calling out his parents' expected complaints before they had a chance to speak.

"I'm happy with myself and what I'm doing. Who needs school," he rationalized after receiving a mark of 40% on a hygiene and health education test. He did equally poorly in geology. He was sufficiently organized to have some friends and a life planned around the pleasures of the moment. His movements had form but, sadly, their guiding star was whimsy. All sessions seemed alike in their lack of purpose. The therapy appeared to me to be a string of initial sessions as goalless as was he.

I decided to try to lend him some self-reflective awareness and to help him create a superego-like goad that would push him to think of today in the context of the influence of his "now" on his "later." With the next session, I told him that I had heard that there was a 26-year-old man waiting for him on the road he planned to travel. I warned him to take care, for the man wanted to kill him because of the things he had done to him. He looked at me incredulously. "What?" he said, "Don't know anybody like that."

"He's here," I said. "You've ruined his life." He seemed to know almost at once that I had used a metaphor. It took two sessions for him fully to realize that the boy he was, the man he was destroying, and the ruined man in search of revenge that would take his life were all one man.

The early adolescent child is just coming out from under the hegemony of the parents. The passivity involved in sustained exposure to adult influence generates anger and exclusion of adults from the private thoughts and adventures of the child. The therapist does not at first stand apart from other adults in the mind's eye of the child. He is tarred with the same brush. Therefore, the therapist must expect slow acceptance into the secret world of the child. His confidence must be won. In the thinking of the child, the therapist may be an agent of the parents. "Does he repeat what I tell him to Mom and Dad?" "Can I trust him or is he a spy?" Extended sessions may have to be spent talking about films, singers, and news events attractive to the child while a relationship is established that will permit the interchange of information of therapeutic value.

Dealing with Parents

In dealing with parents, it is important to determine if the child is so mature that there are secrets to be kept. In that case, the parents must be told that after the first interview with the child, they will only be seen in the child's presence. Thus the child will know all that has been said to the parents by the therapist. As a result the child can be assured that he will be able to speak freely. It has been my impression that the most willing early-adolescent child will present a drift toward impersonal and surface topics if he suspects that his parents are privy to his thoughts through the therapist.

Since early-adolescent children are not willing to share freely, or even able to judge what is important to tell the therapist, some contact with the parents may be necessary. Telephone messages and letters from parent to therapist, as well as family sessions, fill the need nicely. The calls and letters should be reported to the child, in order to bring topics into the therapy. Parent information that is unknown to the child and is of a highly personal nature should be reported when appropriate, watched over by the twin guardians of tact and discretion.

"Interpreting" on the Predicate

It is not rare, before trust has been gained, to find that the therapist's questions about the patient will draw limited responses:

Q. "How are you?"
A. "Fine."
Q. "What did you do this weekend?"
A. "Hung out."
Q. "How are things in school?"
A. "Fine."

If no questions are proffered by the therapist, the early-adolescent child will in many cases offer only silence. This occurs in spite of the fact that at this age the child's experience is vast. There are many things of which to tell that are maturational, developmental, or social. Even if the child wanted his world to stand still, exciting and interesting events are being called forth by biology. There is a technical way around such withholding. It consists of active questioning which will not lead the content of the sessions away from the ideational content of the child. I like to call this technique *interpreting on the predicate*.

It should be recognized that whatever a relating child says must contain sentences consisting of a referent to himself or a past conversational element that is shared by both therapist and patient. In addition, most sentences contain new material in the predicate portion of the sentence (predicate nominative or predicate adjective), or in the object. One of the ordinary pathways pursued by free association follows the predicate. Therefore, with the early-adolescent child who would be silent, a synthetic form of free association compounded of the patient's own ideas can be produced. One need only remember the predicates, storing them if too many appear, and in times of excessive silence make questions out of them.

Let us say, for example, that we are in a session with a silent early-adolescent child. A silent child plus a silent therapist means trouble at this age. I ask questions about such things as what the patient did last weekend, or will do next weekend. I ask about movies seen, relationships between people heard of in school, or favorite television shows. From the child's answers I gather predicates from which to fashion questions.

Which questions? One might be guided in selecting topics from the problem areas and topics to be found in the chapters before and after this one. Oedipally flavored situations, sibling rivalry, strivings for independence are important, as are references to growth and development. Remember that the early-adolescent child's major means of achieving repression is through the countercathectic direction of attention and energies to external events and experiences. For the child at this age people and their experiences are symbols. The child is most sensitive to those events that represent his own conflicts and preoccupations. Through actualization and displacement, he removes the responsibility from himself while he continues to enjoy discharge or master situations vicariously. For the adolescent, gossip is the equivalent of the fantasy of the child in the latency years. Therefore one should look for parallels to the child's conflicts in the distant mirror of a child's selective gossip or his thrice-told tales from the movies.

A girl of 15, who had been sent for treatment by her parents because of a school phobia, went to school immediately after she had started treatment. That she had great problems with separation from her mother and feared growing up could easily be seen from her parents' report that she rejected dating requests from boys while arguing continually with her mother in a style that kept their hostile relationship primary. Through the latter, she kept her mother's control at a distance. At the same time, she forced her mother to be watchful of her. Her mother had to supervise her, for she refused to take any responsibility for herself. She would not clean her room or do her homework without prompting. She both rejected and invited parental intrusion. A prime matter of contention was her large breasts, which she attributed with a sense of blame to inheritance from her mother's family. Her mother could do no right. Yet the girl wanted to go shopping with her and be with her in preference to peers. At the same time, she was in competition with her mother over the mother's inability (in the eyes of the girl) to care for her father properly with respect to religiously mandated customs of the hearth which were especially important for her father, who was a member of the clergy. As far as she was concerned, she had no problems—there was nothing to talk about. She did not know why she was in treatment. The reason for treatment, if there had been one, was obviated by her return to school. There were no problems now. The issue was closed. The basic underlying conflict that led to the school phobia was seen as solved the moment its derivative in action had been erased. How could one approach her conflict and her fear about growing up?

Direct statements and questions availed little. The associations that followed such interventions somehow always brought her back to her favorite topic for study and discussion, New Guinea. For weeks on end she returned to thoughts of this far country as though it were her own beleaguered domain. I searched through the events of the adolescent age and through the physiological prerogatives that seize upon the mind of a child and could find no link to her preoccupation. How could this very distant land be a mirror to her mind? No reconstruction was possible. It seemed as though her interest had proven false the rule that "in therapy, an adolescent's spoken interests contain a kernel of her fear or worry." Finally I gathered the predicates, and asked, "Why are you so concerned with New Guinea?"

She answered quite directly that New Guinea was wonderful as the virgin jungle it was, and that she thought it would be awful if they "caused it to develop too soon."

The Technical Polarization of Interventions in the Therapy of the Early-Adolescent Child

If a child speaks of problems directly, one need not "prime the pump" through such interventions as asking questions or pursuing predicates for their hidden meanings. Therapeutic problems arise when there is silence, or when the child's associations drift away from the self and into the world of countercathected things. Silence may be used as a defense at this age. A child mind can be set to dwell in worlds away from troubles. Interventions are needed to keep the child on the track. Unless there is current anxiety to hold the problem in the mind's attention, problems drift away when an early adolescent talks to an adult. The child did not bring himself for help for the dysfunction that only an adult can see in its inherent dangerousness. The child who did not seek help may not welcome it. Like the dog who bites the hand that helps, the early-adolescent child may turn his anger or disdain on the therapist who offers his skills, as though the therapist were an intruder. He may turn from the therapist to silence, or he may drift in his associations in a direction away from the expected tendency to go inward toward the self or backward in time.

The adult weighs the emotional defect of the child in the balance against the impact of the defect on the future life of the child. The child adjusts for the moment; the parent seeks adjustment that will serve a lifetime. When the child is alone or with friends, troubles and depression loom over their thoughts, and they can talk endlessly of such matters with the assurance that they can be treated as passing things. Adults remind one, children let one go. With the therapist, an adult who reminds the child of the extended implications of a problem, silence tends to supervene. Many adolescents consider it more important to be free of adult influence than to be helped. For this reason, free association can be compromised in the psychotherapy of adolescents. In the early-adolescent child, free association may tend to pull thoughts away from the self and toward the world.

The goal in adolescent therapies is the same as that of adult therapies: insight and change through interpretation, especially of the transference. Adolescents often demand special attention during the early phases of treatment and some adjustments during the midphase. The approach to termination is little altered, though. The technical adjustments required take into account the special conditions, expectations, attitudes, and cognition that mark adolescence, especially the closeness to drive awareness that is produced by the increase of hormone levels and the loss of masking ludic symbol skills. This demands a turning outward of the attention cathexes that scan for free associations, which produces a hypercountercathexis of the environment as a means of drive suppression. Clinically this is manifested in therapy sessions as a tendency to respond to interpretive interventions by associating away from the self after an interpretation in which the self is mentioned. This tendency is intensified in situations of acute and chronic marijuana use, wherein patients will actually respond to interventions by providing extensive lists of things seen or experienced. The emphasis tends in all these situations to speak of things, not selves. Thus, a technical adjustment should be made to move interventions toward an interrogatory pole, which will keep the child's attention on himself.

We now digress to take note of the nature of the interventions in psychotherapy, in order to provide a foundation for explanations of the adjustment required.

There are six basic interventions used during verbally based psychotherapy:

Confrontation—conflicting pieces of information presented by the patient are placed side by side for his response ("You said, you would never marry, now you speak of becoming engaged.").

Construction—that which is currently happening to the patient is verbalized. Both affect and action may be constructed, resulting in two categories of construction, *affect construction* and *action construction* (e.g., "You are angry now.").

Reconstruction—what has happened to the patient in the past is verbalized. Both affect and action may be covered in a reconstruction; thus there are two categories of reconstruction, *affect reconstruction* and *action reconstruction* (e.g., "You were angry then." "Your father threatened you, and you became afraid.").

Interpretation—an intervention is framed using similarities of psychic function of the individual drawn from the areas of real-life events, past experience, and transference. One expects from an interpretation not necessarily confirmation but rather extended associations, which become the source of new information and insight ("Isn't it striking that in your work, your dreams, and in your way of talking to me in the sessions, you fear to speak because you worry you will not be liked?").

Each of the six basic interventions can be presented in one of three ways: They can take the imperative form, as in "Call me if you plan to do something foolish." This form is rarely used. They can take the declarative form. This was illustrated in the above *reconstruction*. They can take the interrogatory, or questioning, mode. This was illustrated by the *interpretation* above.

In adult therapy, declarative modes are preferred. Undue pressure is not brought to bear. The adult patient spontaneously associates with himself as focus and backward in time. For the young adolescent, the lack of structure in the use of the declarative mode permits the associations to drift toward more superficial externals and away from the self. Therefore, the interrogatory mode provides a polarity toward which one can direct the posing of an intervention in such a way that it will enhance the development of therapy along a patient-oriented line.

Adjustments in the Midphase

Symptoms and characterological behavior require insight for therapeutic gain to be made in the adolescent. In this, adult therapy and adolescent therapy are alike. The point of departure that characterizes therapy in late latency–early adolescence is the fact that this phase is normally dominated by change and progression. Development, maturation, and unfolding cultural demands make *change* the watchword of the phase. Psychotherapy must be conducted with knowledge of the average, expectable changes that are taking place concurrently. Developmental gains must be differentiated from therapeutic gains. At times, the work of the therapist is not so much interpretation as it is the encouragement that enables maturational changes to produce developmental results.

In early latency and adulthood emphasis must be placed on holding firm an ego structure which will be able to handle extended periods of status quo. The late latency–early adolescent ego structure must change in accord with internal changes and in response to the ever-changing requirements of self, peers, and society. In addition to the gain of insight and the pedagogical transfers of information that occur when one lends ego, the therapist must aid and enable progress.

At this age progress has many aspects. One of the most important is the development of readiness to achieve removal. This is the transfer of libidinal cathexes from primary objects (parents) to peers. It is a necessary step. After all, parents will not always be around, and members of the new generation must find each other and found their own dynasties. The hope is that removal will be so complete that the drives will find new objects without carrying with them the trappings of neurotic fantasy. Removal may take many years. Its high point occurs in late adolescence. In some societies, in which the family remains intact, removal would be considered pathological. Removal is not linked biologically to the growth period of youth or the stage of adolescence. It is a culture element of societies in which children set up their own separate households.

Early adolescence is an age period in which removal is not a primary feature. Early adolescent psychotherapies deal with the prospective enablement of successful removal in late adolescence. Usually this revolves around an event that occurs in midadolescence and casts its shadow on early adolescence: the break involved in moving from home at 18, as happens when someone goes to live in a dormitory at college, or to work away from home after graduating from high school. Although the patient says that nothing is going on or that he cannot find the reason for anxiety or sadness, the therapist should be alert to anxiety that deals prospectively, at times years in advance, with the upcoming separation. Bursts of depression are not unusual. They represent prospective mourning. This is a form of working through of separation. It is better done if the object of the mourning is identified and the process can be discussed.

Sometimes the source of fear is the threat of new freedom. When away from home, the suzerainty of the parents threatens to be displaced by a hegemony of inner forces and drives. Away from home and with free unsupervised hours to "get into trouble," new and fearedly profane experiences crowd those horizons of fantasy that invest the new life. Lunch hours for "quickies" (brief sexual episodes) are not as common in the lives of college students as they are in the fantasies of high school students. Their presence opens for the child awareness of how inexperienced he is. Anxiety ensues. The child must know how to evaluate danger in new situations. If he has been sheltered or inexperienced, this ego skill may be quite faulty. Look for this especially with overprotective parents.

Another possible source of difficulty in family interaction that may be linked to the separation of ensuing college matriculation or its equivalents is the sense that between now (usually about 16 years of age) and then (usually about 18 years of age) there never will come to pass all of the things that the parents could not provide for, for which the child had hoped. These include clothes, vacations, entertainments, and expensive colleges. Since such resentments are considered to be reprehensible, the content is often suppressed, with the affect retained in consciousness as a resentful mood in search of a precipitant. Usually it is necessary to hear complaints about the precipitant for a while until the underlying material can be elicited.

An important step in maturation and development that rivets the prospective attention of the early adolescent is *sexual initiation*. The first exploratory moves toward sexuality are apt to strip latent insecurities of their defenses and to produce anxieties. It is quite difficult to encourage a teenager who fears his or her own sexuality to talk about sex or to approach a partner maturely without appearing to the child to be seductive. Questions about masturbation or about intercourse experiences are apt to cause children great discomfort. They may, in fact, appear to be near panic; there is little chance that they will tell the truth. It is better to wait until the child gives indications of interest in the topic than to compromise an extended therapeutic situation in its incipient stages by making the child feel seduced and raped by a new intrusive adult. When there is a male therapist and a female child patient in early adolescence, an additional problem exists if a sexual transference is developed in silence. The girls are likely to act out on the sexual transference with peers. Pregnancies can occur. In such situations, it is necessary to ask about dreams and sexual fantasies to achieve discharge through verbalization. Severe situations of the sort require transfer of the patient to a female therapist. Male adolescents with a tendency to feminine sexual identifications may develop homosexual panic as a manifestation of a sexualized transference. Transfer to a female therapist may also be indicated here.

Remedies for Slowed Removal

The most frequent warning signs of slowed "removal" in the making are temper flares and battles involving the members of the nuclear family over schedules and telephones. Parents must often be included in sessions in the early part of treatment if their behavior in this regard is dominated by a need to infantilize the child. In the sessions with the parents, it can be explained that their child will be completely on his own in college, or in the military, or in work life. Some risks will have to be taken if the child is to gain the experience first-hand that will result in a position of safety when confronted with new problems. It is important for parents to let go early enough for the child to prepare himself for life and its joys and dangers.

The parent–child battles in early adolescence may have the appearance of a struggle for independence. As often as not, the purpose is battle itself, not freedom. At its root is a close relationship whose binding glue is intense anger; it is the opposite of removal. Such early adolescents may fight and cry for independence, but rarely take the steps to insure it, such as getting a job so as not to have to ask for money in order to carry out a personal project or plan. At times, parental acquiescence results in loss of interest in a plan that has been fought for. The real excitement for the child lies in the battle with the parents, not with dating a passingly fancied peer. In the battle children tend to see progress if the parent agrees to surrender when demands are made. Winning fights is seen as progress. The parents, conversely, see progress in the breaking of the child's will and the cessation of demands. Actually such "progress" is merely a shift within a battling family between a polarity that consists of fighting on one end and passivity on the other. True progress in removal exists when new and independent life relationships develop with peers.

Remedies for Omnipotence

Many forms of pathological adult narcissism or omnipotence have roots in the unwillingness of the child to give up the latency-age tendency to use fantasy as a means of expressing, mastering, and gratifying drives. In essence, fantasy holds the attention of the cathexes of consciousness. This counters the contributions of maturation, which strip the personality of symbols from within (evocative) as objects for drive discharge and provide the child instead with an organ system for discharge that requires a real object fitted with a partnering organ. Relatedness and compromise are required. If fantasy discharge persists instead, narcissism is reinforced; the object is recruited to help live out the fantasy, and the needs of fantasy usurp the place that would belong to the real world. Interventions, especially confrontations, can be used to enhance the shift to the testing of reality. I have found it possible to open the way to a modification of the force of omnipotence by introducing the concept of the reality one can feel, which must be differentiated from the reality one can touch. Thus one can view each new topic from the standpoint of its place either in reality that can be checked with others, or the felt reality that is informed by need, drive, and fantasy. Working through takes the form of repeated reviews of evidence.

> At 16½, though attractive, the shy but truculent tall blond girl had never been to a party. She was invited often, but feared to go. She held a newly received invitation in her hand and spoke with trembling lips of the fun she could have, but also of her fear that she would be seen as stupid and ugly.
>
> "Why would they invite you if they thought that of you?" I asked.
>
> "The other ones," she said.
>
> "What is your reason for this thought," I asked. "What has been said or done?"
>
> "I just know," she replied. Then she said, "I want to go so badly. I know what I'll do—I'll go early and wait outside and listen to what they say about me. They'll look at my face and I'll hear them talk." She went to the party and did just that. Reality was kinder than her fears. The party was enjoyed.
>
> Some weeks later, she responded to one of my interventions with a groan, saying, "That is the stupidest comment I have ever heard." Then she said, "How can my parents hate me so to put me into a room with the ugliest man I've ever seen and make me stay here for hours?" Apparently her fear of insult was informed by the projection of her own wish to insult. She saw others as motivated as was she, and she feared herself in them.

Eventually, on a deeper level, the feeling of inadequacy that causes one to fear realistic communication with the world, and forces the child to control his contacts by clothing new objects in the trappings of old fantasies which can be controlled, must be analyzed to its roots.

Thinking Disorders

It is wise not to consider thinking disorders to be diagnostic of severe mental disorder during the latency years. Only flagrantly disordered use of predicate identification in hallucinations (see Despert 1948) and loosening of associations that inform disorganized behavior should be used diagnostically. Concrete thinking and even mediate associations, though suggestive (Bleuler 1905) of autism, should only be indicators that further study is needed.

The period of late latency–early adolescence represents a time of emergence during which maturing cognition usually causes the intuitive thought styles of latency to give way to properly ordered thinking. There is a period of years during which certain thinking disorders persist during the transition. They represent remnants of the earlier thought patterns of the latency years. Their persistence into adult life has severe pathological implications.

Early adolescence is a time at which much can be done to resolve and treat thought disorders. Even those associated with process schizophrenias seem to give way. Therapeutic progress during this period is difficult to differentiate from maturational processes. During early adolescence, thought disorders, if identifiable, should be treated through: (1) challenge, (2) ego lending to set examples of correct thinking patterns, and (3) attempts to minimize anxiety, which causes thought disorders to intensify and fix. Since omnipotence is served by disordered thought, thought disorder can be treated through the resolution of omnipotence.

One type of thinking disorder normally colors behavior during the stage of adolescence, and one must be aware of its strength and appearance while doing treatment. It is *inadequate capacity for object–ground differentiation*. It is manifested in a tendency to understand present behavior as justified by affects and drive needs. Life contexts are ignored. (Mis)behavior occurs in a vacuum. Punishment for antisocial or antifamily behavior is not understood as being appropriate or connected and often stirs anger instead of contrition.

Using this form of thinking, one is justified in doing something if one "feels like it." Often the child's poor object–ground differentiation is encouraged by the persistence of this kind of thinking in the parent. A parent with poor object–ground differentiation may prevent a child from going to visit a friend because it makes him or her anxious, not because there is real danger. This does not support the development of reality testing or the process of removal.

During latency, immature (inadequate) object–ground differentiation was necessary. It supports fantasy as a drive outlet and as a technique for the mastery of the past. Even in healthy adults, it continues to work in dreams, with the effect that the outside world is excluded, giving free rein to a secret place for discharge of tensions through fantasy and symbols. In adolescence, its persistence applied to the contexts in which real people as manifest symbols of the inner fantasy life are set, can wreak havoc. It permits the child to live for today without reflecting on the effect of current behavior on the rest of his life or the real lives of the people who currently surround him. (See the preceding section on the therapeutic approach to omnipotence.)

At 11 years of age, the towheaded boy became aware that the cursing, kicking, hitting behavior that he carried on in the classroom, though it gave him momentary power and release, was the true cause of his placement in a hospital school. He had thought that the teachers were mean and intolerant and sent him to be with ill-mannered children as a result of their prejudiced opinion of him. His behavior had been a response to his passions. He had thought that others behaved this way, too. In his therapy, it was seen that he could be calm if his hands and eyes could be kept busy with structured activities. He was given puzzles to do while talking. During these calm periods it was possible to engage him in discussions of causes, motivations, and affects. He could carry this over into other areas of his life and bring experiences into the sessions and analyze them from the standpoint of the web of causality that related in his case to needs in classrooms for discipline. He came to see as the result of a construction ("If you behave, and only if you behave, will you be acceptable in a regular class. The teacher is not the cause of your transfers. You are.") that his behavior, not teachers' affects, were damaging his education and the outcome of his life. Note here that behavioral constancy came late and as a product of therapeutic work.

Once object–ground differentiation is an active force in the mental life of a child, affect- and drive-informed behavior can be differentiated from behavior motivated by the web of realistic and verifiable reality. Once it can be seen that anger is a thing with a source or a potentiator, instead of only a justified cause for behavior, it is possible to place it among those things that can be analyzed and, through knowledge, controlled. Parental moods then come to be seen as something to be coped with rather than responded to in kind.

Clinical Instances: A Primer for the Beginner

This section of the chapter is devoted to information of particular interest to the beginning child therapist. It deals with the nature of psychotherapy and its special characteristics during late latency–early adolescence.

Psychotherapy is a verbal technique for overcoming human discomforts of psychogenic origin. By *psychogenic* is usually meant experiential causal factors with roots in memories of experiences in the past. In working with people in late latency–early adolescence, it is necessary to add to psychogenic factors such age-specific psychological phenomena as delayed or neglected cognitive development, social expectations, and residual defenses that contribute to the production of psychogenic symptoms (e.g., depression and phobia). The complexity of the psychology of the situation makes the techniques of psychotherapy more varied than those ordinarily called into use in dealing with adults.

In standard circumstances, in dealing with adults, psychotherapy has as its primary goals such tasks as making the unconscious conscious, replacing primary process thinking with secondary process thinking (i.e., replacing reliance on the sense of what *feels* real with an awareness of that which can be *tested* and *validated* to form the reality one can touch), replacing id with ego, and developing the ability to love and to work to its highest individual potential. This is achieved in dynamic psychotherapy through bringing into consciousness repressed memory elements that in potentially psychopathogenetic states tend to draw energy away from useful functioning in the world. Instead of being available for the resolution of reality problems, emotional time, energy, and attention are locked into service as caretakers and guards for past affects and memories that are feared, actively forgotten, or proscribed from within or without. Euripides described this state of mind when he wrote,

> "You who sit there in utter misery, look up and show your friend your face. There is no darkness bears a cloak so black as could conceal your suffering. Why wave your hand to warn me of the taint of blood? For fear your words pollute me? I am not afraid to share your deep affliction with you. . . ." (Euripides 423 B.C.)

For some, the source of suffering has simply been concealed. For them, sharing and exploring forbidden thoughts in search of insight is a simple act of will involving the mere uncovering of that which had been willfully withheld. For instance, telling of that of which one is ashamed requires an act of will. The rewards of telling are mastery, organizing one's thoughts, discharge of tension, hope of good advice, and the possibility of gaining insight. In the *Tale of Genji* Lady Murasaki came close to an explication of this when she wrote, in the year 1008, that ". . . even those who wander in the darkness of their own black thoughts can gain by converse a momentary beam to guide

their steps" (Chapter 1, p. 12). Such supportive tasks as giving comfort, and permitting relief of tension through ventilation in the form
of repeated telling about traumas in the service of mastery through
repetition, help to deal with much stressful material once it has been
shared.

There are times and situations in which the source of anxiety and
pain is unknown or repressed and therefore excluded from consciousness. Simple communication is not enough. In these situations, special techniques based upon special understandings are required. Such
techniques are the distinguishing characteristics of dynamic psychotherapy; they serve to unlock the unconscious and bring it to the
surface, where its contents can be defined, discussed, and resolved.
Such unconscious content, which contributes to anxiety, fear, depression, and symptoms, is rockbound away from consciousness in the
adolescent and adult. The repression is less well concealed the earlier
in late latency a child's development can be placed. The older the
child, the more difficult is the task of retrieving the unconscious. It
eventually requires an understanding that surpasses reassurance and
kindliness. The key to uncovering of this magnitude lies in understanding the following: that which is in the unconscious, but is so
actively on the mind that it serves as a potential source of affect and
discomfort, is actually quite capable of distorting the concurrent conscious activities and thoughts of the child. If one speaks or acts in a
way that might influence the child's thinking, the unconscious influence might be lessened. If one remains silent or avoids intrusion into
the thought stream of the child, the persistency of the influence of
unconscious elements is sustained. The symbols, interests, and play of
the child can then serve to carry active bits of the contents of the system
unconscious into manifest play and talks.

S. Freud (1909) was the first to observe this in a child; he had
already studied the process extensively in adults. He noted that all
thoughts and actions are to some extent *psychically determined* by
unconscious elements. As a result, any sequence of thoughts and
actions should not be seen as random, even though they are seemingly
disconnected: there is an unconscious connection between any series of
thoughts. Sequences of thoughts serve to bring the unconscious to the
surface. The process can be encouraged. The less one interferes and the
more isolated the patient is, the greater is the *unconscious motivation*
that is represented by the activity or verbal associations of the child.
This gives rise to the therapeutic principle that one does not introduce
one's own ideas during therapy sessions, and that one directs the early
adolescent (postludic demise) patient to "say what comes to mind to

the best of his ability" or one directs the late-latency (preludic demise) patient to do anything in the playroom he wishes so long as it does not hurt self, therapist, or the room and its equipment. Once this has been done, the therapist takes the position of observer. His task is to figure out from the persistence of manifest (conscious) ideas and themes those distressful experiences and affects in the unconscious that influence the daily life of the child. With the younger ludic child, the use of toys and symbols in play gives the clue. With the late adolescent, subtleties of action and ideas expressed in the verbal associations of the child must be searched for hidden themes.

Let us take some examples. In each case, what is repressed is related to rejection and the child's response to it.

Late Latency (Preludic Demise) Fantasy Play

At the age of 9, she was still tiny. There was no sign of physical development. She spent her sessions quietly drawing pictures of kittens, rainbows, and stars. She answered questions with short and undetailed answers. Little if any personal information could be elicited directly. She had effectively established a countercathectic boundary between herself and the preoccupations that lay beneath the surface of her smug and proud retreat from communication with the therapist. Then one day the therapist asked her to make a series of pictures about the life of the kitten. With a gleam in her eye she began to draw cartoon after cartoon. A story began to unfold. A cat was hit by a car. She was badly hurt and therefore had to be taken to the hospital in an ambulance. Once in the hospital, she recovered quickly. The doctor took an interest in her. He was a fine tall cat with a long, somewhat bushy tail. He took her home from the hospital still on crutches. They married. A baby cat was soon born. The baby cat was very smart. In each class she was swiftly promoted to the next. In this way she grew up quickly. It wasn't long before she became a grownup teenager. One day while out walking, she was hit by a car. She had to be taken to the hospital, where she both healed quickly and met a handsome doctor cat. She didn't bother to draw more, pointing out to the therapist that since the story repeated through cat and kitten endlessly, all that the therapist had to do was to read the cartoon again and again from beginning to end.

One would be hard-pressed to guess that this immature child had so much in her mind about glamorous romances. She did not watch television "soap-operas." Yet the theme of the story was more than a story about cats. It could be used as the basis for exploring her ideas about babies. In addition, erotic transference wishes toward the doctor-therapist could be inferred.

Transitional, Shifting between Play and Talk. (Rarely Fully Reality Oriented)

He was 11 years old and in the second year of therapy for uncontrolled behavior in school, which included bullying other children and cursing out loud in the classroom. On this day he came storming into the room holding tightly to his bag of little metal airplanes.

"Did you buy more airplanes?" . . . "You didn't? Why not? I need lots for my game!"

He unpacked his planes and lined them up on the desk.

"How much would you spend for a car? . . . I mean the most," he said.

"What do you have in mind?" responded the therapist.

"The Mercedes Benz is a good car. Don't you want people to think you are a success?" . . . "How old are you?" . . . "You're old enough to have a nicer car than you have."

He began to fly the planes around. He crashed them into each other and into the walls. He ate a cookie his mother had given him and then dropped the cookie bag on the floor. The therapist made no move.

"I need some of your planes." He went over to where the therapist was sitting and began to move the wastepaper basket away from the tray that holds cars and planes. He suddenly lifted up the basket and spilled the contents all over the therapist.

Said the therapist, "What was that for?"

"I'm trying to see what will get to you."

Notice, the first attempt at provocative defiance was the throwing of the bag on the floor. Failing to elicit a response he escalates the attack. When that fails, he tries a verbal approach. Curiosity about an adult's response to defiance mounts in him. "What would your wife do if you raped her?"

The therapist said, "What does that mean?" The patient knows of rape as a sexual and offensive act. His sophistication does not permit more subtle questioning.

"What would you do if you saw someone raping your wife?"

The therapist said, "Call the police. That is what they are for."

Still unable to provoke an expression of rage from the therapist, he changed the question to "If you meet him after he gets out of prison, what would you do?" Concurrently he spilled a box of rubber stamps on the floor.

The therapist said, "You'll have to pick that up."

With a haughty expression he said, "What if I won't?"

The therapist said, "It's not a question of won't. I'm asking you to act like a gentleman. You didn't mean to spill that, so it isn't one of your games in the therapy." Notice the sharing of therapeutic distance and self-observing awareness that the therapist has offered.

The child picked up the stamps and replaced them with care.

The airplane race began in earnest. For about fifteen minutes, planes took off and landed and raced about. There was a collision of planes. The therapist asked what happened. This is appropriate, because it will add data and certainty to his observations and conclusions. It also checks to see whether the child is using the evocative or communicative mode in the use of symbols. The child went into detail in explaining the accident that had occurred.

Then the patient sat on the couch next to the therapist and told him they were involved in a race and that he was the pilot. They are being delayed for takeoff by the "umpires." "Don't you just hate officials? Give them the finger."

The activity of this child seems chaotic. Yet there are scenarios and themes driving the content from within the unconscious. He had been criticized for his rough behavior during a school game that day. However, the session content was not unusual for him and could not be related to that incident alone. His trouble with others was more the product of his difficulties with aggression control and sexual preoccupations. He wondered how people handle anger. The anger that he had in mind was aggression interpreted with a sexual cast as seen from the viewpoint of a young boy. He was not telling the story of an air race alone. He was expressing anger, defiance, and sexual excitement. His anger as experienced in the session reached such proportions that he attempted to displace it to the therapist. He tried to do this by attempting to provoke the therapist in hopes that he could actualize his own anger in another. He would then attribute the anger to the therapist, while his provocations could be forgotten and as a result, his own aggressions seemingly mastered.

Early Adolescent (Postludic Demise), Primarily Fantasy-Dominated Verbalizations. The final step during psychotherapy in the transition from late latency to early adolescence is the move from the playroom to the consultation room. The child simply feels out of place among the toys and tools for drawing, and may actually initiate the move through a request. If the playroom has two doors, one to the waiting room and one to the consultation room, it is possible to choose direct entry into the playroom from the waiting room or to choose to walk through the consultation room each day on the way to the playroom. If the latter course is chosen during the transition period, the child will find himself confronted with the option of choosing the "talking room" over the "playing and talking room" each session. This eases the process of moving into the consultation room. The child who chooses the consultation room consistently is quite verbal and ready to speak. In fact this is a sign that he has changed his mode of drive expression from play to speech. The timing of the transition varies markedly from child to child. It is usually encompassed by the years 12½ to 14. The shift away from toys toward talk does not mean that now children will speak of their problems directly. Spontaneous introspection into the problems of separation, sexuality, passivity, and mortality will not be shared by the average child for two or three more years at the least. At first speech is used to report on recent events, countercathexes, and reality problems for which an attempt to enlist the therapist's prestige is made.

One should keep in mind that the first task of therapy, which is the uncovering of disquieting unconscious content to be confronted and worked through, runs directly contrary to the primary psychological task of the age period. Shorn of the structure of latency and its tool, ludic play, the early-adolescent personality is busy establishing a new, more adaptive structure for the selective repression of drives and derivatives—*selective*, because some of the drives and their derivatives are prohibited in the adult world, while others are encouraged by social custom and the possibility of finding objects for the discharge of drives in reality. The effect of therapy at this age could be an undermining of the establishment of personality functions that are important elements in support of superego demands, culture, and defense. One must therefore be wise, and be careful to avoid attempts to puncture defenses in a way that would bring stress contents from the system unconscious into consciousness. Telling the child that by saying what comes to mind we can unlock his secrets and uncover the repressed may be counterproductive in a youngster whose developmental goal and current dearest wish is to put and keep his most troublesome thoughts in repression. One should avoid interventions that would interpret and undo defenses in such a global fashion that the development of the mature personality will be impaired; permit the child to associate at his own rate; formulate questions about the stories the child tells at an ego distance congruent with the distance through displacement that the child has chosen.

For instance, should a child be playing out a battle between soldiers, it is possible for the therapist to enter the game as a newspaper reporter whose questions can elicit details and associations that would not be available through direct questions. Direct interpretation of the child's responsibility for the displaced anger and the unconscious wishes that its presence represents should await one's sensing that the child has already come close enough to the material to be able to come to the conclusion by himself without undue stress. It helps little to bring material to a level of awareness at which it could be confronted or worked through if concurrently there is mobilization of so much anger and affect that it would impair communication or muffle reason.

Age 13 seemed a bit late for a child to elect to start his treatment in the playroom. This was especially so for this tall, pleasant-appearing, and slightly overweight young fellow. He seemed to be too big for the room. Toys were dwarfed by his hands. He wanted to draw.

His parents spoke of his problems of sexual identity, his shyness and lonely pattern of existence, particularly emphasizing his "addiction" to television. He was the frequent butt of jokes in school and was teased repeatedly. He had trouble sleeping at night because of his fear of intruders, robbers, and thieves. In the initial sessions he gave brief, unelaborated, positive answers to questions about that which his parents had reported. Within a few days of the beginning of the sessions, he described the rapid disappearance of all symptoms and troubles. In answer to all direct personal questions about himself and his problems, he thenceforth responded with variations on "Good," "Fine" and "O.K." This response covered even those questions which dealt with the normal process of sexual development. His words hid his real feelings. The mere mention of sex caused him to become riled, upset, and apt to call the therapist a pervert or dirty-minded person. He often brought in quotes from friends to reinforce his point of view. In spite of this, his activities in the playroom consisted primarily of the production of television dramas of extended duration which contained multiple references to sexuality, which were accompanied by a knowing look or leer. He drew the pictures of each new character and then handed the therapist the sheet from which to cut out the characters. This help speeded up the process. The characters were then pinned in affinity and marital groups to a cork wall. As the story of multiple affairs, much sadism, few children, murders, divorces, surgery for brain tumors, illegitimate pregnancies, and a few sex change operations unfolded, it was clear that he had watched his television well and had more than the interest of an "actively rejecting prude" in matters sexual. He willingly spun out his stories. However, he refused to see any connection between them and the content of his unconscious mind, or with his problems. After all, they were distant events with no possible relationship to himself. The summer break came and went. With his return, he opted for the consultation room where we could "sit and talk." Occasionally, he drew a picture. There was no attempt made to identify the picture or to connect pictures to make up a tale. The therapist supported this deemphasis on verbalization woven around the pictures in order to encourage verbalization woven around mental constructs. The content of the sessions changed little at first. He was able to talk about a lessening of teasing in school.

"Why do they pick on me? I don't bother them," he would say repeatedly.

"Why are you with people who tease in the first place?" asked the therapist.

"A lot of people are in the lunch room. I mind my own business and don't bother anyone," said he. Then he remembered that he had had a dream the night before, but somehow could recall nothing of it. "I know you psychiatrists need dreams, but I'm sorry I can't tell you about it," was his comment.

He recounted his visit to a movie with his mother where he saw the movie "Superman." The superhero had been teased because of mildness born of forebearance. The session had come to the end of its time. I told him this and bade him good-bye. As he left the room, and with the door half open, he said, "Now I remember the dream." As he spoke these parting words, the gleeful, knowing leer of old returned to his face. He held out the dream as though he had food to offer to a hungry animal. He was teasing as he said, "I could tell it now, but I don't have the time.

Next time." By next time, the dream was forgotten. His provocative way of handling the dream remained with the therapist.
Through teasing he invited an attack on himself. The therapist
recalled the French expression, "le pécheur péché" which conveys the meaning that it is the sinner who is sinned against, and
that the fisherman alone who drops a hook for the fish to bite
runs the risk of being pulled into the sea by his quarry. In the
sessions, his repeated gestures of secretiveness, withholding,
momentary offers of surrender, and then withholding again were
bordered round with hardly concealed excitement. The patient's
similar excited teasing of aggressors in the school had, in a not so
subtle way, set for him a reaping of the wild wind he had so
secretly sown.

The therapeutic task required that his behavior be demonstrated to him, and that the concealed hostility that drove it be
brought to consciousness and analyzed to its source. This could
not be simple in light of the indirect way that he yielded up his
secrets to the therapeutic process.

In the next case, a child went to the playroom after starting in the
consultation room.

He had come to therapy because of bullying of his sister, being
the butt of teasing in school, and massive temper outbursts at
home. At first this wiry 11-year-old chose the talking mode in an
attempt to be grown up. Even after he moved to the playroom, he
did not use toys or drawings as more than things to handle out of
curiosity. He did not develop stories or organize the toy material.
Instead, he used the playroom's space and permissible freedom of
movement as a place in which he could throw a ball up and
down and in general release physical tension. This is a physical
equivalent of the ordinary teenage use of paradoxically calming,
strongly plangent, raucous music. The tension release so
achieved permitted him to converse about his problems with the
therapist much in the way that loud music helps teenagers to
study, or sound-makers, fans, or air-conditioners help them to
sleep.

Theoretically, these activities and sounds can be viewed as projection, actualization, or externalization of internal, potentially disruptive masturbatory excitements.

This case and the next illustrate techniques for bringing topics into sessions when the early adolescent, who is using communicative speech and tertiary elaboration to discuss social issues, sports, and entertainment, chooses to avoid a spontaneous self-reflective exploration of manifest problems. The technique is to ask questions or pick up on topics related to the reasons for which the child has been brought to sessions, and also information about ordinary ongoing events in the child's life. One should ask about school progress, report cards, weekend activities (before and after) if the child does not bring up these topics spontaneously. Parental letters or telephone calls should, within the limits of tact, be brought to the attention of the child, with emphasis on events that reflect the child's problems.

> The boy came clattering into the playroom encased in the 11-year-old's full regalia, including helmet, face mask, and mouth guard, of a football player ready to play. "I have to go right from here to the game."
>
> The therapist evinced great interest in the sport, asking how long the youngster usually is in the game.
>
> "I'm usually in for three quarters," said he. "Trouble is, I may be cut because my marks aren't good."
>
> A discussion of the trouble he was having in school ensued. Then he fell into silence while he played with a ball. Undoubtedly he was comforting himself with something he could do well after revealing his deficiencies. After an appropriate time to let him heal his wounds in this way, the therapist brought up the topic of a call left on his answering machine by the child's mother. He suddenly became angry and had a temper fit for which the mother could find no cause. "He ran out of the house and we couldn't find him for hours. No one knew where he was hiding. We finally found him. He had climbed a tree. He was hidden by the leaves. All the time we were looking for him, he was watching us."

The therapist chose to enter this topic with a parsimonious question that would permit the child free rein in avoiding the topic as well as freedom to expand on it without being forced into a digressive and therapy-blocking defense should the mother have seen events differently from the child. Note the use of the interrogatory form of intervention. The therapist wanted to force an answer. In this way he would focus the child's attention on recognition of the recent unpleasantness as his own (the child's) problem. A question that could be avoided because of insufficient recall for the experience during latency cannot be so easily deflected during early adolescence. In early adolescence, one may expect that the child will remember important events as contrasted to the child in full latency, for whom fantasy defense provides countercathectic repressive forces that result in a dropping from conscious awareness of important experiences.

"What happened on Sunday?" asked the therapist.

"Did my Mom call?" answered the patient.

"Yes," said the therapist.

"It wasn't as bad as she said," demurred the patient in advance of the therapist's information.

"What?" said the therapist.

"I wasn't so angry," the patient replied.

"The tree?" asked the therapist.

"I got angry 'cause I wanted to go with my mother, and she wouldn't wait for me till I was done with the TV," said the boy. "No one listens to me. My sister got a new bike and clothes and stuff and all I got was a book. I ran and went up the tree to calm myself."

"How else do you calm yourself?" asked the therapist.

"I listen to music you wouldn't like. I don't like to go to my room. I get away from people."

"How does that solve the problem?" asked the therapist.

"It doesn't, but I get calmed down," the youngster rejoined.

The therapist then pointed out, "Have you thought of talking to your parents directly about how you feel? Calming things stop anger, but the problems are still there the next day."

The youngster complained in response, "It won't make a difference. They won't listen. They don't care a s--t about me."

In this exchange was revealed the underlying complex of sibling rivalry and feeling of rejection that gave rise to the seemingly cryptic anger reported by the mother. Thus, it was brought to the surface to be worked on. This kind of data should alert the therapist to poor parent-child communication. The youngster had improved markedly from the very beginning of the therapy. This was less the result of therapy than the product of a sense of importance in that his parents now thought enough of him to give him therapy. There was obtained thereby a reversal of the lack of parental attention that he had felt existed.

The following case focuses on the approach to the patient's associations that makes it possible for both therapist and child to bring into awareness trends that are unconscious and that shape the child's life avoidances and sensitivities.

Hilda was 15, frail and thin, with a firm belief that her parents should take no part in her life.

She limped into the session, threw herself into a chair, gave a sigh of relief, and stared at the floor. After four or five minutes of musing while studying the rug, she began an almost imperceptible humming. She tilted her head till she could see me with one eye, while the other eye squinted tightly.

If you object to a patient who starts a psychotherapy session in this way, stay with the treatment of adults. A high tolerance for aberrant behavior is needed in work with early adolescents. They need such behavior to set the session off (isolation) from the rest of their lives, to create a mood, to proclaim their equality, and to gather together their energies for the difficult work of facing themselves.

She opened her associations with "I'm grounded again. My folks finally figured something out. I told them I wanted to spend the night with Jane after the church social last Saturday night. They told me to get home by two. How can I tell George I have a curfew? They figured I'd be with him all night. They said so. I got so mad. What is it their business? How are you supposed to get laid? When I got to Jane's house I got so mad I started breaking things. I kicked the thing in the fireplace. How do you know if your toe is broken? Do you think I need an X-ray?" Looking at her foot. "I couldn't enjoy anything. George was mad. I finally got home at 5:30 in the morning. Can you imagine? They were waiting up for me. The chauffeur was up. The maid was making them coffee. They were eating cake. (Pause) Can you imagine,—They were having a party. When the h--l do they get laid? They grounded me. The worst thing is that now I'm going to be in more trouble, 'cause they haven't got over this and already I got something else to worry about."

Up to this point the therapist sat quietly. The child had by this age acquired much experience in extremes of anger at her parents, and could tolerate it without fear of loss of the relationship with them or danger that unfamiliar levels of anger would activate either the internalization of anger (depression) or the projection of anger (paranoia). However, he should have given second thoughts to the self-injury that the anger produced when she kicked the andiron. The therapist waited out the storm and permitted the patient to discharge affect until she could calm down. When her thought content switched from past concerns to apprehension about the future and she began to slow down her affects, he asked "What's the something else?"

She thought for a moment and began to sift through her concerns. Report cards were due to be sent home shortly. She was due to fail in chemistry. "My average is 85. But the nutty teacher is going to give me an F because I didn't get the lab reports in on time."

There is now enough information for the therapist to recognize and share with the patient through interpretation one of the sensitivities that arouse such rage in her. She becomes angry and defiant when she is forced to match her time schedule to the demands of others. Note the content of the above associations. They follow closely fifteen unbroken minutes of free association during early adolescent psychotherapy. They begin with a period of silence during which she waits to begin the therapy at a time of her own choosing. Then she tells of her rage at her parent's intrusion on her all-night social schedule. Finally, she speaks of school failure as a result of a defiance of academic deadlines. One such incident could be an accident. Two could be a unique and accidental confluence of similarities. Three such associations, including one which was acted in during the therapy call for a therapist to pursue the possibility that there is an unconscious pattern in action. When the therapist pointed out the similarities of theme to the patient, she became quite muted, seemed to think for a moment, and said, "You say whah!" The therapist remained silent. The patient began to talk of her next weekend schedule.

Note how much the patient is involved in the present moment and her affects. In the overall picture, this represents her wish to grant priority to her own schedule. She just cannot see time and responsibility from the perspective of adults. It is not unusual for youngsters to be so involved in current troubles that they miss telling about important events. It is necessary, therefore, that the therapist ask about events of the past weekend that have been ignored or of the next weekend that loom in the near future and are important. The perspective of young teenagers is skewed in that their capacity to place proper emphasis is not weighted as is the capacity of adults. Their object–ground differentiation tends to idiosyncratic personalizations of what is important.

Questions about the child's current affairs and scheduled events often must be asked by the therapist in order to keep himself informed to a level adequate for the responsible conduct of a therapy. In asking such questions, one should be aware that one may be trespassing on the child's priorities and that transference anger may be generated. If the child is angered at such questions, interpretations that refer the anger to its source in the child's preoccupation with control over her own schedule would have been prepared for, in the case of the present patient, by the explaining that she had become angry at being forced to match first the time schedules and then the contents of the session to the presumptive priorities of others.

The complex psychology of late latency–early adolescence is characterized by an underlying developmental theme. This is a period of transition to those cognitive skills that emphasize realistic evaluations of observed phenomena, as opposed to intuitive and self-oriented interpretations. During this period, the needs of others gradually come to influence the planning and decision-making of the child. Concordantly, social demands guide the superego, and the schedules of others come to be respected. As a result of these developmental characteristics, the techniques of psychotherapy must be more varied and pedagogic in aim than those typically used when dealing with adults with settled, adult ego functions. Early adolescents often have to be reminded of social demands that in adults have been internalized. As we have said, the social contexts within which people coordinate their lives through conventions of time and the use of schedules become the topics of interpretations. Age-specific psychological phenomena, such as delayed or neglected cognitive development, must be monitored and interpreted. Often, the behavior of the therapist becomes the pattern upon which the patient bases his identification with social uses and accepted customs.

This 17-year-old was short, thin, and frightened when first seen by the therapist in the disturbed ward of the county mental hospital. He had been admitted the night before. He had lost control of his anger at home and expressed it by smashing the tiles in the bathroom of his mother's home. The police had been called and had brought him directly to the hospital. His affect was appropriate and there was no thinking disorder. He spoke of his life at home with his mother and sister. His father was rarely home, and remained a shadowy figure throughout the treatment. His mother was constantly controlling. No attempt at adaptation to the environment for the children had been made by the mother. School attendance had been spotty. He had never worn a belt or a tie. The main source of his argument with his mother had been his refusal to finish his dinner of *baby food*. His mother served mainly strained food to the children. His sister, who was 12 years old, had never eaten anything but baby food. He had eaten more age-appropriate food on occasion when taken out by a concerned uncle. There was no identifiable mental illness. His uncle arranged for him to be in therapy after his discharge from the hospital. In addition, he obtained for the boy a job soldering connections on prototypes of electronic weapons. He was quite conscientious. He saved his money. He was a messy but accurate solderer. In the therapy he spoke of his rage at the extreme passivity that dominated his position in the home in relation to his mother. He hoped someday to move out and to provide help for his sister. One day, he appeared particularly apprehensive upon entering the consultation room of the therapist. He stared at the therapist's tie. When asked about this, he revealed the following: "The boss on the job has invited me to dinner. I keep looking at you to find out how to dress and what clothes to wear. Looking won't help my problem. Please teach me how to tie a tie. How do you use a fork when you eat?"

Sometimes we take for granted that children know more than they do.

Let us return to the case of Hilda.

She was so taken up with her own needs that she could not consider the needs of others in the organization of time, or their concerns for her whereabouts, safety, or mores. This came to a head during family preparations for a summer vacation. She wished to go on a teen tour. Her family did not object to this. However, they were perplexed by the fact that the tour she had chosen conflicted in time with the wedding of a cousin. They wanted her with them at that time. They suggested that she take a slightly different tour that would fit in with their schedule. Her response to this was "S--t no. I refuse. Why can't they leave me alone?"

"Do you want to go to the wedding?" asked the therapist.

"Sure, but I don't want to give in," she answered.

Her parents eventually hit on a solution. Since the teen tour passed near the distant city at which the wedding was to take place, they offered to arrange to have her leave the teen tour for a few days in order to attend the wedding. "You know," she said, "I have to admit they're being fair to me—to you—but I'll never admit it to them. They worked it out so I won't really lose anything. How did they do that?"

"It's called love. Keeps families together. You've got to give to get," said the therapist neatly summarizing the concept that love means taking the needs of the loved one into account before one's wishes reach the planning stage.

She used this information in a somewhat self-serving way, which gave evidence, however, that she had absorbed the concept. She began with an awareness that she had a right to be treated by her boyfriend in a ". . . loving way. I see him. We have sex. Then I do a slow burn. He leaves me alone for the rest of the day while he gives his pals rides on his motorcycle." She told him good-bye. Then she began a relationship with a boy who "calls every day," builds his free-time schedule around her, and pays attention to her whenever they are together.

The Interpretation of Dreams in
Early-Adolescent Psychotherapy

Spontaneous dream reporting is rare in the psychotherapy of latency-age children. The same material that could find its way into therapy sessions through dream (oneiric) symbols can be expressed in the near-at-hand medium of ludic symbols. Fantasy play serves a function so similar to dreaming that insights into one of these fantasy forms can help in understanding the functions of the other. The early adolescent, having lost the functional capacity of ludic symbols to communicate or to evoke inner moods, must turn to dreams and fantasies, in which reality is manipulated to a form in which it will be able to carry the message of the unconscious into therapy.

Dreams are not so much different at these different ages. Their use, primacy, and effectiveness as discharge or communicative psychological instruments undergo a transition during the period of cognitive changes of late latency–early adolescence. This transition contributes a perceptible difference to the psychotherapeutic interpretation of dreams during early adolescence. In working with latency-age children, dream interpretation yields little if it is based on waiting for the child to associate to individual symbols. If a symbol can be made into a cardboard figure and introduced as a playtoy, the fantasies built about the cardboard figure can be seen as dream associations.

In working with adults, dream interpreters in dynamic psychotherapy use one or more of four techniques. First, there is the technique of asking the patient to look for elements in the events of recent days that the dream reminds them of. This produces links between the dream and unprocessed, stressful events that require more effort for mastery. Second, there is the request that the patient respond to each dream symbol by saying what comes into his head in association to the symbol. Third, there is the technique of avoiding focus on the dream while the therapist seeks enlightenment by considering the content of the *entire session* to the associations to the dream. Fourth, there is the study of the secondary elaboration of the dream as a source of information or confirmation about the core fantasies that identify the sensitivity and predilictions of the patient in his current life. (*Secondary elaboration* refers to the organization of the disorganized melange formed by the dream symbols into a coordinated tale with sense in its relationship of one element to another. It can be differentiated from tertiary elaboration in that the latter creates order for a listener, while the secondary creates order for oneself.)

In early adolescence, it is possible to ask about day residues and to pursue the use of the session as an association to the dream, as is done with adults. Because of the limitation on abstractions during early adolescence, free association to dream symbols is not particularly productive. On the other hand, the pursuit of secondary elaboration (themes that tie together content) can be very useful in giving clues to problem areas and defining goals for the therapy.

A young man of 19 had never lived away from home. He was greatly attached to his mother, and tried his best to substitute for his father as the man of the house. His father and mother were estranged, and the parents had lived apart for years. During a period of expectation prior to his father's return to the home and his parents' reconciliation, he had the following dream:

He was in Russia . . . with his mother . . . and two brothers . . . they ran as they were being pursued . . . his mother fell a couple of times . . . each time, he picked her up.

Each individual unit of the dream was inquired about. There were no associations other than those that expressed wonderment at the flimsy relationship that the units had to him. The family was originally from France. Although the dream consisted of symbols selected from realistic representations, it was fantastic in content when considered in the context of the patient's life. No day residue could be uncovered. If viewed as a symbolic representation of an oedipally involved young man, one can see parallels to his current life situation and problems. He escapes to a strange land with his mother. Someone pursues (guilt—the father?). Her falls represent her ambivalence as conceived by the boy. He reinforces their flight by helping her up. What has been done by the dream interpreter is to guess at the core fantasy that predicts and shapes the boy's fate. The oedipal fantasy is chosen from the usual currency of fantasies active at this age in young men who have failed to achieve removal, because of the similarity of elements between the manifest dream and the oedipal fantasy (i.e., the child is allied with the mother against a pursuing father). There is no certainty that this is the operative fantasy; however, in the absence of associations to the dream, the oedipal fantasy can be used as the basis for theories and interpretations. Should this tack steer the patient's thought toward confirmatory associations and unlocked memories, the guess will be worth the risk of losing time.

With this model for the handling of the early-adolescent dream in mind, let us examine the dream of a 15-year-old girl.

The vital facts of her life at the time of the dream were that she was sexually inexperienced and thought of sex as repulsive. Still, she was excited by boys and attracted to them, and was being courted by her first boyfriend. She lived with her mother and half sister. Her mother often referred to sex as an unnecessary burden. Her father, to whom she had been close as a companion and confidante, had been divorced by her mother when she was 10. He had moved to Europe two years before the dream. Her mother had recently remarried. Her stepfather paid little attention to her; she stated that he only ". . . takes me out or talks to me as part of being with my mother."

She started the session with the statement, "I don't want to see my boyfriend anymore and I don't think he wants to see me. What a nerd. That goofball. Can you imagine—he wanted me to unzip his pants! In the movies yet. What does he think—I'd know what to do? I don't know nothing. I never did nothing. He keeps nagging, nagging. If I even think about it I get antsy. I get this sandy feeling in my mouth and my throat gets all up and full and feeling funny. What does that mean?" (pause) "Oh God! don't say that!"

"What," said the therapist.

"You know . . . (slight pause) . . . Oh, I could throw up! You know, and if you don't know I'm not gonna tell you. (Note the typical softness of repression that marks the transition period from latency to adolescence. Bereft of repression-supporting fantasy symbols and not yet fully protected by the countercathectic defenses of adolescence, the contents of the repressed unconscious come to consciousness spontaneously as well as at the behest of interpretive psychotherapeutic work.) "Why does there have to be boys? The whole d--n thing is disgusting. You like dreams. I had two last night. I only remember one," she said.

She then recounted the dream that follows. The dream, though quite long as presented here, has been edited. One of the characteristics of the typical early-adolescent 15-year-old's dream is its immense detail and length. This is a characteristic that is shared with the latency-age child's dream during treatment. Often the entire session is occupied by the dream recital. This characteristic shapes the potential for dream interpretation at this age. Focus on individual dream elements is difficult. A search for a day residue becomes like a search for a needle in a haystack. In broad overview, secondary elaboration includes the influence of all the dream elements it has been forced to provide for in the synthesis of a story that can make the dream as a whole seem related, internally consistent, and relevant. Note that the softness of repression that characterizes the period of transition between late latency and early adolescence also makes confirmation of interpretation and subsequent working through more accessible than is customary with adults.

The dream resolves into three segments—

Segment one: "I was walking alone near the train station. I went into the station to get a drink of coffee. I saw my father there. I went over to him and said 'Hello.' He gave me a hug. I told him to come back to the house. He said he couldn't. He stayed with me at the train station."

Segment two: "We were talking. He was holding my hand. Some foreign looking men came over to us. One of them gave the sign. You know it? They tickle your palm with their finger. It means I want to lay you. Imagine with my father right there. He didn't make a difference."

Segment three: "Then I was in a car. My father wasn't there. I was driving. I couldn't drive. I went from one side of the road to the other. I almost went over the side a couple of times. Then I woke up."

The theme of the dream that ties it together is the presence or absence of her father. Each segment of the dream is distinct in content from the other. The child calls attention in each segment to the presence and the absence of the father. With or without him she is alone and unprotected in the world, either from her own uncontrolled drives, as in driving the car, or from the approaches of men.

Questions about the individual dream elements were met with blank responses. The total context of the session during the time preceding the dream dealt with some of the problems reflected in the dream, such as controlling the drives. However, the total status of her mental adjustment, which included depression, feelings of loss, and a sense of desertion by her father—which were available from her life history—was introduced into the session through the symbols of the dream.

The therapist said, "You feel your father left you to deal with life alone."

She became angry and tearful. She felt ". . . so alone. I want a boyfriend 'cause there is no one to be with at home. I used to have girlfriends. But they have boyfriends. If my father was here, he'd take me out like he used to. I got this boy. He's kind. But he wants what I don't know to do. I think my father is there and telling me to be a good girl. It don't help. Dating isn't the funnest thing when that happens. I'm so ugly. I won't get another boy. I know. Life sucks. Why live when everybody is unhappylike. I don't want to live. I feel terrible." She spoke about her feelings of being deserted by her father. The depression that lay beneath her earlier manic-like excited associations could no longer yield to the pressure of denial. She became aware of her anger at her father and verbalized her fear of establishing close relationships with boys in which she could be hurt again. She began to withdraw into a defensive nihilistic denial of the value of life. If all were valueless, then the hurt in comparison would be of no importance. At the end of the session, as she went toward the door, she began to take out a cigarette and said, "What's the use of living, if it's so hard and you're only going to die anyhow?"

The therapist pointed at her hand and said, "Why enjoy a cigarette now if it's going to be all burned up, useless, and thrown away in a few minutes?"

"You got a point there," she said.

Transference in Early Adolescent Psychotherapy

Transference as used in psychotherapy refers to an expansion of a psychoanalytic concept. In psychoanalytic theory, transference describes the recall of a past experience through a reliving of its content or a derivative memory which in the here and now takes the form of an action or fantasy that involves the person of the therapist. The recall can be expressed through events that are part of a psychoanalytic situation. Should the action or fantasy be modified by defenses to produce a symptom, the resultant syndrome is called a *transference neurosis*.

In psychotherapy, there are a number of phenomena considered to be transference also. The form, shape, and usefulness of these phenomena during late latency–early adolescence differ according to the nature of the past experience relived and the level of maturation of the cognitive structures that both shape the manifestations of transference and provide the capacity to achieve insight and understanding.

All transference manifestations have in common the psychotherapeutically useful characteristic that the therapist can use the patient's transference experience during the session as an incontrovertible example of a character trait of the patient. In the presence of cognitive maturity that will make insight possible, such examples can be used to anchor verbal interventions to recent experiences. When the therapist links the mutually observed transference experience of the patient with related and similar experiences reported by the patient during present or previous information-gathering therapy sessions, a psychotherapeutic intervention called an *interpretation* can be produced. One expects the patient to respond to interpretation with recollection of information that can be used in the therapy to understand many aspects of the patient's current behavior. The latter process is called *working through.*

It is possible that while a patient reviews and reports pertinent events in his life, he may gain intellectual insight into his idiosyncratic patterns of behavior. This provides only moderate therapeutically induced leverage in the direction of mastery of these patterns. Fantasy play contributes mastery through discharge and also, to a small degree, through increased awareness of such patterns. Insight involving drives and the resolution of neurotic conflict depends upon the appearance of new data during free association that follows a transference interpretation. Once this activity affords the patient experience of the origins of today's behavior patterns in drive-impelled memory traces from the formative years of life, it becomes possible to turn the exploration of current psychopathogenic patterns of behavior into therapeutically effective working through of problem areas. Note that the same verbalizations on the part of a patient can be either conversation or psychotherapeutic working through. What makes for psychotherapeutic working through is the existence of awareness that the behavior in question is a repetition, on the time plane of the present, of patterns whose potential for causing difficulties has been seen both in the transference and in recall of early years. Essentially, one shows the patient during working through that a single episode of a given behavior does not serve the rationalization to which it is assigned by the patient. Rather, the rationalization (i.e., secondary gain) is an afterthought that hides the now demonstrated fact that the behavior serves an internal and secret scenario which in turn mediates the needs of drives from ways and days that once were lost in the tomb of time.

The Fantasy Components of Early Adolescent Transference. The fantasy components of transference in early adolescence are derived from past experiences. These past experiences consist of:

> Early maternal care—the child is primed to relate to the kindly ministrations of the therapist by past experience of being able to turn to mother and have injuries soothed. The prior experience could be called the "band-aid" stage. This contributes to "positive transference." This produces a state of expectant cooperation. Its existence should not be pointed out to the early adolescent unless it interferes with the treatment.

A 16-year-old girl with an acute phobic reaction found that she could travel anywhere as long as she had with her a pill which her therapist had given her. "It's like you are there with me," she would say.

> Traumatic experiences—These are such as occur when the therapist is identified with a hostile relative.
> Early infantile wishes that have never been fulfilled—These are exemplified by wishes for tender caresses, that have been thwarted either by an emotionally distant parent or by the establishment of internal prohibitions in the child to the expression of these needs as a result of inhibiting and drive-expression-limiting behavior on the part of early caretakers

of the child. This is the only manifestation of early experience that can occur during the psychoanalytic situation that can properly be called transference. Rarely can this be seen in psychotherapy. This rarity gives rise to the broadening of the concept of transference to include most reliving of any early experience in the psychotherapeutic situation. Infantile wishes that have not yet come to the surface—The child has not yet reached a stage in which it would be appropriate that they appear. These include phallic-stage wishes in an anal-stage child. The therapist is the first or primary object to which drive derivatives are directed simply because of the circumstance of being present at the time the drive manifests itself. Such transference is not a characteristic of early-adolescent psychotherapy.

Phase-appropriate wishes, both pregenital and genital—These are wishes (e.g., oedipal wishes) that have broken free of the fantasy defenses of latency, and following the shift of symbols away from fantastic referents and from the primary love objects (the parents), settle for a moment on the therapist while on their way to peer objects and lasting relationships. This phenomenon is primarily a characteristic of the psychotherapy of early adolescence. It can be viewed as a phase in the process of removal (Katan 1937). *Removal transference* touches the therapist as it brushes by on the way from the parents to a peer. There is a remarkable similarity here to the "transitional object in statu nascendi" described by Winnicott (1953). A growing need comes from the increasing pressure of the drives as the result of weakening of symbol-based defenses and stronger hormonal influences. The therapist's role as the armature around which transferences are formed makes him the perfect target for removal transferences. These transferences are particularly perilous events in early-adolescent psychotherapy. The peril arises from the fact that the transferences serve as formative testing grounds for ensuing real-life experiences. Erotically tinged removal transferences can usher in sexual acting out with peers. In addition, libidinal energies needed for the therapy may be withdrawn from the therapist when an erotically cathected peer appears. This could result in the decathexis of the therapist and a premature termination of the patient–therapist relationship.

The Structural Immaturities that Produce Early Adolescent Pseudo-transference. Because of structural immaturities, there are psychotherapy situations involving the therapist that *appear* to be transference. The patient appears to be making fun of the therapist in what seems to be a transference. In actuality they are not the recreation of prior experience; instead, they are the products of the misunderstanding of the use of verbal communication. This is likely to happen when the child feels that he can claim that something is a likeness of something else, when actually it is not in any way a likeness. A prime example of this is the use of words as though they were capable of producing realities at the moment they are spoken.

> Ptah was 11 years of age. Strong of face and lean of limb, he actively voiced his preference for the playroom because "I feel more comfortable here." Yet he did not play out tales with the toys. Rather he threw a ball or kicked a sack. In his mind he played out competitive ball games with peers or showed off to me his peerless skills. He was willing to talk freely about his problems with aggression control, which made life difficult for parents, neighbors, and schoolmates. His concomitant fear of thieves who might come at night (projection of aggression) was amply documented by his parents. When they were brought up, he discussed them freely. This resulted in a resolution of his fears, since he was able to confront his anger as his own and thus master the need to project anger. There was marked improvement in his persecutory fantasies; they dwindled to a minor element in his symptom configuration. Soon he ceased to speak of his aggressive behavior. Therapy sessions threatened to become part of a fitness program for him. Then his mother called to tell me that he had broken a window. When his mother's report was mentioned to him, he flushed and said, "She told you that. Damn! She told you that. Why did she have to tell you that. What a fool. If she tells you that how can you believe me? Now you know that, I have to stay here longer. How long do I have to stay here now?"
> Even though his mother wished the aggression to be brought into treatment, the child felt that if I were to say he was better, he would be "better" and could stop treatment without the bother of working through his aggressive behavior. "My mother says that when you say I'm done, I'll be all better." He interpreted this in the light of his own attitude toward words. He felt that my word would be accepted as truth just as he expected his words to be

accepted as truth. He had no conspiracy with his mother. Yet he depended on her for silence in support of his manipulative use of words to render his cause plausible.

It was explained to the boy that words cannot create reality, they can only reflect it. "When you say something, I don't listen for your words. I listen to what you are trying to tell me. It has to fit in your whole world, or I know it isn't true. Your world has your mother in it. What she says helps me to see the whole picture. You wouldn't be here if she wanted to help you fool me. If you could make up real things just by saying them, you would be very powerful. People who think they can do that get into trouble because they make up their own rules. Lots of times there is no room for such people. Then they get picked on and disliked."

While the therapist was alternately "naying" and weighing the introduction of the proverb "If wishes were horses, beggars would ride" to a child whose thinking had not reached the level of abstract operations, the boy blurted out, "I used to think I came from another planet. I was so sure, that I must have asked my mother if I was adopted a hundred times. That's why I always wanted to play 'Star Wars' when all the other kids wanted to play cops and robbers. I was waiting for my family to come and get me."

In the session, the therapeutic activity is twofold: First, it serves to modify the omnipotent use of words as magic instruments with an existence independent of the reality that all people test and share. In a second and larger sense, one of the processes that support the hypercathexis of fantasy in preference to reality is being confronted and undermined. Early adolescent reactive narcissism is being undermined.

In the course of a session, the child is being led through a recapitulation of the cultural evolution of man's use of words from the use of words as things to the use of words as representations of things and concepts in memory (Sarnoff 1987a). The therapist must have sufficient cultural background to appreciate the role of culture in developing cognition. With this background, he will be able to recognize as normal those developmental levels in late latency–early adolescence that represent pathology when found in adults. This patient, for instance, is using a cognitive thought pattern that would be markedly pathological in the daily thinking of an adult. In the latency-age child, the abilty to use words as realities strengthens the fantasy-forming

defenses (the structure of latency). These defenses depend on the creation of fantasies that have sufficient sense of reality to permit drive
discharge. Once the child begins to enter the object-related world of
drive discharge that marks early adolescence, such styles of thinking
must leave the area of personal life. They may persist in the passive
experience of political, religious, and ethnic myths. Persistence in the
child's personal life leads to strong fear fantasies and may presage
omnipotent thinking in adolescence and adulthood. Such use of words
as things and the creation of personal realities unaffected by the
presence and needs of others must be attended to if the child is to
become capable of relating to others and falling in love as an adult.

In Western culture, the capacity to create matter, situations, or
truths through the use of words is limited in attribution to deities, or
those who have been deified. In ancient Egypt, before there was Neph-
this, before there were Osiris and Seth, there was a god who made all
the things of the earth by speaking their name. The Bible says in the
Gospels, "In the beginning was the word." In children, such belief in
one's own speech is a warning of a spillover of the normal narcissism
of latency into adolescence. In adults, when "one regards as a likeness
what is not a likeness" (p. 297) (i.e., the equation of words and reality),
it is a sign of mental illness (Aristotle, circa 340 B.C., 451 A 10).

The therapist's experience of normal thinking in adults becomes,
unfortunately, the model for comparison in his observations of children. As a result, pathological deviations in adult thinking become for
the therapist the only recognizable childhood deviations in thought.
Because children are evolving adult thinking patterns, there are to be
diagnosed in addition maturational lags in thinking, whose origins
are to be found in styles of cognition that precede modern thought.
The labyrinths of the human psyche extend beyond the perigrinations
of a single human experience during a single lifetime. Modern cognition is the product of eons of insights and codifications, and integra-
tions of these insights into socialized patterns of thought. These in
turn become the basis for the maintenance and continuity of social
institutions. The thinking of children contains elements of outworn
ways of thought that are normally challenged by the precept and
example of parents, peers, and teachers. In this way the path is cleared
for the potential for more effective and acceptable forms of thought to
mature. Nowhere is this more sharply in evidence than in the organizations of memory and in definitions of truth.

Quite accurately, the therapist was able to tell that the patient's
creation of an image of himself solely for the therapist was neither a
"cute" saying by a child, worth repeating to others, or a transference

based on libidinally charged memories in search of expression. His knowledge of the evolution of thought forms caused him to diagnose instead a cognitive developmental lag or fixation. The works of many thinkers (Cicero, Aristotle, Piaget, Freud, the *Ad Herrenium*, quoted in Yates 1966) contributed to this understanding. The therapist was aware that what his patient told him was an anemnesis rather than a history or memory. If we define history as the story of what has happened as reported by many observers, we recognize the possibility of reality testing the recall of past events. If we define memory as all that the patient is capable of retaining of an experience, we recognize that under even the best of circumstances the whole truth is not available to the patient. And if we define anemnesis as a recollection which is an ". . . excogitation of true things, or things similar to truth to render one's cause plausible . . ." (Cicero, p. 8, quoted in Yates 1966), we shall recognize that anemnesis can be a conflation of memory elements with the primitive thought process that creates truths out of words. This produces the immature cognition of the patient.

A therapist who is equipped with such knowledge about cognition and thought is removed from involvement in conversation in therapeutic sessions. In addition, he is able to recognize that situations that involve the therapist are not automatically transference when one is dealing with children in late latency–early adolescence. Instead he is able to view from a distance the processes of thought of the patient, recognize deviations, and devise therapeutic strategies with which to confront them.

Recruitment and Metamorphosis through Transference

Because *removal transference* (defined on p. 206) is an early step in the establishment of object relations during late latency–early adolescence, the therapist is often in a position to make therapeutic inroads into the patient's personality through his behavior and thought style rather than through interpretation and insight.

She was tall and willowy, winsome and wiley, and wise beyond her 16 years in the ways that women sway men. Her father, who was fascinated with her, could easily be made "to see the light" when she became flirtatious. She had been sent to therapy because of an unexplained drop in grades that was directly relatable to clouding of thinking following marijuana use. A pout had crossed her face when she was told that the therapist would not call her parents to tell them that it was all right for her to sleep over at her girl friend's house the following weekend. As she got up at the end of the session, the pout turned into a sweet smile. She advanced toward the therapist. He moved back slightly and offered a handshake. "I only wanted to give you a hug and kiss good-by," she said.

"Kisses and hugs are parts of a different kind of situation. Therapy has to do with thinking. Let's talk about it more next time," said the therapist.

She had tried to recruit her therapist into the interpersonal inter-actions of her fantasy world, but had received from him a pattern upon which to base a character metamorphosis.

At the age of 10, it had already become clear that the gracile young lad who spent hours in the playroom playing out brutal combats with toy soldiers felt no need to work diligently in school. His low marks had placed him in a remedial classroom where he was separated from friends whose level of intelligence and perspicacity he shared. He met with them after school. He felt left out of their school talk and was beginning to suspect that they were talking about these matters as a mean way of leaving him out of things. He had come to therapy because of the disrup-tion of the household that resulted from his constant provoca-tions and fights with his mother. His mother contributed to the problem, for she had difficulty in containing herself when he refused to clean up after his dog, left clothing on the bathroom floor, or left his socks and toe pickings on the living room cocktail table on the evening of a party she was giving for socially prominent people she had hoped to impress. As often as not, he reported that he was unable to do his homework because the fights with his mother upset him so that he could not settle down to study. He spent his time in the sessions playing out robberies and war games using toy soldiers. He spoke often with the therapist; however, psychotherapeutically effective communi-cation was shied from by immersion in play. The therapist equated the games with fights with his mother. The child made no verbal response. He just played on. The therapist began to think that he was a very nice boy with a nagging mother and no internalized tendency to become a partner in sadomasochistic wrangling. There was marked improvement in his behavior at home. This could be attributed to discharge of tension through displaced playing out of battles in the playroom.

Concurrently, something strange was happening in the office. Not always, but often, the toilet paper in the bathroom became tied up in a knot. Sand deformed the soap. Emergency lighting fixtures became disconnected. Other children, taking heed of the events, began to engage in similar pursuits, so that identifying the culprit was difficult. It's hard to place blame on a child for a type of destructiveness when there is someone who already has admitted responsibility for a similar disruptive pattern. One day, no other suspect had come to the office, and a telephone had been disconnected and a wad of paper placed in a light fixture, incapacitating the bulb. At the next session the therapist described the problem and asked if the patient "knew anything about it."

The patient repeated the description of the misdeeds and then said, "That's mean."

The therapist remained calm through the session. He checked the office before and after the child's visits. It became clear that he was the source of the problem, but not the only culprit. The therapist mentioned each damage to equipment and explained how he knew the child was at fault. "Gee!" said the child, "you don't get angry like my m---- (his words dwindled to a hum)."

"It's not something to be argued about. It's something to be settled."

After that the patient's contribution to disorganization of the office disappeared. Concurrently, he began to work on his lessons in the professed hope that he could regain his academic position and rejoin his friends.

One can construct the theory that he was in the process of transferring his internalized sadomasochistic patterns of discharging his drives from the family to peers and school. In the process of moving his conflicts from home to the world, he included the therapist. Through provocations that disrupted the therapist's reality and set examples for other young patients to follow, he recruited the therapist into a relationship in which his removal transference could be expressed. Instead of finding a partner in this life expression for the battles of the toy soldiers, he found a calm model who both diverted his energies toward useful interactions and provided him with a pattern for the handling of provocations that might come his way.

His foray into sadism had resulted in the attempt to recruit the therapist into a mutual acting out of the transference. The resulting interaction provided for a model that could produce a metamorphosis of behavior in the direction of the exploration of new realities in place of the persistence of old patterns for drive discharge.

One of the most important differentiating characteristics of psychotherapy during late latency–early adolescence is the chance to get at therapeutic targets early in the life of the patient. Often the patient is seen just as new styles of thought are being introduced or are just beginning to dominate. During early adolescence, libidinal and aggressive drives are transferred onto the therapist on the way to the world. One might say the therapist catches them on the way. All such transferences and the patterns upon which they are based still have the potential for transience. Secondary gain has not yet had a chance to lock a pathological pattern into place. As a result, therapy during the transition has great potential for producing change. It might be better to say "Shape the personality to start with." This chance to influence is based on the fact that during adolescence the child's personality is first hatching out of the shell that had been provided by the inward turning and narcissistic cathexes of latency. Since one can observe during therapy the initial experiencing of self–world confrontations without parents and without the structure of latency, one is in a position to guide, interpret, and set examples while the structure of the personality is still flexible and more open to influence than when locked into place by an interdependence of defenses and secondary gains. In this regard, one should be especially watchful of the vicissitudes of anger during therapy in these years.

The First Experience of Anger Free of the Structure of Latency in Early Adolescent Psychotherapy

During the period of transition between latency and adolescence, the organizations of defense that have supported latency fall away. The mechanisms that supported them are organized into new systems which focus away from the egotism of latency and toward the altruisms of adult life. Anger, which had been siphoned off into displaced fantasy elements through the mediation of the structure of latency, is now present. The buffer of symbols is weak during the transition. Later, displacements, sublimations, even fantasy and symptoms will be available to be interposed between the self of the child and the people of his world. During the transition, raw anger begins to stir and—for the first time for many of those who have been called by their parents "The best-behaved child I have ever known"—rage begins to disturb their adjustment. Depression, projected anger, anxiety, unrest, and irritability in the face of passivity mark the period. They are signs of attempts to forge a piece of the personality that can be used to modulate the impact of an affect that had been well contained during a healthy latency and now bursts forth into a state of exposure to the elements that cries for emergency relief and the development of a long-term personality structure to deal with it.

When children in this state (the struggle can contribute to discomfort and psychopathology from 11 years of age to the early 20s) come to psychotherapy, the problem is not how to get them "in touch with their feelings." Rather, it is to help them to deal with their feelings and how to handle or avoid levels of anger that they have never experienced before. The therapist is not protected by the presence in the patient of years of experience in dealing with such feelings in financially successful and independent adults. The children who are introduced to such unguarded anger for the first times cannot be depended upon after they have left the session to activate defenses which will result in "resetting" of the personality and a placing of anger on "hold" until the next session. The inadequately defended anger persists, mounts in fury, gives rise to fulminating rage and obsessing about remembered hurts and slights of childhood at the hands of parents and siblings, and draws vitally needed attention and energies from studies and work. Often the anger spills over into raging fights with parents, withdrawal from parents, and even suicide attempts.

"I feel a dread within me. It comes over me from time to time. I feel depressed and frightened. I love my parents so that I can't stand coming here. Why are you emphasizing my mother so much? Why are you making me hate her?" This was said by a 17-year-old girl whose fear of leaving the house with her friends had started when her friends began talking about going away to college, and her parents told her that she would have no choice but to go to the college they had chosen for her. Her father, an attorney, had sufficient funds to send her to any college, and their choice of a college of their religious denomination seemed arbitrary in light of their lack of involvement in religious affairs. "They want me to marry a boy of the same religion, I think," she said wistfully in the early sessions. As she said this, it seemed to be more of an observation than a pivotal source of anger at passivity in the hands of overcontrolling parents.

In the early sessions, she reported fears of leaving the house because of feelings that she would become upset and not be able to handle the feelings if her mother were not with her to comfort her. This gave the therapist a clue. Such a longed for, comforting companion is often at the center of the conflict as a symbol or source of the repressed problem.

"What are the feelings that you have that you fear?" asked the therapist.

"I get sad. I feel alone. I'm afraid I'm going to die. It's awful. Sometimes I feel I want to kill myself—I mean, go to sleep for a long time so I don't have to have these feelings for a while," she replied.

"The feelings are present always?" the therapist asked.

"No, only now and then. Most of the time I'm afraid they will come on and that's bad too," she stated. "I can hardly study. I spend so much time listening to records about lonely people. Gee, I wish I had a boy friend." This is another clue to the therapist. Removal was not sufficiently far advanced for the patient to have disengaged her conflictual energies from her parents. He knew that he should look for the source of the conflict in the relationships at home. He noted that questions about a boy friend led to answers that dwindled quickly.

In one session she came in reporting that she was depressed. "Depression is anger turned on the self," stated the therapist. "When did the depression start?"

"On Saturday afternoon."

"What happened on Saturday?" the therapist asked.

"I had a fight with my mother," answered the girl. "I wanted to go out and I couldn't get my makeup. She spends three hours in the bathroom when she has to go and nobody is allowed in there. Why did she have to use the one with my makeup? She sometimes isn't thoughtful. When I told her I wanted to go out, you'd think she would be happy. I wanted to go out and I *wasn't* scared. She wouldn't let me go 'cause she was going out to the library and she wanted me to stay home to make dinner for my father."

She began to feel angry at her mother and spoke of the angry feelings, which were new to her. As is so typical in these situations and at this age, the child was able to feel forbidden feelings of disappointment because of failures of the parents to offer material, financial, or educational advantages that had led to unspoken envy of peers throughout the latency years. Each new session or two brought a new episode of depression, which in turn when analyzed brought into focus another situation in which her self-bound angry reaction, through its lack of expression, had encouraged the mother to take advantage of the child's apparent passivity. It wasn't long before the child could ". . . identify the start of the anger that starts the depression.

Now when I get depressed I try to figure out what makes me angry and then I tell whoever is pushing me around to stop it. Only I use a lot tougher language." "Sometimes it's my brother. . . . Sometimes it's my parents. . . . I get scared when I get angry at them. I'm going away. I'm going to need them and miss them, but I can't control getting angry."

Then, one day when the defiance of her mother reached a level that "sounded as loud and bad as when my parents fight," she experienced an urge "to pick up a knife and stab her, or was it me." Now we have come to a turning point in the treatment. An intervention was needed in order to set a course that would permit the resolution of the emotional family situation without interfering with therapeutic progress. To go on with the therapy could relieve the depression and free her from the close and sadomasochistic relationship with her parents, which would surely sap the emotional energies that would make it possible for her to have a boy friend. To stop would leave these problems untouched and leave the relationship with the parents in a sorrier state than when she had started the therapy. To continue the therapy without change could intensify the situation to the point that a severe and dangerous acting out could occur. Suicide attempts and termination of college careers are not unusual in these situations. It was then that she said "I feel a dread within me. It comes over me from time to time. I feel depressed and frightened. I love my parents so that I can't stand coming here. Why are you emphasizing my mother so much? Why are you making me hate her?"

Said the therapist, "I do not choose the topics. I follow your associations and sometimes ask you to expand on them. The feelings that come up here are not brought up for you to act on them or revenge old wrongs. They are brought into focus so you can understand where your fears and angers come from and free yourself from them." These became the guiding principles of the therapy. It then became possible to see that the fights drew her closer to her mother and were being used to counter the feelings of distance and loss that her ensuing departure from mother and home for college promised.

The first experience of anger after the passing of latency has been our topic in this section. Mentioned, but not emphasized, is the strong role of passivity that is both superimposed by the parents and sought out defensively by the child who is frightened of a world of other peers whose sole role in the life of the child is to serve as recruits to play out roles that parallel the neurotic interactions learned from the parents. Often a child is afraid of sexual and other new life situations because of expectations to know more than he or she can ever know, and from fear of attacks by potential partners for lack of sophistication. "What will I do? . . . What does he (or she) expect of me? . . . If I say no, will he be angry?" The projection of anger into a situation that is seen as indicating humiliating passivity is great in a child with little experience of expressing anger. The reactive anger the child fears is brutal. For the therapist, it is wise, rather than to explore the source of the anger alone, to add supportive comments that will permit the child to understand that there is no need to remain in any relationship that is so uncomfortable. After all, peers are not parents. One is not bound to a person with whom the shared history goes back a few weeks. The reality that others cannot expect any more from them than that for which they are ready can sometimes be conveyed by the reassurance that "sophistication is a cumulative thing and that people who would reject one cruelly for its lack are better done without."

During the transition phase there is a strong push toward object-relatedness. The world arena for the discharge of the drives presents a hitherto open field within the boundaries of which the child can explore. Except for those who project their hostilities into the world newly found, this is a time of great excitement. The transitional child either greets the new world in an object-related, reality-oriented way or enters through the bridge of projection into a world that is known through assigning it the role of persecutor in areas with which the child has had some experience. The most angry and troubled children turn their energies away from the object world. Their energies become involved in their own bodies. They distort their body image, as in anorexia nervosa or become, in rare cases for this age, hypochondriacal. These develop delusional fantasies about their body parts or organs. Intensifications of symptoms come in times of increased anger and feelings of passivity. They reflect feelings of dread at things that could give rise to bodily disintegration, which is the ultimate paradigm of passivity. The problem of passivity and aggression can be addressed directly only after the body delusion has been decathected. Directing attention to the problems of passivity and aggression—similar to that pursued in the case of the girl with the new-found rage at her mother—sometimes works. Most often, the patient becomes infuriated at the failure of the therapist to join in the preoccupation with the patient's body. At that point, the only possible course is to treat each somatic complaint as though it were an element in a dream.

In essence, one agrees that the patient's sense of reality makes the symptoms seem real. However, by following them back to their roots, their origins can be found beyond the boundaries of reality and they can be devalued. Once they are established as semidelusional and, as such, derived from memory sources with roots in early experience, it becomes possible to seek out the situations and affects that are being avoided and unmastered as a result of the countercathectic function of overemphasis of body parts and their disordered function. The following case is one of therapeutic handling of an example of passivity directly.

Passivity in Early Adolescence

One of the primary sources of angry defiance in early adolescence is the experience of passivity at the hands of others who, either by attitude or position in life, take charge of one's life or give orders.

> A girl of 13, who limped because of an incapacitating bone pain for which no physical cause could be identified, reported a "hysterically funny" time at a big family party the Saturday night before her early Monday morning therapy session. The most fun came when the children began to ". . . cheer wildly at the grandparents. They get so uncomfortable and embarrassed when we do that."
>
> The therapist sensed that here was a role reversal, frequently seen at this age, and of importance psychotherapeutically. He said, "You turned the tables."
>
> "Most of the time you can't kid them," she answered.
>
> "You are taught democracy, but when it comes down to it in your home, you get upset when you see how small your vote is," said the therapist.
>
> She became heated in her discussion as she added, "My mother says, 'clean up your room.' I say 'Why?' She says, ''Cause I'm the adult.' Then I say, 'But Mom, it's not fair.' Before you know it we are having a small fight and I'm calling my friend to tell her what my mother is doing."
>
> In this way a discussion of the patient's reactions to passivity is developed.

This interchange is perhaps the key to the conflict of generations that occurs in Western culture with its democratic traditon. In societies in which more authoritarian theories govern the relationship between children, family, and the state (such as the traditional Chinese, Greek Catholic, and some early primitive societies), conflicted early adolescence with its defiance and rebellion is not so much in evidence. In Western cultures, democracy is so honored that even totalitarian countries call themselves "people's democracies." Our children are taught to revere the principle of equality among men. When they are old enough to think that they can function independently, they demand a vote in their daily destinies. Unfortunately for them, they find themselves confronted by "the tyranny of a gerontocracy, of old men who initiate the young men and forcibly impose the tradition of the tribe" (Harrison 1921, p. xxxvii). Our children, raised in the tradition of democracy, discover that living in a family does not permit the development of an organization consisting of presidents alone. Some must lead. Others must follow. The therapist would do well to be ever alert for signs of conflict reflecting this strain in the associations of our patients.

This interchange between a father and son indicates the proper handling of this area of strain between the generations:

> The son was 9 years old, wiry and with a will of his own. That day, his father had decided against a trip to the city to attend a baseball game, in spite of the pleadings of his son.
>
> In response to this, the boy said: "The trouble around here is that every time I want something, maybe I get it, maybe I don't. Every time you want something you get it."
>
> The father said, "That's right. It's because I'm older; I'm in charge; I'm the father."
>
> "It's not fair," said the boy.
>
> "Who said things are fair?" said the father. "The fact is that I'm older, I work for the money. I've been around longer than you. So, I know more about what is important and how to make decisions. . . . But don't fret. Soon, when you grow up, you'll be the daddy; you'll be working; and then you'll make all the decisions. It's just a matter of time."

It is helpful to point out to the child that there is a progression of the generations and an orderly transfer of power to be traversed, all to his benefit. Sometimes children who have taken high school biology enjoy hearing that they and their parents have the same genes. The current situation comes from the fact that the parents got them first. Soon enough the children will get to use them on their own.

Summary

Most adolescent problems can be dealt with using a therapy closely akin to that which is used with adults. Late Latency Early Adolescence comprises a distinct phase of transition between the ego structure of latency and the adultiform ego organizations of adolescence. During Late Latency Early Adolescence, there are transitional characteristics to the child's experiences which require special handling. These experiences include removal, thought disorders, omnipotence, the involvement of parents, and the persistence of evocative polarities in symbolic usages. The latter is of special concern since it limits free association. Such impairments of the therapeutic usages of free association are dealt with separately in Chapter 10.

Chapter 10

Adolescent Masochism

Latency-age masochistic fantasies persist into adolescence.* They acquire a manifest form dictated by progressions and regressions in object relations and cognitions that are specific to the phase of adolescence. To understand the nature of the manifestations of masochism in adolescence, it is necessary that one understand their origins in the previous phases from which they have emerged. The manifestations are masochistic braggadocio, masochistic perversions, adolescent shyness, aspects of prepubescent schizophrenia, incipient masochistic character traits, and the misuse of free association during psychoanalytically oriented psychotherapy sessions. The genetic complexes of origin that give structure to the forms of adolescent masochism may be studied through a review of the life phases of masochism.

The Life Phases of Masochism

Masochism, the passive experience of aggression accompanied by painful and excited affects, appears in all of the stages of human life and development. Its manifestations change with each age. Variations of intensity and modifications of the form of masochism result from phase-related alterations in object relations and cognition. Each developmental period contributes a unique step in the march of manifest masochism. A description of the steps follows.

---

*This chapter is an expanded version of a paper presented in December 1983 to the "Vulnerable Child" Study Group of the American Psychoanalytic Association at the Association's midwinter meeting.

Primary Masochism (The First Months of Life)

In the very earliest months of life, there is objectless, unbridled aggression. This takes the form of screaming, crying, and thrashing about, which only hurt the crying child, who alone suffers whatever discomfort there is to feel and is exhausted in the end. Parents, as witnesses, may feel pain at the sight of the pained child. Their pain does not intrude upon the psychic reality of the child and does not take part in the interaction.

The masochism of this age is called *primary* (as in primary narcissism), for in his world of feebly perceived boundaries, there is no concept of an object and the child is limited to himself as persecutor. In later years, regression to this level of preobject relations colors those clinical states in which there is little relatedness to the therapist and in which symbols are used to evoke moods rather than to communicate.

Protosymbols (The End of the First Year of Life)

The introduction of the parents as primitive persecutors awaits the development of *protosymbols,* which consist of bodily sensations (affects) or organs of the child's body, which symbolically represent other affects or organs. As cognition matures, they may be used to represent parts of the parents. Through such protosymbols, aggression aimed at the parent can be experienced as turned upon the self.

With the development of self–object differentiation, the fused libidinal and aggressive energies of the child can be perceived by the child as directed outward, toward an object. Should the parent withdraw from contact or from view, the child can persist in contact with the parent through an internalized memory of the parent. This internalized image is called the *introject.* The aggression that had been directed toward the object accompanies the introject. It, too, is directed inward toward the self of the child. This produces a paradigm for the experience of self-directed aggression. It is called *secondary masochism.* This becomes the basis for the patterning of relationships in which masochism involves objects. Intensification of the secondary masochistic experience by actual aggression on the part of the parents enhances the masochistic fantasies that will color the relationships of adult life. The resulting heightened tolerance for such relationships permits people to enter them without challenge.

A protosymbol creates, in psychic representation, a synthesis of self and parent. The child's aggression, directed toward the protosymbol, is experienced as directed toward the self (i.e., masochistically).

Since the parent is the only reality object of which the child is aware, the parent is fantasized to be the source of the pain. Actual parental aggression, either spontaneous or stimulated by the child, can be adapted by the child as an actualization (i.e., appearance in reality) of these fantasies. In this way, a real event can be recruited to serve as a fantasy derivative. This activity intensifies between 15 and 26 months, and gives a provocative character to children's behavior during this period. This gives rise to its name, the "terrible twos." In adolescence, the child's response to the passivity that is felt when strivings for independence clash with parental power is often a derivative of the experiences of this earlier phase.

Psychoanalytic Symbols (26 Months)

At 26 months, there is the development of repression and its concomitant in thought content, psychoanalytic symbols. There is some lessening of the actualization. This is the result of the use of fantasy to drain off some of the child's aggression. Sadomasochistic (anal-sadistic) fantasies persist (Blanchard 1939). They tend to be expressed with siblings and peers in place of parents. At this point, children begin to experience masochism as the sadism of symbolized whole objects that has been directed at the sufferer. This step in cognitive development produces changes during the prelatency period.

The Prelatency Period (26 Months to 6 Years)

The considerable use of symbols to interpret the environment causes the child's relation to actualities to be primarily intuitive. Memory emphasizes the use of affect and sensation. This produces recalls of totalities. External characteristics, rather than the abstract, intrinsic nature of things and situations, are used to recall the past and interpret the present. As a result, logic is not brought to bear to correct misapprehensions, such as those produced by regressions to the cognitive world of primary masochism.

During this period, masochistic fantasy may undergo three vicissitudes:

1. Aggression and cruelty from parents, caretakers, or peers in actuality may reinforce the aggression that fuels it.
2. Mastery through fantasy may dissipate it. Fantasies that use psychoanalytic symbols can effectively dissipate latent fantasy and drive. These symbols populate persecutory fantasies, animal

phobias, and fears of amorphous attackers in the dark experienced when going to sleep.

3. Whether masochistic fantasy is reinforced or dissipated, it is subject to the modifying effects of the phallic phase. Progression through phallic-phase interests (competition, object-relatedness, penetrative urges, oedipal concerns) and parentally encouraged progress in cognitive development that aids in the neutralization of drive energies (i.e., acquisition of verbal conceptual memory organizations) can modify the manifest strength of masochism. There may result a lessening of the anal-sadistic energy cathexes of the masochistic fantasies to the benefit of more mature functions.

Latency (6 to 12 Years of Age)

As the child passes through the sixth year of life, the threatening nature of oedipal concerns calls regression into action as a defense. As a result, anal-sadistic drive energies are recathected.

This does not result in manifest masochism. Ego mechanisms of restraint mask it during this period. Provocative aggressive stimuli from the environment are buffered by the fantasizing function of the ego, which produces defensive play fantasies, and these discharge drive and master conflict on a symbolic level (see Sarnoff 1976). As a result, the child appears to be calm, cooperative, and educable. These clinically observable traits dominate behavior from 6 to 12 years of age, the latency period.

Play fantasies routinely contain highly symbolized sadomasochistic content. Cops and robbers, war stories, kidnappings, and cruel elements in fairy tales are examples of this. Manifestations of masochism during this age period are primarily in the form of fantasy experienced internally or projected into an interpretation of relations with peers. The older the child, the more realistic is the source of the symbols called upon to represent the masochistic fantasy.

Failure of the ego structures of latency permits the appearance of manifest derivatives of masochism. Foremost among these are playground teasing, night fears, and paranoid accusations of peers during periods of stress.

Adolescence (Adolescent Masochism in Manifest Pathology)

The *onset* of adolescence is heralded by an intensification of the anal-sadistic drive organizations which have been blunted by the defenses of latency. For the most part, the defense structures of latency hold masochistic fantasies and trends in check rather than process them. Therefore, children enter adolescence with latent masochistic fantasy content little changed from what it had been in the phallic phase. In early adolescence, the fantasies are manifested in thinly masked derivatives which use reality elements rather than toys as symbolic representations.

One of the clinical characteristics of the psychological shift to adolescence is the loss of potency of toys and other play symbols to serve as substitute objects and tools for the discharge of drives and the mastery of conflict. There is thus an increased use of parts of the body, and of people and peers, to express, experience, and manifest masochistic fantasies. Manifest fantasy fails to serve this need; the world of reality and its parts are then recruited to provide an arena in which masochistic fantasies can be lived out. In this way, the masochistic fantasies that had fueled the play fantasies of latency are carried over to become the foundations for masochistic character formation.

One of the tasks of adolescence is disengagement of the drives from anal-sadistic discharge patterns and from character traits derived from them. This is done either through removal (Katan 1937) or the resolution of the oedipal conflicts, which, as we have noted, motivated the regressions that intensified masochistic drive activity during the latency years. This process of resolution can often be recognized in the masochistic derivatives seen in adolescence.

In *early adolescence*, the thinly masked *masochistic derivatives* can be seen for the most part in masochistic braggadocio, masochistic perversions, and prepubescent schizophrenia. In *later adolescence*, the failure of resolution of masochistic trends can be followed through the clinical study of such derivatives of masochism as incipient masochistic character traits and through an explication of the way masochism intrudes upon the use of free association during psychoanalytic sessions.

Causative Factors in Adolescent Masochism

Traumatic and painful experiences are common in early childhood. Early trauma and persistent masochistic fantasy make a child vulnerable to the development of masochistic traits in adolescence. This sets the stage for the appearance of similar character traits in adulthood.

There are other determining factors in addition to early life trauma and masochistic fantasy—which, after all, are universal—that have clinical significance for manifest masochism. These other elements lead to specific forms of masochism and, in some cases, even determine whether masochistic elements will dominate lives. Patients in general have tales to tell of pain at the hands of the parents. Parental behavior that is interpreted as cruel does not account for those who are free of symptoms although they have the same parents as those who are afflicted. Among the additional determining factors that encourage manifest masochism during adolescence, developmental variants in the cognitive organization of the mind stand out.

There may be inadequate shift from evocative to communicative symbols; and in the developmental march of symbols, the choice of objects for representation—which shifts away from fantasy objects toward the self briefly before it goes on to enlist peers in the roles of persecutors and lovers—may remain fixated on the self as object. Projection undergoes many and marked vicissitudes, providing a multitude of variants in the defenses used to express aggression (Sarnoff 1972). Furthermore, there are remarkable variations in the characteristic way of dealing with introjects in early adolescence. These changes in the cognitive styles of defense organizations contribute to the characteristic appearances of masochism in adolescence.

Masochistic Derivatives in Early Adolescence

Masochistic Braggadocio

Early in this century, and late in the last, there existed at the University of Heidelberg in Germany highly regarded social organizations known as dueling clubs. Ostensibly they served those who wished to learn fencing. In the broader social context, they served to identify the elite. Since the end of a duel was reached with the inflicting of a wound that drew blood, members of these clubs could be easily identified through the permanent scars on their faces, which proclaimed proudly to the world that they had been cut and had bled. Even in our own day, such a culturally adapted proclamation of borne pain is seen in fraternity pins that identify those who have undergone hazing.

This late-adolescent expression of masochism (a tendency to brag of suffering) finds a parallel in early adolescence. It is at this younger age that there is an attempt to process and master painful and traumatic experiences through reevocation through words. A verbal context is used which makes the person's suffering seem heroic. I call this behavior masochistic braggadocio. There is a kind of Heidelberg scar mentality to this reaction. The image of manliness or courage is generated by this pseudo-strength display.

One child, upon returning to analysis after the summer break, said, "In camp we really had it tough. We walked for miles without stopping. I got blisters so big that they bled." The affect was pride. He sought to evoke and to awe. There was nothing here that would serve the search for insight. I wondered as he spoke if the child was complaining or bragging.

Looking more deeply into the psychology of the youngster who told of the blisters, there could be found a characterological context in which any form of pain or discomfort (experienced or remembered) was avoided rather than confronted. Experienced pain was bragged of as a counterphobic means of mastering this fear of pain. Painful future activities were evoked prospectively. Placing himself in future danger was a form of advanced bragging rather than future planning.

He once called an end to his treatment (with his father's consent) so that he could join the high school football team. Both he and his father agreed that participation in sports would affirm his masculinity and counter doubts about his gender identity. He planned to miss many sessions and possibly to interrupt treatment. He missed but one session in the process. On the day of the second session to be missed, he arrived unannounced in my waiting room at his usual time. When I asked him what had happened, he told me that he realized when the first few plays were run right through his position that it hurt to be a football hero. He was interested in glory but not discomfort.

One of the elements that potentiate adolescent vulnerability to masochistic conflict resolutions is a failure in the development of the symbolizing function. There is a failure in negotiating the developmental shift from evocative to communicative symbols in expressing drive manifestations. The more primitive evocative symbols continue to evoke feelings and memory of trauma in the service of discharge without mastery. They are not used for communication, or for reparative mastery. They are not viewed from a therapeutic distance. For therapists who have worked with adult cases, such activity is familiar: it occurs in repetitive traumatic anxiety dreams.

The person in late latency–early adolescence who repeats masochistic patterns endlessly exhibits clinical failure of mastery through repetition. The cause of this is attributable to a regression to the objectless "primary" masochism of the earliest days of childhood.

This works together with the fact that for these people the symbolizing function has not matured to the point that symbols can be used for communication.

A communicative level of symbol use supports the discharge of drives and the mastery of trauma in a corrective reality context. It also reinforces the guarantees of the autonomous functioning of the ego in relation to the id. Failure to achieve a communicative level in symbol formation results in symbols (evocative) that can only evoke inner moods and past events over and over again.

In adolescence, evocative-mode symbols used during free association in psychotherapy attempt to draw sympathy from the therapist and evoke prior painful affect and ego states instead of serving psychotherapeutic goals. A form of repetition compulsion is produced. In the psychotherapy situation the therapist is converted from a helper, aiming his skills at adjustment and the future, to a witness to past pain that the patient proudly shares. What does the patient derive from this situation? Narcissistic injury is overcome. The masochist's narcissism is served when he can present his pain as an experience without equal. The pain of recent experience is thus mastered at the expense of the long-range goals of the therapy.

Masochistic Perversion

The following case (presented in Sarnoff 1975) illustrates variations in masochism associated with developmental changes in the symbolizing function. There is a march of symbols used as the protagonists in persecutory fantasies and their derivatives that accompanies the transition through latency and adolescence. These are:

In early latency
    Persecutory symbols experienced in fantasy
At the end of latency
    Parts of the body used as symbols to express masochistic fantasy
In early adolescence
    Enlistment of real people as symbols to express masochistic fantasy
During maturity
    Using symbols to communicate reality

As the presentation unfolds, consider the effect on the psychopathology of the adult should the source of symbols be fixed at one of the above points in the developmental line, rather than progress.

George was 16½ years old when seen. He was the son of divorced parents. His mother had left the marriage when she learned that his father had teased, beaten, and tortured the child for no apparent reason whenever he was left alone with the boy. The patient could recall these incidents as occurring when he was but 2 years old. The boy lived with his mother after the divorce. His latency period was characterized by unexceptional evening fears early on and a strong capacity to develop states of latency (see Sarnoff 1987a). When the boy reached the age of 11, he developed erections every time he saw himself or another boy without a shirt on. He could produce an erection by standing nude before a mirror. He responded to these erections by making cuts into the skin of his back with a knife. The appearance and flow of blood was accompanied by a release of feelings similar to orgasm. When he had achieved physiological ejaculation and orgasm readiness, he found that it was possible for him to masturbate successfully with a fantasy about a girl. He reported no cruelty in this fantasy. When he began dating at the age of 16, he sought to hide his relationship with the girls whom he had chosen for their common characteristic of full, voluptuous figures. These characteristics, as he viewed it, lowered him and caused him to feel embarrassed in public.

This pattern is not unusual. It has been described elsewhere in the literature (Werner and Levin 1967). The pattern starts with early exposure to a sadistic parent. This reinforces anal-sadistic fantasies, which are maintained in repression after 6 years of age by latency defenses. At age 11, as the latency defenses weaken, a masochistic masturbation fantasy becomes consciously manifest. In it there is actively and passively relived masochistic submission to the sadistic parent of infancy. The fantasy is not confined to mental expression. The representations chosen as symbols are not fantastic or distorted images. They are real, of the same sex as the child, and acted out with real objects (knife and self). With the onset of ejaculation, the representations become real people, who serve as sadistic heterosexual objects.

In consonance with the developmental march of symbols, the manifestations of masochism change with growth, demonstrating for each stage their own characteristics, and varying degrees of visibility and implied degree of pathology. The developmental events of adolescence can uncover previously undetected fantasy structures, such as those that produce masochistic behavior, and can make visible structural weaknesses and aberrations in ego formation. These weaknesses and aberrations, in turn, often persist when adolescent development is blocked, or they may become less virulent when normal development causes their expressions to be clothed in less distressing guises.

Adolescent Shyness and Prepubescent Schizophrenia (Pathological Relationships with Introjects)

In both adolescent shyness and prepubescent schizophrenia, adolescent masochism appears to be a manifestation of the persistence in memory of parental introjects.

Adolescent shyness is a common condition, occurring primarily in early adolescence. It is characterized by an avoidance reaction to contacts with peers or adults in authority on account of false beliefs. The contents of these false beliefs are feelings of inferiority or defect, which the child feels would become known to, or recognized by, others and would result in the child's rejection.

Prepubescent schizophrenia is a rare condition, with onset usually after 11 years of age. It is a variety of childhood schizophrenia, of relatively late onset. The cardinal signs of this condition are delusional thinking involving pain and aggression directed toward self or others, poor peer relations, and an absent history of projected introjects (night fears or phobias) during early latency.

Introjects and Adolescent Masochism

The paradigmatic model of a masochistic relationship can be seen in the context of a punishing parent confronting and disciplining a defenseless child. The conduit that carries this context from early childhood through latency and then into adolescence and beyond is the introject. The introject refers here to the product of the human tendency to respond to loss by reevoking the memory of a departed loved one. Departure can refer to brief partings, deaths, or loss of the *sense* of the presence of the object if engendered by cognitive maturation that changes the way things are seen. This last type results in apparent changes and losses in the environment. The memory of the lost one becomes a source of replacement. If the lost one was primarily experienced in the context of a masochistic relationship, then duplicates of such relationships may be sought as a means to recapture that which was lost. Thus, remembrance of things past can be experienced in newly generated words and experiences. The persistence in memory of parental introjects in the context of early traumatic situations becomes the source of multiple actualizations patterned after the original. When these actualizations place the adolescent in the passive role of the child, the situation is called masochism.

When the child internalizes a relationship, the seed of an introject is produced. Such an introject may grow to become the raw material of fantasy. Thenceforth, the youngster will have a pattern after which to fashion his relationships with later significant, and sometimes loved, objects.

The impact of such masochistic paradigms on later relationships is especially strong when there is exaggeration of parental aggression. This can occur when the child projects his own aggression into his interpretation of the parent's behavior. For instance, if a child in the early-childhood situation projects his own anger onto the parent, the parent's aggression will be exaggerated in the memory of child, with the result that parental aggression in the model situation becomes more marked. At the least it will be remembered as such. Should the child then base his parental introject on this false image of the parent, he will acquire a distorted (fantasy) base upon which to draw when a need for re-evocation reshapes his world. This major factor in intensification of adolescent masochism is called *projective identification* (identifying with parents whose anger is perceived to be stronger than it really is as the result of projection of the child's own aggression onto the parent).

Distortions in early parental introjects can lead to a distortion of self-image as well. When the introjected parent is seen as hostile or cruel, self-image declines. This is especially so in those instances in which the child sees all the manifestations of thought or ideas within himself—even those derived solely from the image of the parent—as personal characteristics without origins external to himself. This psychic self-perception makes a child vulnerable to the occurrence of adolescent masochism, especially in the form of adolescent shyness. In that condition, the avoidance is the product of a projection of a low opinion of oneself into the thinking of peers.

Other factors can create vulnerability to masochism in early adolescence. Among these factors is cathexis of the internal fantasy in preference to reality. This leads to distortions in the perception of the world and impairs object relations. Another factor is ego impairment in the ability to differentiate self-image from the hostile internalized parental imago (Mahler 1955). Those factors lend power to the ability of the child to intensify introjects—colored by parental aggression—to the point that memory becomes strong enough to overwhelm the child's interpretation of reality, in later life.

The Phenomenology of Adolescent Masochism

In conducting a psychotherapy that deals with masochism in adolescence, it is important that the therapist realize, and interpret to the patient, the fact that situations that are feared in advance or are repeatedly experienced subjectively as painful are interpretations of reality rather than reality itself. Although people and situations vary, the content of the fears and complaints of the patient are consistent, and are marked by sameness. Latent fantasy, which takes its shape from internalization of a child's relationship to a hostile punishing parent, becomes the model for masochistic relationships. In adolescence, when the discharge of drives shifts from manifest fantasy formation to actualization (living out of fantasy), peers are recruited to serve as symbols of the punishing introject.

As symbols that are more human and real-appearing come to be tolerated better with the move into early-adolescent cognition, real people can be recruited to serve as manifest symbol representations. Reality interactions with others begin to take on the masochistic cast prescribed by the persistent child–introject relationships in latent fantasy content. Clinically, this may be seen in the preference for painful experiences in the presence of potential comfort that occurs in the real life of adolescents. The well-trodden paths of masochism give the security of familiar territory. The child tends not to stray far from the path. The devil that one knows feels safer than the angel who comes as a stranger. Should the pattern become fixed, the fantasy, now characterological, will influence the pattern of object relations in adult life.

Adolescent masochism may be viewed as a living out of the relationship that existed between the prelatency child and the hostile introject. What appears to be reality takes form from the ways of the introject (the parent remembered).

A Comparison of Adolescent Shyness and Prepubescent Schizophrenia

In adolescent shyness, a masochistic confrontation is feared and avoided. In prepubescent schizophrenia, the masochistic fantasy is experienced with psychotic intensity, while the sense of reality is strongly linked to fantasy at the same time that reality testing is suspended.

A third situation exists: In this situation, peers are interpreted to be, or induced to be, cruel. (This is *masochistic characterological behavior*). In reality situations, cathexis of inner fantasy diminishes, permitting a certain amount of cathexis of reality. Relationships develop with real objects. The relationship is colored by the same driven need to relive the past through interactions with new objects that occurs in the peer relationships of prepubescent schizophrenics, who complain of being treated badly. Again, peers are interpreted to be or induced to be cruel. In the child with masochistic character traits, delusions are not present. The impact of the model role of the introjected hostile parent who punishes in fantasy is the same. The pattern of behavior is lived out with real objects rather than experienced as fear fantasies. (Notice in this regard that among the cases to be presented, J.D. contains elements of both and may be considered a transitional case, whereas L.L.L. is dominated by an aspect of activity that is confined to his inner world.) However, in adolescent shyness there is fear of pain at the hands of real objects. In adolescent shyness, there is a nearly delusional fear that entails real people.

Adolescent Shyness

Adolescent shyness is characterized by an avoidance reaction to contacts with peers or adults in authority. This avoidance is related to feelings of inferiority or defect. The child feels these would be known or recognized by others, and rejection would result. Although object relationship is avoided, real objects are recruited to serve in the child's fear fantasies. A shift to a real object in the outside world as the symbolic representation of that which appeared as the persecutor in the typical latency-age persecutory fantasy occurs in early adolescence. This sets the stage for turning the manifest form taken by drive derivatives from persecutory fantasies to masochistic character activity. Adolescent shyness as reflected in the following case is an early manifestation of this dynamic.

Vicky went away to summer camp for the first time at the age of 12. She became quite depressed and frightened for fear that people would not like her or would find her boring. She spoke of herself as boring. She had projected her opinion of herself to others. When younger, she activated feelings of boredom when she needed to suppress memories of aggressive scolding on the part of her mother. In effect, her view of herself as boring was a defense against an aggressive identification with her mother. An introject had been formed that she could not differentiate from herself. A sense of being boring was substituted for aggression. In this way she defended against an activity which would have made her too much like her mother. Her attempt to individuate herself from her mother was furthered by her projection of her mother's aggression onto her peers, who were seen as aggressors.

Andrew, at the age of 11, clowned in school to hide his fears he would be rejected by peers as he was repeatedly rejected by his psychotic mother, who had beaten him and had yelled at him since he was a child. He shouted down and belittled teachers. Analysis revealed that this behavior mirrored his mother. He identified with her as the aggressor and then had great difficulty differentiating himself from this internalized image of his mother. He then projected this image of himself derived from the maternal introject into the minds of teachers and peers and clowned to defend himself against their criticism, which in reality was his own. His provocations often enlisted his teachers and peers in hostile activity in the mode of his mother. His sufferings cast his early adolescence in a masochistic light.

These youngsters tend to ascribe to others the view they have of themselves. In turn, they confuse their self-image with the early hostile mother imago. The hostile mother imago is intensified by introjection during teenage separations, making the situation worse. Because of this dynamic, separations provoke crises. In this way there is created a masochistic context to accompany the sullen mood of loneliness that is part of teenage separation experiences.

Prepubescent Schizophrenia

Perhaps the most striking clinical context in which to study the effects of the relation of introjects to adolescent masochism is found in prepubescent schizophrenia. In this late-onset form of childhood schizophrenia, poor peer relations, delusional thinking, and an absence of the normal neurosis of latency are characteristic. In contrast to normal children, who begin to project introjects by the age of 4, these youngsters begin to project introjects at the age of 11 (Bender 1947). Hallucinations in childhood schizophrenia are internal in apparent point of origin during latency and external in apparent point of origin in adolescence and adulthood. In those with this late-onset form, auditory hallucinations are experienced as coming from within their bodies, as is typical of younger childhood schizophrenics. They experience internal persecutory fantasy objects, which are derived from introjects; however, the symptomatology is often blurred by the presence of masochistic object relations. They begin to get into scrapes with others, since they are entering upon the age at which for them peers can first be used as symbols. In essence, at this age the memory of the introject can be evoked through employing a peer or other person in the environment whose characteristics allow him or her to be used as the armature around which the masochistic fantasy is shaped. This manner of dealing with objects characterizes masochistic object relations.

Typical of the type of prepubescent schizophrenic who is persecuted from within and without is J.D., aged 12. He suffered severe pain when he tried to walk because of an iron bar that pierced both of his heels and impeded walking. If he suppressed this hallucination, he suffered severe stomach cramps, which were attributed by his family to allergy to macaroni. He also had fugue states in which he dissociated himself from his classroom and found himself in a cave 150 feet below the surface of the earth. Here he sat before a devil and a crowd of accusers. The devil bore a strong resemblance to a girl in his class who picked on him in the school bus. His father rejected the "theory" that the boy's difficulties were emotional in origin and encouraged his son to beat up the girl.

Note in this case the concurrent existence of painful body-oriented hallucination, persecutory fantasy, and masochistic relationship with a peer.

A pattern formed of the latter two symptoms is sometimes also seen in latency-age children when there has been a breakdown in the mechanisms of restraint.

L.L.L. presents us with an example of a prepubescent schizophrenic child with a cruel commanding internal fantasy object, which he cannot separate from himself, but which he tries to externalize. No external persecutors were created. L.L.L., who was 12, was hospitalized in the children's unit in a hospital in Beijing, China when seen. His head, face, and nose were covered with scabs, scars, and abrasions. All were self-inflicted. A shy boy, with few friends and difficulty speaking because of a malformation of his palate, he began to show signs of behavioral change at

the time of the exams which decide one's life course in China. He
was heavily sedated. Antipsychotic drugs had been used to no
avail. The current drug regimen was undertaken to keep him
from injuring himself and those around him. He hit himself and
others as the result of verbal commands that came from the
"Monkey King" who resided in his stomach. He repeatedly went
to the toilet where he attempted to expel the Monkey King. (The
Monkey King is the main character in a Buddhist fairy tale,
Journey to the West. He has prodigious skills, and in an ani-
mated film version available to children in China, "Havoc in
Heaven," is a successful challenger of authority and passivity.)

Note the misinterpretation of his own anger. He could not differentiate his aggression from that of an introject and tried to expel it.

L.T.L. was 15. For two years, he had irregular school attendance.
He experienced his flatus as offensive (contrary to the usual
experience of sensing narcissistic extensions of oneself as above
reproach). He felt that the odor remained about him, and interpreted movements of people away from him as signs of their
rejection of his emunctory odor. He needed to see but a few
people walk in a direction that took them away from him to
confirm his negative image of himself.

L.T.L. presents us with an example of a transition step in the
continuum of symptoms that starts with the internal persecutor of
childhood and ends in the imagined external persecutor experienced
in adolescent shyness. The internal persecutor is clearly delusional. In
this transition step, a negative product of the rejected self is considered
to be the object of a delusional rejection by the world. The symbol of
self-degradation is bizarre and irrational. In this continuum the masochistic experience of adolescent shyness can be seen as the healthier
pole. In that situation, the person who does the hurting is identifiable
as someone known, and the reason for rejection ("I'm boring," "I'm
not pretty enough," or "I deserve it. I'm hateful and bad.") is rationalized to the point that it can be understood and seems logical.

Placement of the Introject about the Margins of the Psychological Boundaries of the Self

These cases present in direct and exaggerated form the dynamics by
which youngsters deal with introjects during early adolescence.

This relates in turn to the dynamics of masochism. Adolescent masochism can be interpreted to be a manifestation of a placement of the persecutory introject outside the self and materialized as a peer in the *location continuum* of persecutors developed in the child's psychic reality. What are the primary locations on this continuum? The introject can exist within the psychological boundaries of the self. It can exist in the interface between self and the object world. It can be assigned to feared fantasy objects. It can be interpreted into the actions of well-known peers. The variations in location of objects utilized as sadists in adolescent masochism are derived from these placements.

Within the psychological boundary of the self, introject placement takes four forms. In the first instance, the introject remains within the boundary of the self and takes the form of the demanding contents of the superego. These contents serve to find fault with self and provoke guilt.

In a second instance, the introject also remains within the boundary of the self. Despised portions of the self, which are experienced intensely in adolescence, generate low self-esteem. They can be recognized to be a misunderstood remnant of the hostile parental introject of early childhood. The part of the self that cannot be separated from the introject becomes the object of rejection. The remainder of the self rejects the introject. (In adolescent shyness, the rejected introject is projected onto fantasied persecutors beyond the boundaries of the self. See below.)

In a third instance, the hostile introject can be placed within the boundary of the self in the form of an angry delusional internal fantasy object. Such an object can be experienced as the source of insulting command hallucinations from within (e.g., the Monkey King).

In the fourth instance, the introject can serve as one of the hostile fantasy elements in the individual's latent fantasy life. (When the fantasy is actualized through placement in a person recruited from beyond the boundary of the self, the early-childhood relationship that contributed to the content of the introject becomes the basis for adolescent masochistic experiences involving peers.)

At the psychological boundary of the self, the introject can be represented by any body product that leaves the body. It should be noted that none of these objects need be the seat of an introject placement; however, they can be used. In fact, it is remarkable that there are so many examples that one can find of the use of body products as animistically endowed beings or part-beings, which can in turn be used in persecutory fantasies, wanderings, fantasies of vulnerability, and fantasies of the extension of power. Hair trimmings, nail trimmings, excreta, flatus, "the soul," semen, and menstrual blood have all been used as vehicles to carry the power and the vulnerabilities of the self as shaped by parental introjects.

Beyond the psychological boundary of the self, the characteristics of introjects are invested in heard external voices, peers, persecutors, and lovers. When externalized, the voice of the conscience may become the voice heard in dreams and delusions as well as the voice of conscience and the sense of guilt felt by some when a policeman comes into view. Peers, persecutors, and lovers, when invested with the attributes of the hostile introject and related to in the context of a primordial paradigmatic painful relationship to the person introjected, become the protagonists in the life of the masochistic character.

Masochistic Derivatives in Later Adolescence

Incipient Masochistic Character Traits—Psychotherapeutic Considerations

The selection of cases for psychoanalytically oriented psychotherapy in adolescence requires as a prerequisite the existence of an internalized conflict, coupled with a capacity for object relations. Thus the best candidates for such treatment are those who involve some real objects in the masochistic experiences they report. Children with adolescent shyness have a better prognosis than have the prepubescent schizophrenic children who maintain their introjects within or on the borders of the self. Where outside figures are recruited to play out the masochistic fantasy, the development of transference neuroses may be looked for and therapeutic gain expected. To the extent that outside figures are involved, the patient can be said to have incipient masochistic character traits. It is obvious that in the conduct of a psychotherapy with such people strategies should be devised to involve objects in the world in activities of the patient and in the patient's associations. It is necessary to encourage free associations that pursue insight to replace the misuse of free association through a self-oriented constant retelling of ominously similar masochistic adventures.

Adolescent Misuses of Free Association

Psychoanalysis and psychoanalytic psychotherapy will progress if free association can occur. A problem arises if the patient uses free association (an opportunity for unlimited communication with the analyst) to serve purposes other than the search for insight. Often the patient seeks to relieve tension by communication aimed at the evocation and immediate mastery of a recent traumatic situation. Typical of this is a recounting of an accident or a recent fight. At times, the past is searched and recalled memories are used to justify, rather than modify, current behavior. Typical of this is the patient who says "I have a right to be mean, look how mean people were to me." All too many are primarily interested in drawing sympathy from the analyst or creating a sad mood through memories that will serve as a comforting evocation of a lost, albeit painful, relationship. The analyst may be turned into a witness to pain bravely borne rather than the person engaged to help the patient to understand and resolve the problem of masochism. The use of evocative symbols in free association is a manifestation of a predisposing tendency to repetition compulsion. Such behavior is a "more grown-up" form of masochistic braggadocio. Its clinical manifestation is the domination of one session after another with repeated tales of discomfort and apparent complaints. All this is achieved at the expense of pursuit of insight and long-range therapeutic gains. Therapeutic intervention requires a strategy that interprets this characterological "acting in" of repetition compulsion-based behavior.

Conclusions

Not all children exposed to cruelty while young or occupied with sadistic fantasies in early childhood are at risk for masochism during adolescence. There are a multitude of factors that determine this outcome. Foremost among these are: evidence of pathological placement and psychic representation of introjects; failures in progression along the developmental march of symbols; repetition compulsion, and narcissistic hypercathexis of the sensation of reality at the expense of reality testing.

Psychotherapeutic interventions must be aimed at the correction of these factors. The presence of these influences makes a person vulnerable to penetrations of the anal-sadistic phase memories that intrude upon and shape the relationships of late adolescent and adult life.

Masochistic fantasies themselves may be transmuted during the transition from latency to adolescence. These transmutations occur as the result of cognitive reorganizations that distort the memories of childhood. Such alterations of latent fantasy content affect the life experiences that are shaped in part or whole by fantasy.

The styles of recall of the memory of the actual infantile experiences and the infantile fantasies of the child are modified with the transition to adolescence. For instance, the various placements of the introject provide a variety of possible protagonists and plots for remembering the sadomasochistic past through the realities and experiences of the present. If there is a cognitive impairment of the ability to differentiate self from introject, or a limitation of the ability to assign the introject to a placement in the world beyond the self, the recall of the infantile experiences will take place with more emphasis on delusion and less on the creatures of the object world.

In latency, the capacity to reshape fantasy in the service of the discharge of drives was limited to the use of symbols as the organ for discharge. Within this limited mental activity, the child could create symbols to be used to represent the primary objects of fantasies. A remnant of the cathexis of symbols as the organ for the discharge of drives persists into adolescence. The sweep of objects available to be used as symbols is markedly enhanced. In those who can achieve normal object cathexes and can place introjects beyond the boundaries of self, the symbolizing function turns more toward the world. It increases the available representations that can be used as symbols. Peers, loved ones, and reality objects (such as houses, jewels, and money) that can be controlled and manipulated into scenarios, are enlisted in the service of the need of the fantasizing function of the ego to hide and distort original memories (repression). To the extent that these elements are compliant, the fantasies in which they participate adhere closely to original sources. Less flexible symbols cause shifts from passivity to activity or from object to subject for the protagonist. Thus a fantasy of being bullied may be lived out as a fantasy of bullying if the available objects are weak.

There weighs heavily in the balance of those elements that produce vulnerability an inability to turn attention cathexes away from memory and fantasy so that the child can invest reality with the right to call the tune. This source of vulnerability to masochism in adolescence must be pursued, understood, and analyzed if progress is to be made in psychotherapy.

Chapter 11

Epilogue: Late Adolescence into Adulthood

The psychotherapy of late latency–early adolescence requires a component of alertness on the part of the therapist to the need of the patient to prepare in advance for the tasks and troubles of the transition period between late adolescence and adulthood. When reflective self-awareness is turned toward the effect of the resolution of early adolescent problems on the future, late adolescence and early adulthood are the periods of the future involved. The tasks and troubles of the latter period involve adult sexuality, resolution of identity, the choice of a career, marriage, and parenthood.

This chapter is devoted to a description of such tasks and troubles from the point of view of a younger person gazing ageward. It is meant to round out the developmental presentation of this book and to give background within the context of the book for the therapist who needs to know what is on the patient's mind, though not necessarily in focus and perhaps rejected as unimportant by the unwary child.

Developmental Tasks of Late Adolescence and Adulthood

Internal

Among these are acceptance and resolution of adult sexual drives and goals in response to maturational progress and social demands. This includes:

Intercourse
Pregnancy
Choice of a mate
Dating

There is a shift from drive-dominated, omnipotent behavior without well-articulated goals to reality-oriented, goal-directed behavior.

External

There is a need for delay of sexual gratification and marriage in response to social and economic demands. This is expressed in:

Economic dependence on parents of an individual capable of
self-support and parenthood
Education for life work

Timing of Tasks

By the age of 18, there are available on a maturational level the capacity for realistic evaluation of others; reality-bound object relations; the capacity for object-bound sexual relations; sufficient judgement for independent functioning, and physical size and strength for self-support and marriage. Psychological factors can have slowed the development of any of these elements. For instance, neurotic inhibition can delay the onset of sexual activity. Experiential factors may have deprived the adolescent of realities against which to hone skills. For instance, military service or a college with an unbalanced ratio of boys to girls may delay dating or integration into the community. Social factors can cause a delay in implementing the possibilities made available by appropriate development at this time. For instance, the individual who is ready for marriage may have a career ambition that requires that marriage be delayed in order to complete necessary education.

By the time this age is reached, we must consider, in addition to maturation and development, delayed implementation of developmental potentials. As throughout adolescence, the exact age of occurrence of events in the unfolding of psychic life from late adolescence to adulthood is difficult to set. For example, parenthood may happen at 14 or at 40. There are usually certain limits upon the earliest possible date, and there are usual ages for certain occurrences. These criteria will be used for setting the ages at which the events to be described occur. In this way we shall draw an approximate description of the timing of a typical picture of psychic life from late adolescence to early adulthood.

The emotional tasks of the final stages of adolescence consist of the resolution of financial and emotional dependence on the parents. Concomitant with escape from dependence there is a minimizing of passivity problems. A lessened influence of rebellion against passivity and the introjective human response to separation enhances the reassertion of parental imagoes and increases mainstream socialization, producing acceptable and mature social behavior.

Separation Problems

Successful separation increases identification while completing removal. By the time a child is 18, a number of separations have occurred. He may have gone to camp or even to a preparatory school. Whatever the situation, parental supervision and dependence on adults are fostered and continued by individuals who function in loco parentis. At 18 the first true break with parental domination and direct influence occurs. It is at this age that custom dictates the possibility of truly independent function and decision-making. Here the break with home can be made in circumstances that are socially dictated and are considered appropriate. The usual situations that afford the new freedom are going to college, moving to one's own apartment, and joining a military service. In those who stay at home, weekends, summer vacations, and trips provide the situations in which independent function can manifest itself. There is no specific change in the general structure of the ego when this occurs. There is little concomitant resolution of the action- and life situation-informing core fantasies. These, as always, remain the same; they transmit a potential for characterological patterns of behavior and the roots of neurosis or emotional sensitivities. However, within this context of sameness there is often a general ego strengthening (during the age period 18 to 20) in the ability to gather life elements into a context which includes future needs.

The approach of high school graduation, with the demand for self-reliance that is implied, seems the social concomitant correlated with this cognitive move at 18. When it occurs at 20, usually between the sophomore and junior years of college, the social concomitants are pairing off with a sexual partner ("living together") and focusing on an area of specialization that will support one's career choice. A certain amount of organization of schedule, neatness, and taking into account the needs of another come into play with living together. It is not unusual to see grades improve at this stage in school, and formerly casual students become interested in medical school or the like.

The move away from the parents is accompanied by a developmental shift in the personality structures related to the superego. Three types of responses are seen on the surface. The unprepared person may be overwhelmed by the new freedom, and seek withdrawal from all new challenges. He becomes less independent and less involved with more mature activities than he was at home. Others maintain their standards and rate of progress, much in the way that they had functioned in the parental home. Still others "let go," and act on core fantasies which would have been manifested in promiscuity, or a drop in work skills, or in political activities foreign to the family attitudes, had they not been stifled by the direct influence of the omnipresent parents. In essence, for these youngsters, parents provide an external superego. Control and ego ideal in these children were still external when they were at home. Parents when present set the precept and example that guided the child's life. Once the child is free, the ego function that has to do with the implementation of superego demands is no longer constrained to respond to the strong control of the parents, and derivatives of the core fantasy which might be odious to the parent begins to appear. Internal and external prohibitions dissolve.

An 18-year-old girl from a strict and controlling family becomes promiscuous while on a trip to Europe.

Some late adolescents respond to separation by repeating the infantile response of seeking closeness. The infant who was hit by the mother turned to the mother. A 12-year-old who is growing up nicely can be slowed in her growing away from her mother if her mother begins to fight with her. Sometimes promiscuity is an attempt on the part of the child to replace the lost closeness with the mother by substituting physical closeness with peers. For some, the reaction to separation upon going to college precipitates disorganizations at this age that are manifested in depressions and anxiety. In the psychotherapy of late latency–early adolescence, those youngsters who have been infantilized and have shown a tendency to adjust through intensifying their relationships with their parents should have the topic of separation introduced so as to avoid decompensations upon separation from the family in late adolescence. Especially pertinent are a need for closeness, a need to have someone support one even when one is wrong, the use of parents as an object to relate to when others reject or withdraw, and unresolved resentment of parental failings (Often there is resentment of parents' inability to provide material things that others in the neighborhood had. Expressing such resentments is forbidden; they live on, if unexpressed, as generalized and disorganizing anger.).

A boy of 18 went away to school in another state. He did well until he was criticized by a teacher. Hurt, the boy would have turned to his mother for comfort as he had done in the past. Separated from her, he was frustrated in his turning to her and deteriorated in his appearance, neatness, and school capacities. The parents resolved the problem by bringing him to a college that was close enough to home so that he could continue to live with his mother. He promptly recovered his former skills.

Living away from the parents is an important step in the growth of a late adolescent. It permits the development and elaboration of personal patterns and tastes.

Career Choice

It is during the period from late adolescence to early adulthood that the ultimate choice of a career must be made. Whatever the decison is, it must be implemented in deed.

In childhood years, choice of a career need not have had much to do with reality. At first, the child, admiring the father, wants to follow the parent's chosen field. As the child's world widens in prelatency, he seeks jobs that are highly visible and of which children are in awe. The fantasy and excitement associated with such activities as fireman, policeman, or airplane pilot take center stage. Girls wish to become wives and mothers during prelatency.

With the coming of latency, the child's vistas expand to include people whose professions bring them into contact with children. Doctor, nurse, teacher, coach, lifeguard are added to the professions that the children want to pursue. The jobs favored by the child reflect his or her fantasies. They are played out in make-believes and may be accompanied by breakthroughs of excitement. In high school (midadolescence) the private fantasies of the child that involve fantasies of adult life still retain excitement as a determinant. Publicly proclaimed ambitions are a different matter. A boy with a low average cannot hope to be taken seriously when he announces that he wishes to be an atomic physicist. Personal limitations have to be taken into account. The private fantasies that go underground are not given up. They become the bases for disappointment and depression in adulthood. There is some measure of unreality in the revealed choices of the high school senior. Rarely does one find such skills as refuse collector, chimney cleaner, plumber, or gardener among the occupational choices listed in a high school yearbook.

At the time of high school graduation, some decision has to be made. Whole areas of occupation are denied by exclusion from college. For those who do not go to college, at age 18, the life career is beaten into shape between the hammer of hope and the anvil of reality. What jobs are available? What are the skills of the individual? Are there ethnic or religious qualifications that make one path easier than the other? At first the sights are set high. Then little by little there is compromise until means of earning a livelihood are assured. The original dream (to be a doctor, to be a baseball player, to be rich) are not forgotten.

Often the youngster puts his dreams away for a while, or he thinks he does. "I'll take this job for now, while I'm looking for something better," or "I'll get a job now and I'll go to night school and get good marks so I can get a better job." "When?" "In a couple of years, after I've finished paying for my new motorcycle."

In dealing with the child in late latency–early adolescence in regard to the topic of life work and career, the therapist represents reality to the child. Academic potentials are explored. The reality of goals is assessed. Omnipotence, narcissism, and grandiosity, manifested in career ambitions that exceed potential or willingness to invest time and work in necessary education, need be analyzed. At times, an evaluation of life career ambitions reveals these pathological states to a degree otherwise unexpected. Ambitions can be confronted with the requirements of the ambition as compared with the attributes of the child. Popular singers who earn millions of dollars singing songs they have written do not spring from among those who have no training in music. One's level of education and the earning power of one's occupation dictate later life style and the nature of entertainments shared with friends.

A man who had worked for 17 years as an assistant to a house painter at times created financial difficulties for himself. He insisted on maintaining friendships with individuals who earned more money than he. He claimed that they formed his appropriate peer group, and that it was a matter of pride that he be with them. At the age of 18 he had been offered a tryout with a major league baseball team. He had not gone for the tryout—he had had to run an errand for a friend that day. He felt that if he had gone, he would have become rich and famous. Actually, he had not gone out of fear of rejection. Had he been turned down, his self-esteem would have been shattered. In this way he bartered uncertainty and the possibility of fame and fortune for the surety of a fantasy that he could keep alive.

So it goes with the fantasies that people turn to when they bow to subjugation under the harsh realities of the world, with its impersonal bosses and placement tests. Such fantasies become a refuge in times of discontent. People withdraw to them and dwell within them. They pursue each facet and enjoy each gleam of hope, like some potentate withdrawn to his treasure room to meditate upon the cast and color of his jewels.

For people with the necessary skills to attend college, college affords a "breather." There is more time to explore, ponder, and prepare for the future. The same requirement to face the need to find oneself occurs with college graduation that had beset the recent high school graduate. Education improves the job potential. The jobs they can get are better; however, in spite of the gain, for many the breather is a pitfall. Youngsters reprieved by four years of college from the need to make life decisions must now confront what they were ill prepared to face four years before. Acceptance of sexual maturity and family responsibilities can be avoided by extending schooling. In dealing therapeutically with college-bound youngsters, assessment of active delay of maturity through extending education can reveal fears that need resolving. Often, graduation is delayed by dropping out for a year, or graduate school is selected to delay the need for further mature function. One should especially beware the group who do not know what they wish to do in life and seek therapy in a state of anxiety. People with problems of object–ground differentiation (a thought disorder related to inability to focus on main ideas, which can be detected and treated in early adolescence) can often be protected by the tracks and disciplines of a college, only to decompensate and become nonfunctional upon graduation from college.

Youngsters who are well organized and goal-directed use college as a means of improving their position in life. Even these, who have adequate personality skills, however, face pitfalls. Many have to accept disappointment, in that they had failed to acquire skills required for a desired job, or are seeking jobs with requirements beyond their level. Somehow it is part of the human spirit to suffer from the "divine discontent" that makes a man pursue ever-higher goals. Few are satisfied for long with what they have. In the hands of the inventive and creative, this is a vital part of the evolution of career and culture. The introduction of new ideas and things, of new viewpoints and art depends on this. To the person who is only capable of handling a workaday high-level activity, but no more, it is a taunt.

A girl at 22 had just graduated from a private college. She obtained a job with a magazine doing editorial work. It was a nine-to-five job. This was according to her plan. She was saving the nights for the writing of a great novel. "The problem is," she complained, "I'm too tired to do anything much creative by the time I get home." In her late twenties, marriage and children made further incursions on her time. She never wrote the novel.

It requires much drive and self-discipline to do the workaday things that keep one alive and still have time to be creative. Some individuals prefer not to work at regular jobs, so that they can pursue their artistic and inventive bent. Others accept a pattern of regular daily work and home chores while keeping their private fantasies in reserve. The healthiest group accepts the reality of their limitations, devoting all their energies to the here and now of enjoying and enriching their lives.

Sexuality

Living away from the parents presents the adolescent with an arena in which freedom is obtained, among those who are physically mature, to achieve full resolution and adaptation in the area of sexuality. The period of breaking away (late adolescence–early adulthood) is a time of courting. The courting period begins during the later part of high school and continues until the late 20s. Divorces, deaths of spouses, and good psychotherapeutic results introduce later courting periods into the lives of individuals. In European countries, courting is extended to the mid-30s. In some primitive cultures marriages are arranged with selected mates, in the early teens. In American culture today, people are expected to find their own mates.

One divorcee of 28, who was searching for a husband, set the end of courting at 23 for women and 26 for men. Her observations were that "men who are interested in women are married by the time they are 26."

This estimate, which was made at the time of the writing of the first draft of this chapter in 1968, has been altered by social changes, such as the extension of the period of education for women. In 1986, the relative position of a "time to panic" if not married has shifted back about four years, to 27 for women and 30 for men. Age 30 has always been a source of second thoughts in this matter.

A woman who came from the Far East and had experienced a marriage of convenant was amazed at American courting procedures. She felt that a father in America must be a cruel man to force a girl to find a husband instead of providing her with a well-investigated person from a suitable family.

The timing of courting is an example of cultural relativism. Obviously it is a cultural matter determined by the mores of the land. Its interest for us lies in the fact that in our culture it comes at an age by which all normal people have *matured* to the point that they have the potential for sexual gratification and performance. This does not mean that they have all *developed* to this point. The experiences of adolescence that are heterosexual and are encouraged by the parents need contain no sexual activity. As long as the boy or girl goes out and is popular, the parents are happy. In fact, many parents prefer to deny that there is any sexual activity in their children. The sexual expectations come from within the child and from within the group.

During the age of courting, the situation is somewhat different. There is pressure from social mores to undertake a course of activity that will lead to marriage, sexual intercourse, and parenthood. From both the standpoint of expectations of the community and the need for the continuation and preservation of the human race, there is no possibility of faking it. "Let's not and say we did" works with "post office," but not with courting and marriage.

Individuals who are maturationally and developmentally ready, marry early. Others delay because of educational requirements. Still others utilize the period of courting and marriage as the time for working through sexual adjustments. Sexuality is encouraged and expected. The time is ripe for marriage, but the psyche may not be. Through dating and courting and the first years of marriage an attempt is made to work out sexuality and neurotic interactions. This occurs, of course, in those who are dissatisfied with themselves. There are individuals who are quite satisfied with their limitations and the underlying gratifications that they derive from them. These people become those with adult character disorders, whereas those who are anxious about their failure to function as others do become neurotics and character neurotics if they are not able to resolve their problems. A possible outcome of the set of adolescent ego structures used as a means of adjusting to sexuality is the preservation of an ego structure that will introduce neurotic character patterns into adult life. Thus, the passing of adolescence is often associated with the precipitation of neurosis.

Love in courting and in marriage consists of benevolence toward the partner and pleasure derived from the partner with justice all around. Where this does not exist, there is present the distorting intrusion into the interactions of everyday life of the contents of prelatency core fantasies. Where there are cruelty, selfishness, and withholding, an element of neurotic interaction exists in the relationship. Experience and the working through of problems, either as a couple or with outside help, results in the resolution of the problem through disentangling the marital relationship from the neurotic core fantasy. Failing this, psychiatric treatment can be used to vitiate the strength of the fantasy.

One form of neurotic interaction is the use of intercourse and marriage as a special symptom. The demands of society put great pressure on young adults. That one is a virgin is considered a fact to be hidden. In response to taunts, and the projection of one's own dissatisfaction, individuals may plunge into intercourse and marriage in order to prove themselves. Often, this results in chaos if the individual is barely at the level of sophistication at which the complexities of the situation can be handled.

Recently, newspapers all over the country told the story of a bride who ran away on her wedding night.

A young man of 24 was taunted by fellow workers for actions which belied his wish to avoid adult sexuality. He dated an experienced female to whom he confessed his wish to share an asexual relationship. In response to the taunts and to prove himself, he found a young woman of 24, who was also a virgin, and involved her in a relationship that led to intercourse. After the establishment of the sexual relationship, he met her family. He found himself involved with a person and a family who were unsuitable for him.

A boy of 17 was driven by the need to prove that he could have intercourse, as his older siblings did. He dated an older woman who worked in a restaurant in which he did odd jobs. She consented to intercourse. He proved himself. The price was high. She cheated him of his entire summer earnings on the basis of a falsely claimed pregnancy.

For these people, intercourse and marriage are not real events and aspects of life. They are concrete pieces on a playing board, which when won are the special symbols of strength and capacity. They are then exhibited like a Heidelberg scar. They are a message to the world, having little to do with the inner life and needs of the individual. This is soon learned by these individuals when they realize that the turmoil from within and the limitations from without have not been cured by a gesture. Intercourse and marriage provide a resolution for only three problems: they help with the need for companionship, the need for sexual outlet, and the need to fulfill social expectations. Inner loneliness, neuroses, psychosis, depression, etc. are not resolved by sexual affairs and marriage. Rather, they become a rich medium for the growth and efflorescence of the acting out and rationalization of these conditions.

A woman of 26 who had never been able to achieve sexual activity with a man and had been hospitalized many times for psychotic episodes married a man who admired her chastity and felt that he could cure her problems. In their relationship, he played the role of a psychiatrist in competition with the psychiatrist of his first wife, who had helped her deal with her problems. Although his second wife tried, she was unable to accept his closeness or to continue to have intercourse. They were divorced within a few months.

A woman of 24 who had had a number of affairs in which her close attachment to her girl friend had forced a breakup, finally married a man who she felt respected her because he did not make sexual advances. After the marriage she learned that the reason for this was the fact that he was impotent. The marriage was annulled. He explained his action on the basis of his belief that if he got married, it would make everything all right.

Courtship and sexual affairs—and, often, living together—are seen psychologically as extensions of dating by the participants. As such, they are relationships with fairly straightforward effects on their participants. They are what they are. Marriage is something more. Marriage has a mystique. Marriage is for most of our population an introduction to becoming a member of the world of parents and community leaders. Among peoples with complex religious rules governing daily activity, there is a marked difference in the attitude toward a woman who is sexually active and unmarried and one who is sexually active and married. In some groups, the woman who was once married has sexual freedom, while the woman who has been sexually active, though never married, is requested to repent.

> A woman of 24 came from an orthodox religious family. Her father discovered that she had been promiscuous and was currently engaged in a sexual affair. The father counseled her to marry her unsuitable partner, with the thought that divorce could settle the problem if the marriage didn't work out. Once married, he reasoned, and then divorced, she would have a better opportunity of making a good marriage later in her life. The woman declined the suggestion. She realized that there is more to marriage than a tool for assuaging the pain engendered by interpretations of a particular spiritual group.

Never underestimate the psychological impact of marriage.

With increasing intensity during late latency, adolescence, and early adulthood, maturation puts a demand on the individual to resolve the problem of the sexual drives and to find a means for their implementation. During latency and early adolescence, this must be done in an atmosphere of guilt. There is little cultural sanction. Indeed, there is disapproval of sexuality at these stages. In late adolescence and early adulthood, the need for adult sexual techniques hurries the learning and accommodation process for all save those orthodoxly religious ethnic groups that insist that sexuality must await marriage. Some degree of sexual experience is expected of one during late adolescence. The world of ethical men and women gives tacit consent through silence, and suddenly everything is allowed.

The young participants may be accepted as sexual beings, but they may not be quite able to accept themselves in this role. The superego is complex, and may not change with the changing winds of mores. Sexual permissiveness as a rule of society does not guarantee guilt-free sexuality. It is therefore important for the therapist of adolescence to pursue the reactions of the sexually active person to sexual experience. The superego is manifested in many ways. Little that the adolescent says should be taken at face value. A person who claims to have no problem with sex, but avoids it to protect himself or herself from syphilis or AIDS may be covering frigidity and anxiety in regard to sexual function. A man who avoids dating because he cannot afford it may be displacing concerns from areas that relate to impotence.

With the onset of early latency, there was a massive increase in the strength of superego prohibitions and the extent of their contents in relation to sexuality. Incest feelings, sexual drives, masturbation, and infantile sexuality as well as genitality fill the list of the things proscribed. With growth there is a continuous buildup of nonsexual superego contents until adulthood. These are derived mostly from later identifications.

Concurrently with the buildup of ego-ideal components in the areas of life activities, ethics, and styles of behavior, there is a softening of the superego in the area of sexuality. The first softening occurs at age 8, when masturbatory activity is reinstated. In early adolescence, dating and kissing and caressing are part of an indication of a further softening of the superego as a matter of custom. Up until marriage there is a gradual change in the expectations of society. The demands of the superego, derived from the attitudes of the parents, do not change so quickly. There is always a gulf between what is done and permitted and what the individual feels is right. This gulf is filled with guilt. When society gives permission for sexuality, only those whose development has reached a point at which their superego will permit it can be free from guilt and adverse reactions. In others there is inhibition and difficulty in letting go. It may take months to resolve the problem of accepting the role of sexuality in one's life even in marriage.

There is often a nonspecific dissolution of inhibition accompanying the period of sexual adjustment that follows initial sexual experiences. It may become quite prominent early in marriage. This can take the form of a ribald sense of humor, a tendency to talk about personal matters openly, and, most commonly of all, a release of the inhibition of oral drives. Thus, smoking may increase and, certainly, eating does. It is common to hear someone say to a newly married man, "You've gained weight. Her cooking must agree with you." It's not the cooking, it's not sex either—it's the nature of the man. To explain this merely on the basis of generalized disinhibition would be to set aside our understanding of human behavior on the basis of psychoanalytic insight. As we have described before, the stress of facing sexual responsibilities can lead to a regression away from the stress area. There may be a shift in the object of the drives from the area of sexual interest to a cathexis of fantasies involving anality and orality. Thus, in the early stages of marriage and in situations of "living together," disinhibition can be coupled with regressive intensification of early infantile sexual activities (e.g., eating for gratification).

Parenthood

Marriage is the culmination of the series of social events and influences that produce the modifications of the ego ideal required to make sexual relations comfortable. The natural issue of this series of events is parenthood. Let us concentrate briefly on the aspects of psychological development and maturation that are served by parenthood. Parenthood is the fulfillment of all human maturation and development.

If there were still flightiness and uncertainty in the career plans of a man, they are put firmly on course by the appearance of a pregnancy. Sometimes, even uncertain affairs become marriages when the catalyst of gestation is added to them. Pregnancy also stirs into action the prelatency fantasies of the expectant parents. A new object appears on the horizon. The man who was threatened by rivalry with his father is threatened by the appearance of a son. The Oedipus complex can be reversed in more than one way. It can be that the father has hostility toward the son out of fear of replacement in the mother's affections. Often men will verbalize this consciously. Greek mythology, which gave the Oedipus complex its name, was not itself aloof to this insight.

Chronus devoured his sons so as to prevent their replacing him. Eventually Zeus (a son who had escaped) castrated him and replaced him.

The capacity of women to bear children stirs up in men an envy (parturition envy). This finds its manifestations in creativity, in *couvade*, and works of genius. *Couvade* refers to sickness and even labor pains experienced by a man when his wife is in labor. In the Guarani Indian group of Paraguay *couvade* is a culturally sanctioned activity.

In women, the effect of pregnancy and parenthood is more intense than in men. When children come, home becomes the major activity of a woman. This is a most important prospective topic for the therapy of a thoughtful early-adolescent girl who has a career in mind. Career plans must be modified and the traditional female role developed more fully. The interaction with a new object is intense. At first this new being is clearly definable as a part of the mother's biology. In keeping with this, the child is viewed as fulfillment of the desire to add to the sexual parts of the body. Dynamically speaking, the fetus may become a symbolic penis. When the child is born, there is a repetition of earlier experiences of loss. In those who feel this strongly, postpartum depressions and psychotic episodes may occur. The suckling child, with its completely carefree manner and lack of inhibition, serves to stimulate by sympathy the mother into less inhibited sexual behavior in her marriage. This serves as a key to an understanding of the role of the birth of a child in the development of sexual capacity. Some women are able to give up inhibitions and have orgasms only after childbirth.

Fulfillment and Disenchantment

Completion of the Superego through Identification

Maturation after the age of 25 is primarily related to an improvement in reality testing, intensification of obsessional defenses, and a strengthening of the superego.

No matter how skillfully an individual has tried to soften the disparity between aspiration and possibility with the use of secret dreams, fantasies, and rationalizations, by the time one reaches 30, a note of hopelessness intrudes should one have fallen short of the goal. There is a strong awareness that the dreams are only dreams and there is not hope, time, or energy for fulfilling them. Time and energy must go into support of the family. Spouses demand attention. Children demand the companionship of the parents. Jobs are not available. And last, but not least, there may not be talent enough within the individual to succeed if all other factors were favoring him or her. Actors and artists who had surrendered security for a chance at immortality, and failed, turn their tired steps toward commerce, production, and areas of the arts that require tenacity, skill, and devotion but not great talent. With the realization that the cherished fantasies of late adolescence will never come true, hopes are put aside.

In this regard, 30 is a particularly difficult age for women. The woman who had had thoughts of a career, which was set aside for childbearing and motherhood, finds that children require more attention at 5, or 15, years than they did at one year. In fact, there is little time to pursue one's own interests. Sometimes time can be bought through the hiring of a surrogate mother, a child caretaker.

Two lawyers in their 40s, married to each other, pondered their impossible schedules. With two children, their lives consisted of professional activities admixed with PTA, shopping, lessons, and transporting and picking up the children. They sat down to list the tasks involved in the day's work. They carefully assigned each activity to lists containing activities near home and near work. Eventually, the needs of the couple came into focus. All at once they defined what was required. "What we need," they said, "is a wife."

Those who are masochistic and tend to be depressed, and further-more live within a marriage in which every difference of opinion is utilized as an excuse for outbursts of temper and aggression, cry the loudest at the state of affairs that ties a woman down and does not permit her to fulfill her potential. The more mature make use of what time they have to entertain and advance themselves.

To have everything—home, children, and career—is the goal of many. Few people, either men or women, can achieve this. Industry, careers, progress up the executive ladder demand devotion. Profession-alism demands the full attention of the professional to the client.

A lawyer in her late twenties awakened quite early in order to catch a plane to Chicago, where she had to make a deposition at 10 a.m. She represented a large law firm. As she kissed her sleep-ing infant child good-bye she realized the child had a high fever and required immediate medical attention.

Caught between family obligations and the demands of executive advancement, a woman in her early thirties discovered that those who had made it to the top in her concern had sacrificed family for career, and that no special rules had been created to advance her in the cut-throat competition for power.

Here reality testing must take the form of acceptance of one's life in place of the hopes and strivings of adolescence. Psychotherapy in early adolescence aimed at bringing future planning into line with potential lessens the strength of future negative reactions. When one turns a life corner and says "Is that all there is?" when life falls short of one's dreaming and the years have slipped away, a sense of humilia-tion and hopelessness descends on one. This is the age of disenchant-ment. The pragmatic imperative (reality) has made itself felt. As a result of disenchantment in hopes and dreams, more time and energy become available for simple pursuits and hobbies. Fulfillment is sought along realistic lines in areas where pleasure as the goal replaces fame. Community activity, courses, bowling, or reading become the sublimations of this age. In effect, the ego ideal shifts to a position that is less removed from the capabilities of the individual.

There is an intensification of the sense of responsibility. This is a developmental step associated with a maturational shift in the structure of the ego. Obsessive–compulsive defenses become more in evidence. Ego energies are devoted more and more to these defenses. Future planning, saving, job security, less physical risk taking, and collecting become the focus of one's planning. There is an increase in the use of mechanisms of defense, whereas acting out formerly was in evidence.

A woman of 30 presented herself to a university clinic. She complained of a severe fear of open places that incapacitated her. She was unmarried. She described herself as having been a "man's woman." That is, she had made herself available to a number of men of her acquaintance in the jazz music field for sexual intercourse under conditions of "equality." She was now living with a girl friend. She had obtained a job. She had stopped her promiscuous sexual activities. She had said it was "time to settle down." She then developed the phobia.

This case illustrates, in exaggerated form, the commonly manifested intensification of the effect of the cultural ego ideal on the life of the individual that begins at 26 and is completed in the early 30s. This does not reflect a change in the ego ideal. These people always knew what was expected of them. That part of the ego that implements superego demands had had insufficient strength to override the demands of the id in its relations to the world. Now, with a reorganization and intensification of the use of obsessional mechanisms it is strong enough to divert these drives into symptoms.

In the case of individuals whose revolt in adolescence was related to a flight from passivity, the shouldering of adult responsibilities removes them from the position of passivity and the need for flight. Passive fantasies may be manifested elsewhere. The characterological structure needed to deal with them in adolescence and early adulthood no longer contributes to the form of adult character. These people, too, start to settle down. The old ego ideals of adolescence now have little to recommend them. As years passed, there was a gradual accretion of bits of culturally conservative, ethical, moral, behavioral, and cultural attitudes and techniques. These were acquired at the very time they were rejected—in early adolescence. Now they are recalled from memory and mobilized as a part of the ego ideal of adulthood. The individual settles down into a conservative style of living. What seems to have been a recent identification with the parental figures is actually an intensification and organization of patterns to live by that were always available, and were acquired from the parents over the years.

The children we have followed in this book have traveled far down the long road that ends with comfort in identification with the parents, maturity, and the threshold of middle age. They can make their own way as we leave them. Maturation has ceased and development has become an individual matter. They are now aligned with their forebears. Their battles are through. The turmoil of uncertainty is behind them. They now join the shuffling multitude in the long march to eternity.

References

Anonymous (date unknown). *AD Herennium*. Harvard University Press, Boston: Loeb Classical Library, 1954.

Anthony, E. J. (1959). An experimental approach to the psychopathology of childhood: sleep disturbances. *British Journal of Medical Psychology* 321:19–37.

Aristotle (c. 340 B.C.). *On Memory and Recollection*. Boston: Loeb Classical Library, 1975.

Bender, L. (1947). Childhood schizophrenia. *Journal of the Academy of Orthopsychiatry* 17:40–56.

Blanchard, P. (1953). Masturbation fantasies of children and adolescents. *Bulletin of the Philadelphia Association for Psychoanalysis* 3:25–38.

Bleuler, E. (1905). *Dementia Praecox or the Group of Schizophrenias*. New York: International Universities Press, 1952.

Blos, P. (1962). *On Adolescence*. New York: Macmillan.

Bryant, W. C. (1903). *The Poetical Works of William Cullen Bryant*, ed. H. C. Sturges. New York: Appleton.

Chambers, W. (1985). The assessment of affective disorders in children and adolescents by semistructured interview. *Archives of General Psychiatry* 42:696–703.

Chandler, L., and Roe, M. (1977). Behavioral and neurological comparisons of neonates born to mothers of differing social environments. *Child Psychiatry and Human Development* 8:25–30.

Coren, H. Z., and Soldinger, J. S. (1967). Visual hallucinosis in children. In *Psychoanalytic Study of the Child* 22:344–356.

Darnton, R. (1975). Writing news and telling stories. *Daedalus* 104(2):175–194.

Di Leo, J. H. (1970). *Young Children and Their Drawings*. New York: Brunner/Mazel.

—— (1973). *Children's Drawings as Diagnostic Aids*. New York: Brunner/ Mazel.

Despert, J. L. (1948). Hallucinations in children. *American Journal of Psychiatry* 104:528–537.

Deutsch, H. (1944). *Psychology of Women*, vol. 1. New York: Grune & Stratton.

Duncan, H. D. (1968). *Symbols in Society*. New York: Oxford University Press.

Euripides (423 B.C.). Heracles. In *Euripides II*, ed. D. Grove and R. Lattimore. Chicago: University of Chicago Press, 1956.

Faima, C., and Winter, J. S. D. (1972). Gonadotropins and sex hormone patterns in puberty. In *The Control of the Onset of Puberty*. New York: Wiley, (1974).

Fein, S. (1976). *Heidi's Horse*. Pleasant Hill, CA: Exelrod.

Fenichel, O. (1945). *The Psychoanalytic Theory of Neurosis*. New York: Norton.

Ferenczi, S. (1911). On obscene words. In *The Selected Papers of Sandor Ferenczi*, vol. 1. New York: Basic Books, 1950.

—— (1913a). A Little Chanticleer. In *The Selected Papers of Sandor Ferenczi*, vol. 1. New York: Basic Books, 1950.

—— (1913b). Stages in the development of the sense of reality. In *Sex in Psychoanalysis*. New York: Basic Books, 1950.

—— (1925). Psychoanalysis of sexual habits. In *Further Contributions to the Theory and Technique of Psychoanalysis*. London: Hogarth, 1953.

Frazer, J. (1922). *The Golden Bough*. New York: Macmillan, 1951.

Freud, A. (1926). *The Psychoanalytic Treatment of Children*. New York: International Universities Press, 1946.

—— (1949). Certain types and stages of social maladjustment. In *Searchlights on Delinquency: New Psychoanalytic Studies*, ed. K. R. Eissler, New York: International Universities Press.

—— (1958). Adolescence. *The Psychoanalytic Study of the Child* 13:255–268.

Freud, S. (1914). On narcissism. *Standard Edition* 14:73–104.

—— (1918). The taboo of virginity. *Standard Edition* 11:191–208.

—— (1919). A child is being beaten. *Standard Edition* 17:172–204.

Goodman, J., and Sours, J. (1967). *The Child Mental Status Examination*. New York: Basic Books.

Harrison, J. E. (1921). *Epilogomena to the Study of Greek Religion*. New Hyde Park, NY: University Books, 1962.

Hart, M., and Sarnoff, C. A. (1971). The impact of the menarche. *Journal of the American Academy of Child Psychiatry* 10:257–271.

Herjanic, B., and Campbell, W. (1970). Differentiating psychiatrically disturbed children on the basis of a structured interview. *Journal of Abnormal Child Psychology* 5:127–134.

Hoffer, W. (1978). *Early Development and Education of the Child*. Northvale, NJ: Jason Aronson.

Jacobson, E. (1964). *The Self and the Object World*. New York: International Universities Press.

Katan, A. (1937). The role of "displacement" in agoraphobia. *International Journal of Psycho-Analysis* 32:41–50, 1951.

Kestenberg, J. (1961). Menarche. In *Adolescence*, ed. S. Lorand and H. I. Schneer. New York: Hoeber Medical Division, Harper & Row.

——— (1967). Phases of adolescence, Parts I and II. *Journal of Child Psychiatry* 6:426–463, 577–611.

——— (1968). Phases of adolescence, Part III. *Journal of Child Psychiatry* 7:108–251.

Kramer, H., and Sprenger, J. (1489) *Malleus Maleficarum*. London: Pushkin Press, 1951.

Krauss, R. M., and Glucksberg, S. (1977). Social and nonsocial speech. *Scientific American* 236:100–106.

Krystal, H. (1965). Giorgio de Chirico—ego states and artistic production. *American Imago* 23:210–226.

Kuhn, F. (1948). *Man in Structure and Function*. New York: Alfred Knopf.

Laufer, M. (1968). The body image, the function of masturbation, and adolescence: Problems of ownership of the body. *Psychoanalytic Study of the Child* 23:114–123.

Levine, M. (1951). Pediatric observations on masturbation in children. *Psychoanalytic Study of the Child* 6:117–127.

Machover, K. (1958). Personal communication.

Mahler, M., and Gosliner, B. J. (1955). On symbiotic child psychosis. *Psychoanalytic Study of the Child* 10:195–214.

Murasaki (1008). *The Tale of Genji*. New York: Modern Library.

Piaget, J. (1945). *Play, Dreams and Imitation in Childhood*. New York: Dutton, 1951.

Puig-Antic, J., and Chambers, W. (1983). The clinical assessment of current depressive episodes in children and adolescents. In *Childhood Depression*, ed. D. Cantwell, pp. 157–179. New York: Spectrum.

Pumpian-Mindlin, E. (1965). Omnipotentiality, youth, and commitment. *Journal of the American Academy of Child Psychiatry* 4:1–19.

Reinach, S. (1903). L'art et la magie, à propos des peintures et des gravures de l'age du renne. *L'Anthrop* 14:265.

Rutter, M., and Graham, P. (1968). The reliability and validity of psychiatric assessment of the child, part I: Interview with the child. *British Journal of Psychiatry* 114:563–579.

Sarnoff, C. A. (1972). The vicissitudes of projection during an analysis encompassing late latency to early adolescence. *International Journal of Psycho-Analysis* 53:515–522.

—— (1975). Narcissism, adolescent masturbation fantasies and the search for reality. In *Masturbation from Infancy to Senescence*, ed. I. Marcus and J. Francis. New York: International Universities Press.

—— (1976). *Latency*. Northvale, NJ: Jason Aronson.

—— (1987a). *Psychotherapeutic Strategies in the Latency Years*. Northvale, NJ: Jason Aronson.

—— (1987b). *Symbols in Psychotherapy, Sexuality, and Sublimation*. Manuscript in preparation.

Stekel, W. (1911). The interpretation of dreams. In *The Psychoanalytic Study of the Child*, ed. A. Reich, vol. 6, p. 84. New York: International Universities Press.

Werkman, S. (1965). The psychiatric diagnostic interview with children. *American Journal of Orthopsychiatry* 35:764–771.

Werner, H., and Levin, S. (1967). Masturbation fantasies—their changes with growth and development. *Psychoanalytic Study of the Child* 22:315–328.

Wilson, C. P. (1979). Personal communication.

Winnicott, D. W. (1953). Transitional objects and transitional phenomena. *International Journal of Psycho-Analysis* 34:89–93.

Wu Cheng'en (1575). *Journey to the West*. Beijing: Foreign Languages Press, 1982.

Yates, F. A. (1966). *The Art of Memory*. Chicago: University of Chicago Press.

INDEX